Popular culture, globalization and Japan

D1600515

Japanese popular culture is constantly evolving in the face of internal and external influence. *Popular Culture, Globalization and Japan* examines this evolution from a new and challenging perspective by focusing on the movements of Japanese popular culture into and out of Japan. The book argues that a key factor behind the changing nature of Japanese popular culture lies in its engagement with globalization. Essays from a team of leading international scholars illustrate this crucial interaction. Drawing on rich empirical content from a series of interdisciplinary perspectives, this book looks at the complex movement of Japanese popular culture as it traverses international borders. Chapters on music, *manga*, media studies, and a range of contemporary popular cultural artifacts illustrate the problematic and complex relations between flows of ideas into and out of Japan.

Presenting current, confronting and sometimes controversial insights into the many forms of Japanese popular culture emerging within this global context, *Popular Culture, Globalization and Japan* will make essential reading for those working in Japanese studies, cultural studies and international relations.

Matthew Allen is Associate Professor of Japanese History at the University of Auckland. He has published widely in Asian Studies, anthropology, psychiatry and history journals.

Rumi Sakamoto is Senior Lecturer in Japanese in the School of Asian Studies at the University of Auckland, New Zealand. She has published on a variety of topics, including Meiji enlightenment discourse, the 'comfort women' issue and Japan's perception of 'Asia'.

Asia's Transformations

Edited by Mark Selden, Binghamton and Cornell Universities, USA

The books in this series explore the political, social, economic and cultural consequences of Asia's transformations in the twentieth and twenty-first centuries. The series emphasizes the tumultuous interplay of local, national, regional and global forces as Asia bids to become the hub of the world economy. While focusing on the contemporary, it also looks back to analyse the antecedents of Asia's contested rise.

This series comprises several strands:

Asia's Transformations aims to address the needs of students and teachers, and the titles will be published in hardback and paperback. Titles include:

Chinese Society, 2nd edition
Change, conflict and resistance
Edited by Elizabeth J. Perry and
Mark Selden

Ethnicity in Asia
Edited by Colin Mackerras

The Battle for Asia
From decolonization to globalization
Mark T. Berger

**State and Society in 21st Century
China**
Edited by Peter Hays Gries and
Stanley Rosen

Japan's Quiet Transformation
Social change and civil society in the
21st century
Jeff Kingston

Confronting the Bush Doctrine
Critical views from the Asia-Pacific
Edited by Mel Gurtov and Peter Van
Ness

**China in War and Revolution,
1895–1949**
Peter Zarrow

The Future of US–Korean Relations
The imbalance of power
Edited by John Feffer

Asia's Great Cities

Each volume aims to capture the heartbeat of the contemporary city from multiple perspectives emblematic of the authors' own deep familiarity with the distinctive faces of the city, its history, society, culture, politics and economics, and its evolving position in national, regional and global frameworks. While most volumes emphasize urban developments since the Second World War, some pay close attention to the legacy of the longue durée in shaping the contemporary. Thematic and comparative volumes address such themes as urbanization, economic and financial linkages, architecture and space, wealth and power, gendered relationships, planning and anarchy, and ethnographies in national and regional perspective. Titles include:

Bangkok
Place, practice and representation
Marc Askew

Beijing in the Modern World
David Strand and Madeline Yue
Dong

Shanghai
Global city
Jeff Wasserstrom

Hong Kong
Global city
Stephen Chiu and Tai-Lok Lui

Representing Calcutta
Modernity, nationalism and the
colonial uncanny
Swati Chattopadhyay

Singapore
Wealth, power and the culture of
control
Carl A. Trocki

Critical Asian Scholarship is a series intended to showcase the most important individual contributions to scholarship in Asian Studies. Each of the
volumes presents a leading Asian scholar addressing themes that are central
to his or her most significant and lasting contribution to Asian studies. The
series is committed to the rich variety of research and writing on Asia, and
is not restricted to any particular discipline, theoretical approach or
geographical expertise.

Popular culture, globalization and Japan

Edited by Matthew Allen and Rumi Sakamoto

LONDON AND NEW YORK

First published 2006
by Routledge
2 Park Square, Milton Park, Abingdon, Oxon, OX14 4RN

Simultaneously published in the USA and Canada
by Routledge
711 Third Avenue, New York, NY 10017, USA

Routledge is an imprint of the Taylor & Francis Group, an informa business

Typeset in Times by
Taylor & Francis Books

British Library Cataloguing in Publication Data
A catalogue record for this book is available from the British Library

Library of Congress Cataloging in Publication Data
A catalog record for this book has been requested

ISBN10: 0–415–36898–7 (hbk)
ISBN10: 0–415–44795–X (pbk)

ISBN13: 9–780–415–36898–8 (hbk)
ISBN13: 9–780–415–44795–9 (pbk)

Contents

PART II
Becoming global   115

Acknowledgments

We would like to thank a number of people and organizations for their help in producing this anthology. Of course, we are very grateful for the support of the series editor, Mark Selden, and for all the authors who contributed to the project. We are grateful, too, for the support of the School of Asian Studies at the University of Auckland, New Zealand. We'd like in particular to thank the generous and endlessly talented Chairman Zhang for his support of this project, and Chris Payne for his outstanding research work in the early stages. We would also like to thank the University of Auckland for its generous staff research grants programme.

Finally, we would like to express our appreciation to our respective partners and children, who gave us enough space and time to complete this project. Thanks Fiona, Peter, Sam, Ngaire, Billie and Leif! We could not have finished this without your cooperation and support.

Note on Japanese names and words

Japanese names appear in Japanese order, with surname first and given name second, with the exception of individuals who are known in reverse order, usually because they live outside Japan and/or publish in English, e.g. Kazuo Ishiguro rather than Ishiguro Kazuo.

Japanese words appear in italics, with macrons indicating long vowels, except with words commonly used internationally, e.g. Tokyo rather than Tokyô.

Notes on contributors

Matthew Allen is Associate Professor of Japanese History at the University of Auckland. His books include *Undermining the Japanese Miracle* (Cambridge University Press, 1994) and *Identity and Resistance in Okinawa* (Rowman and Littlefield, 2002). He has published a number of chapters in collected editions and articles in anthropology, psychiatry and history journals.

Romit Dasgupta lectures in Japanese Studies and Asian Studies in the School of Social and Cultural Studies at the University of Western Australia. His research interests are in articulations of genders and sexualities in Japan and Asia, and in expressions of in-between and diasporic Asian identities. He has published in the journal *Japanese Studies* and in the edited collections *Japanese Cybercultures* and *East Asian Masculinities* (Routledge, 2002). He is the co-editor of *Genders, Transgenders and Sexualities in Japan* (Routledge, 2005).

Hugh de Ferranti is Associate Professor of Japanese Studies at the University of New England, Australia. He researches Japanese historical, traditional and contemporary music culture. He is the author of *Japanese Musical Instruments* (Oxford University Press, 2000) and co-editor of *A Way a Lone: writings on Tôru Takemitsu* (Academica Music, Tokyo, 2002).

Todd Joseph Miles Holden is Professor of Mediated Sociology in the Graduate School of International Cultural Studies (GSICS) at Tohoku University. He has published extensively on globalization, identity and gender in television, advertising, news, Internet, and cell phones. His latest book is *medi@sia: communication and society in and out of global cultural context* (Routledge, forthcoming). Learn more by visiting *http://www.intcul.tohoku.ac.jp/~holden/index.html*.

Koichi Iwabuchi is Associate Professor in the School of International Liberal Studies at Waseda University, Japan. He has widely published on media, popular culture, globalization and transnationalism in Asian. He is the author of *Recentering Globalization* (Duke University Press, 2002) and the editor of *Feeling Asian Modernities* (Hong Kong University Press, 2004) and *Rogue Flows* (Hong Kong University Press, 2004).

Mark McLelland is Lecturer in the School of Social Sciences, Media and Communication at the University of Wollongong, Australia. He has published widely on Japanese gender, sexuality and the media and is the author of *Queer Japan from the Pacific War to the Internet Age* (Roman and Littlefield, 2005) and co-editor of *Japanese Cybercultures* (Routledge, 2002) and *Genders, Transgenders and Sexualities in Japan* (Routledge, 2005).

Yoshitaka Môri is Associate Professor in Department of Musical Creativity and the Environment at Tokyo National University of Fine Arts and Music. He has published on media, politics and cultural studies. He is the author of *Bunka=Seiji: gurobarizêshon-jidai no kûkan-hanran* (Culture= Politics: space–rebellion in the age of globalization) (Getsuyôsha, 2003) and has also edited a collection on the 'Korean Wave' in Japan (*Nisshiki Hanryû*, Serika Shobo, 2004).

Matthew Penney is a Commonwealth Scholar and doctoral candidate at the University of Auckland. He is currently carrying out research on images of war in Japanese popular culture. His recent article 'Rising sun, iron cross – military German in Japanese popular culture' has appeared in the journal *Japanstudien,* Vol. 17, Dec. 2005.

James Roberson is Professor of Anthropology at Tokyo Jogakkan College. He is author of 'Uchinâ Pop: place and identity in contemporary Okinawan popular music' in Laura Hein and Mark Selden (eds) *Islands of Discontent*, Lanham, MA: Rowman & Littlefield (2003) and of *Japanese Working Class Lives* (1998). Together with Nobue Suzuki, he is co-editor of *Men and Masculinities in Contemporary Japan* (RoutledgeCurzon 2003). His current research focuses on the cultural politics of identity and music in/out of contemporary Okinawa.

Rumi Sakamoto is Senior Lecturer in the School of Asian Studies at the University of Auckland, New Zealand. She has published on Japanese national identity and cultural studies. Her recent publication includes 'Civilising Japan: Zizek and the national other', in *From Z to A: Zizek at the antipodes* (Dunmore Press, 2005), and 'Comfort women, national apology and feminist politics', in *Asian Futures, Asian Traditions* (Global Oriental, 2005).

Yukako Sunaoshi is Associate Professor at the Faculty of International Communication, Gunma Prefectural Women's University. A linguistic anthropologist and sociolinguist, she has published on critical intercultural communication (e.g. in *Language in Society*) and language and gender (e.g. in *Japanese Language, Gender, and Ideology*, Oxford University Press, 2004).

1 Introduction

Inside-out Japan? Popular culture and globalization in the context of Japan

Matthew Allen and Rumi Sakamoto

It has become something of truism that in recent years 'Japanese' popular culture has spread its influence across the globe. This book addresses the relationship between Japan, popular culture, and globalization in ways that problematize the ownership of 'Japanese popular culture'. The chapters in this anthology all examine movements of popular cultural ideas and artefacts into and out of Japan, and are new takes on forms of popular culture that extend beyond the current Eurocentric notions of what it is that informs the production, distribution and consumption of 'Japanese popular culture'; that is, Japan as the Oriental or exotic Other.

By opening discourse that moves beyond the stereotypes about Japan that are commonly traded in within the academies and media of Europe, Asia, Australasia and the United States, we can ask significant questions about how 'global' influences cross borders. Using Japan as a case in point, we demonstrate that movements of ideas, technologies and products across borders influence both local and 'global' ideas and practice. From literature to art, from anthropology to history, from music to gay studies and from sports to media studies, authors in this anthology canvass a broad range of topics which employ the triplet of Japan, popular culture and globalization. In particular, authors focus on the dynamism of the processes; that is, all recognize that culture and popular culture are part of a highly mobile and transformative process that spreads beyond the borders of any single nation.

Globalization and Japan

In 1997 Mark Schilling wrote that from within Japan it was recognized that Japan had a 'strong presence' in the global economy but was perceived to have no international cultural presence (Schilling 1997: 9). This reflects a similar view of Japan's cultural global capital to that penned by Frederic Jameson, when he wrote, on Sony's acquisition of Columbia Pictures and Matsushita's buyout of MCA, that '[despite Japan's importance for the global economy], the Japanese were unable to master the essentially cultural productivity required to secure the globalization process' (Jameson 1998:

67). In recent years this has changed. Following the expansion of communications, the development of new technologies like cellular phones and the now almost redundant Walkman, and the prominent acquisitions of global film and music production and distribution houses by Japanese interests in the 1980s and 1990s, the explosion of international interest that began with *manga*, *anime* and video games and the increasing interpenetration of ideas, capital, culture and economics throughout Asia have led to things Japanese occupying a very high profile on the global stage. From *Hello Kitty* merchandise to *Pokemon* with its associated marketing, from the acclaimed films of Miyazaki Hayao to the less acclaimed but hardly less popular *Sailor Moon*, Japanese popular culture occupies a prominent place in today's increasingly connected globe.[1]

Scholarship on cultural globalization has advanced over recent years from early accounts of globalization as homogenization to more sophisticated interpretations. Its early variations included globalization as the West-centred advent of modernity into the rest of the world (Giddens 1990; Axford 1995; Spybey 1996); globalization as homogenization by the capitalist forces of multinational and transnational corporations; and globalization as American cultural domination, i.e. as a version of 'cultural imperialism' (Schiller and Nordenstreng 1979; Thomlinson 1991). Global processes of homogenization may be given a positive twist (celebrating the 'end of history'; see, for example, Fukuyama 1992) or a negative one ('McDonaldization of the world' and its clashing of local cultures). But, either way, in this schema the world is seen to be converging into a single, monolithic space under the juggernaut of global capitalism. Such arguments, which tend to assume an unproblematic relationship between economic and cultural spheres, equating economic and cultural forces, are not very convincing seen from outside the United States. In Japan, for example, although McDonald's can be found at every corner of its big cities and American and British popular music is a staple of Japanese youth, diverse and celebrated *local* forms of food, music, films and other cultural elements are also thriving, and there is also increasing influence pouring in from other parts of Asia. In terms of the outflow, too, despite Japan's place as the second largest economy in the world, the influence of Japanese technology in media and communications, the recent and rapid expansion of its popular culture abroad, and its location at the forefront of trends and fashions in Asia, clearly, the world is not being 'Japanized' either.

Rather than the homogenization thesis, then, what seems more useful is another set of more recent scholarships on globalization that proposes more complex models of interconnectedness and unevenness (Piaterse 2004; Appadurai 1996; Thomlinson 1999). According to these writers, what emerges through the process of globalization is not a uniform 'Global Culture', but increasing differences and complexity of locally inflected meanings due to hybridization and indigenization, which often contain conflicts and contradictions. In this book, we demonstrate that local differentiations and creative processes of adoption and adaptation with inflection are indeed happening around Japan-related popular culture. The process of cultural globalization understood this way also often involves a tension or even antagonism with a national desire/agenda, assumes a complicity with it or exhibits a total indifference to the national, depending on the what, who and when of each concrete case. Still, there is no doubt that multiple and often unpredictable interconnections are creating new situations and cultural hybrids rather than reducing human experiences to a monolithic mode.

One aim of this anthology is to provide a forum in which we can clarify some of the issues that emanate from the ascription of national characteristics to popular cultural artefacts, and the implications of assuming cultural 'ownership'. There is ample evidence to support the view that popular culture and globalization face a conundrum of ownership and location; for example, in Korea during the ban on Japanese popular cultural imports (1945–2004) *anime* from Japan was routinely imported and dubbed into Korean, and its Japanese origins were effectively disguised. Resolving, or at least highlighting, this conundrum of 'belonging' was one of the reasons for the decision to put together this volume. The eleven chapters that follow focus on Japan and its relations with the 'outside' world to demonstrate the dynamism that accompanies flows of popular culture between Japan and the globe. Collectively they show that the relations between Japan, popular culture and globalization are inside out, upside down and back to front. Most importantly, they are not simply about 'Japanese' popular culture.

This volume thus problematizes the 'Japaneseness' of Japanese popular culture by focusing on the intersection of globalization and popular cultural products associated with Japan. Instead of assuming that because it (be it *anime*, computer games or *Pokemon*) is produced in Japan, there must be something Japanese about it, we examine, through concrete case studies, how the production and consumption of each cultural product takes place both inside *and/or* outside Japan, at the conjunction of multiple forces and cultural influences. Importantly, this is not simply about Japan and the Other. It is not about simplistic resistance to and acceptance of popular cultural influence as a whole where only two forces meet (local and global, inside and outside, national and foreign). Our central thesis is that there are many 'insides' ('localities') and many more 'outsides' ('extra-localities'), which inform the production and consumption of 'Japanese popular culture'. The 'Japan' in 'Japanese popular culture' is always already dislocated, contaminated, cross-pollinated and criss-crossed.

The authors in this volume (many of whom themselves have multiple connections with places and cultures) engage different levels of the production, reproduction, consumption and re-consumption of aspects of popular culture. Each chapter provides a detailed case study, with close attention paid to the multiple forces and influences that overdetermine how a popular cultural product is produced, reproduced, interpreted, hybridized, indigenized and so forth. Each considers specific places and audiences, and political, economic, historical and cultural contexts. This is because we believe that only concrete and empirical studies can bring forward the complex process of producing meaning around the triplet of Japan, globalization and popular culture today. While discussions of globalization can often be highly abstract, this book attempts to add empirical content to the concepts related to globalization, such as 'interconnectedness', 'deterritorialization', 'compression of the world', 'intensification of consciousness of the world', 'hybridity', 'global flow' and so forth. This volume attempts to link theory to empirical studies, fleshing out theory and bringing out the unevenness of globalization processes.

Writing Japanese popular culture

Postwar Japan saw little academic interest in 'popular culture', with a few exceptions such as Tsurumi Shunsuke and Yoshimoto Takaaki, who wrote on *taishûbunka* (mass culture) from a perspective of mass/subculture as a reservoir of mass mentality rooted in everyday life and a potential site for popular resistance (Tsurumi 2001; Yoshimoto 1984). Since the 1990s, however, a number of scholarly works on popular culture have emerged. They are largely by younger-generation sociologists and media studies scholars who are familiar with poststructuralism and other theoretical tools for analysing cultural texts (e.g. Azuma 2001; Ueno and Mouri 2002). This coincided with Japanese universities' strategy to secure enough students in the time of '*shôshika*' (declining number of children) and sharply decreasing enrolments by opening new courses on *manga* and other popular culture, followed by publication of books based on 'lecture notes' from these often highly successful courses (e.g. Abe 2001; Shimizu 2002). Studies of popular cultural texts for mass consumption such as *manga*, *anime* and TV drama are now gradually finding their way into established academia, if still at the margins.

Of particular relevance to the themes in the volume is another group of works that look at Japanese popular culture in Asia in the context of cultural imperialism and/or globalization (e.g. Igarashi 1998; Chin 2000; Ishii 2001; Iwabuchi 2001). This approach is understandable as nowhere is the interconnectedness of globalization more true, and nowhere more contested, than in Asia. Because of Japan's past status as the colonizer/aggressor in Asia, there is wariness over the popularity of Japanese popular culture in many parts of Asia. Is popular culture simply a new way of culturally subjugating people in Asia? Or has globalization finally done away with the notion of the 'centre' and 'oppressor', instead offering a global flow of consumer goods with little or no Japaneseness attached? For some, especially those who promote 'soft power', the 'Japaneseness' of Japanese popular culture is hugely important. Aoki thus suggests that performing 'Cool Japan' serves 'the national interest' because it helps reduce anti-Japanese feelings in East Asia (Aoki 2004), whilst Ogura argues that Japan needs an active 'cultural diplomacy' of exporting 'Japanese spirit' via popular culture (Ogura 2004; see also Hamano 1999; McGray 2002).

Japan's international prominence, and its high profile in entertainment, fashion, literature and art, has also attracted English-language interest in Japan's relations with popular culture. John Treat's *Contemporary Japan and Popular Culture* (1996), D. P. Martinez's *The World of Japanese Popular Culture* (1998) and Timothy Craig's *Japan Pop: Inside the world of Japanese popular culture* (2000) all testify to this renewed fascination with things popular and Japanese. On one hand, their focus on the popular has certainly challenged the ubiquitous image of homogeneous, corporate Japan typically found in *nihonjinron* literature in the 1970s and 1980s, and offers a more differentiated view of Japanese society and culture. On the other hand, however, many such works seem to retain the local/global (national/international) dichotomy and the assumption that Japanese popular culture is essentially a 'national' culture. Effectively, many of these works seem to share assumptions about the nature of the 'essentialized Japan'.

The issue of the 'essentialized' Japan is a recurring theme in this anthology. Although the images of Japan as a country of tea ceremony and Noh theatre or of workaholic salarymen may have given way to those of Japan as quirky with a nerdy *otaku* subculture,[2] such new images are still understood to be something uniquely Japanese, especially in the English-language literature. Insofar as the 'Japaneseness' of Japanese popular culture is uncritically assumed, the basic logic – that it is the myth of the nation that retrospectively gives the unity to Japanese popular culture – remains the same. The same can be said about Japanese-language scholarship on Japanese popular culture, much of which focuses on Japanese popular culture in Asia in the context of Japan's cultural and economic hegemony in the region. While such works do usefully challenge the thesis of 'globalization as homogenization as Americanization', they seem uncritical of the assumption of Japanese popular culture as essentially and originally Japanese 'national' culture, which then travels intact to Asia.

Underscoring our inquiry, then, is how we can usefully engage the concept of globalization with specific relation to Japan and the production and consumption of popular culture. Although the issue of globalization has received considerable intellectual attention over the past decade or so, globalization and Japan's relationship with it have been relatively understudied. While Eades, Gill and Befu's contribution, *Globablization and Social Change in Contemporary Japan* (2000), contains some excellent work and Iwabuchi's *Recentering Globalization* (2002) breaks new ground in its theoretical location of Japan in the global community, few coherent studies have yet been produced in either Japanese or English that engage and ground Japan and globalization. This volume hopes to redress this through authors' individual engagement with the triplet mentioned above: globalization, popular culture and Japan.

We are also interested in the new cultural forms of 'local globalization' and 'global localization' that are emerging. In today's world, with increasing physical, monetary, linguistic and popular cultural mobilization and dissemination, the notion of any society free from the influence of others has become moot. And this means more than just saying that all 'national' cultures are under some global and external influence. Rather, locality is often fundamentally restructured and re-imagined through enmeshing global elements; but, simultaneously, global influences may also be restructured and re-imagined on the ground in socially distinctive ways. As a result, differentiating the local and the global is not always possible or useful. It seems to us that the concept of 'locality' itself must be reconsidered in the context of the movements of people across borders, the establishment of diasporic communities, linkages between the new and old homes, and significant restructuring of notions of belonging. Ideas associated with claims to 'ownership' of 'original', 'indigenous' and 'traditional' culture, which are used to reify the production of nationalism and cultural identity, would appear to have less and less explanatory power in understanding what is really happening.

Structuring accounts

The book is divided into two parts. Part I, 'Reconfiguring Japan', looks at what happens when Japan-originated cultural icons travel to other parts of the world. The chapters in Part I encompass a range of topics, all of which look at issues of global importance, with a focus on the movement offshore (to America, Asia, Australia, New Zealand) of icons that are identifiably Japanese. Each chapter introduces specific cases and each author engages the complexities of globalization in varied and interesting ways.

The section starts with Koichi Iwabuchi's chapter (Chapter 2) on the movement of Japanese popular cultural icons to Asia and the recentring of Japan in the region. He opens discourse on how historically driven concepts of national belonging can be overdetermined, particularly in Asia. The chapter looks critically at the privileging of 'America' as the centre of globalizing trends and proposes that by closely examining some of the intra-regional flows of popular culture in Asia, and the history of relations between Japan and its former colonies, we can see how these contribute to the formation of the feeling of 'living modern in East Asia'. Like other authors in this volume, he incorporates the wars in the Pacific and in Korea into his rhetoric of how history influences contemporary cultural flows. In the context of America-driven cultural globalization that has engendered the proliferation of global mass culture, he demonstrates how these flows forge transnational connections both dialogically and asymmetrically in terms of production, representation, distribution, regulation and consumption.

Matthew Allen's chapter (Chapter 3) focuses on the popular US animation series *South Park*'s representations of Japanese history, Japanese animation (*Pokemon*), Japanese culture, Japan's marketing of its culture and its (or the animators') obsession with cross-cultural comparisons of penis size. While the creators of the series display some very amusing insights into Japanese society and customs, they also insist on representing Japan as absolutely alien, comically incomprehensible, subtly manipulative, cunning, underhanded, imperial and intrinsically violent. The products that come from Japan are seen to be similarly manipulative, violent *and* addictive. Such representations of Japan have considerable historical precedence, especially during World War II, when Japanese were demonized by United States propaganda experts. *South Park* raises issues of how Self and Other are represented. In particular, the demonized images of Japan and empire are reinvigorated, this time within the context of the globalization of animation and related merchandising, exposing insights into the impact of the local on the global and vice versa.

In his essay on *Bishônen* in Chapter 4, Romit Dasgupta problematizes the issue of a global 'queer' within the context of interfaces between transnational cultural flows and configurations of 'queer' subjectivities in the Asia-Pacific region. Following Audrey Yue's account, he investigates what she names transnational 'Queer(N)Asian' identity, which often works to disrupt comfortable East/West, local/global binaries. In particular, he focuses on ways in which movements of 'diasporic' and/or regional popular culture engage with 'local' queer identities in crafting identities which are neither purely 'local' nor 'global'. This chapter discusses one specific example of this interface in a 'Queer(N)Asian' context – the 1998 Hong Kong production *Bishônen*, a film which draws on the genre of Japanese *shôjo manga* representations of male–male intimacy, in articulating a diasporic/transregional 'Queer(N)Asian' identity.

In Chapter 5 Hugh de Ferranti looks at how an Australian performance group, TaikOz, has adapted Japanese musical 'tradition' to present Japanese *taiko* drumming to Australian audiences. The compound name of the nationally renowned TaikOz (*taiko* – Oz) suggests that their intention from the first has been both to introduce *taiko* performance to Australians who otherwise know nothing of Japanese music and to achieve popular commercial success through appealing to mainstream Australian tastes. *TaikOz* draws on *kumidaiko*, a form of drumming that has been practised outside Japan by groups whose majority membership is Americans of Japanese and Asian descent, and which became emblematic of Asian-American identity in the 1990s. In the case he analyses, though, the make-up of the group differs, consisting primarily of classically trained Australian-European percussionists dressed in Japanese-style clothing. His analysis of presentational strategies suggests how TaikOz, and *taiko* drumming itself, has in the space of just a few years become one of the most vivid and recurrent images of 'traditional' Japan for Australians today.

Yukako Sunaoshi's chapter (Chapter 6) on the audience for Japanese *manga* overseas provides insights into who consumes these artefacts of

Japanese popular culture, how they consume them and why they consume them. She interviews local diasporic Asian *manga* readers, mostly students living in Auckland, New Zealand. It appears that most of her sample group are already culturally mobile, linguistically sophisticated and have expectations of service provided by *manga* rental shops and libraries, commonly owned by Chinese and Korean immigrants. She finds that, as part of the process of globalization, many students had been exposed to either Japanese *manga* (translated) or local versions of *manga* in their home country and have continued to read them, often somewhat nostalgically, while overseas. On the other hand, she finds that a localized process of globalization is occurring; that is, *manga* become a communicative tool for 'Asians' to cross cultures and bond with other 'Asians' in a predominantly Anglo-European society.

Part II, 'Becoming global', examines what happens when popular cultural influences from outside Japan are brought to Japan and generate impacts on Japanese society and culture. All of these chapters problematize the simplistic reading of global influence over local culture as an encounter between two separate entities, and instead emphasize the difficulty of locating popular culture in one society or another. Moreover, they emphasize, as do the chapters in Part I, the multilateral flows of cultural influences in the production and consumption of popular culture, thus questioning the validity of a simplistic binary vision of 'inside' and 'outside'.

In Chapter 7 Todd Holden coins the phrase, 'sportsports', a wordplay on 'sports exports' in examining how Japanese sports stars who are successful overseas – particularly in the United States – are received, written about and generally consumed in Japan. He critically assesses whether they hold the same status in their host society as in Japan. The parochial interpretations of the 'global success' of Japanese sports stars provide us with some meaningful insights into the nature of the increasing interpenetration of global and local narratives. Holden argues that Japan is currently in the midst of a 'career': one defined and driven by 'sports exports/sports imports' and fuelled by media such as news, entertainment programming, advertising and the Internet. The effect of this flow – of sports talent and its parasitic informatics – is expressed in Japanese media in terms of conceptions of inside and outside, local and global, nation, Self and Other. By investigating 'sportsports', he documents multiple societal effects of the impact of these sports stars' careers overseas.

Rumi Sakamoto, in Chapter 8, looks at some 'border-crossing' literature written by ethnically non-Japanese authors in the Japanese language, within the context of globalization. Although literature has been relatively slow in crossing national borders and creating hybrid forms, the equation between the national community, national language and national literature is now being challenged by these authors. Focusing on four autobiographical novels, she offers a reading of how each author distinctively articulates identities that are 'in-between' and 'neither here nor there'. Although they are all writing for the Japanese market in Japanese, depicting a 'hybrid' existence at the intersection of two or more cultures, each author is positioned differently in relation to the mainstream Japanese society and its dominant myth of homogeneity. The chapter, then, examines 'border-crossing' identity not as an abstract and generalized principle of hybridity but in its specific forms of articulation in concrete and specific historical and political contexts.

Mark McLelland draws on his extensive research experience with Japanese gay culture to examine the impact of 'Western' mores on the production of gay values in Japan in Chapter 9. Employing an historical perspective, he interrogates some of the assumptions commonly made about 'transcultural reductiveness', and proposes that *both* Western and non-Western cultures of gender and sexuality have been, and continue to be, mutually transformed through their encounters with transnational forms of sexual knowledge. Sexual knowledge is neither a local nor a global phenomenon, he argues, but is rather a hybridization of values, moving beyond the local essentialist and global homogenization discourses. By examining the emergence of one Japanese sexual category – that of the *gei bôi* (gay boy) – he demonstrates that sexual identity is a product of hybridizing global processes and is neither simply a continuation of a premodern category nor a product of direct import from the 'West'.

Chapter 10, by Yoshitaka Môri, examines the relationship between contemporary Japanese art and visual pop culture in Japan by looking at practices of young artists, including Takashi Murakami and Makoto Aida, who have recently been successful in the Western art scene. They have explicitly referred to the influence of subculture such as *manga, anime* and video games as well as 'authentic' fine art, and have tried to delineate the specific historical conditions under which Japanese art has developed since World War II by employing, in distinctive ways, the concept of 'Japaneseness'. Mouri addresses two issues: first, the way in which the young artists started to apply pop culture methods to their fine art practices and how they became successful in the West; second, he reconsiders how these artists were able to appropriate specific 'war paintings' imagery in their art works, arguing that these paintings from World War II were crucially important to the development of postwar Japanese artists. He demonstrates new ways of understanding the relationship between Japanese art and pop culture, high culture and popular culture, and modernity and postmodernity.

In the next chapter (Chapter 11) Matthew Penney focuses on the work of Saotome Katsumoto, the popular anti-war artist, writer and illustrator. He shows how Saotome embraces images of both 'victim' and 'victimizer' in dealing with Japan's controversial past, an issue that has had considerable (and contentious) resonance in recent years. He argues that Saotome incorporates a breadth of approaches, making selective use of the 'universal' and the particular, as part of his strategy for entertaining and educating Japanese readers. Penney moves against the grain here of much Western writing on this topic, and demonstrates convincingly not only that Japanese history has a self-critical reflexive cast in the medium of popular culture, but also that there are substantial and deeply rooted elements of critique which underscore the current superficial representation of Japan's interpretation of its own history. Saotome, he argues, with his very large readership, uses 'universal' ideas rooted in particular utilization, and symbols and images coming from the outside in, to deconstruct and reconstruct Japan's past wartime experience. This does not negate the value of 'local' and 'global' as concepts, but rather shows the extent to which local discourse and narratives have been questioned, probed and broadened.

In the final chapter (Chapter 12) James E. Roberson has contributed a thought-provoking account of the development and representation of Okinawan popular music both as a form of 'ethnic music' and as one of Japan's contributions to 'world music'. He argues against the externally composed aural hegemony on 'Okinawan music' which is homogenizing, apolitical and ahistorical, and which suggests that authentic 'Okinawan' music is either that which is 'traditional' and relatively unchanging or is 'modern' in its exotic hybridity. Resisting this approach, in this chapter he restores history to 'Okinawan' music, inserting other musical genres into the mix of musics in and out of Okinawa. This is done by dislocating Okinawan musics in the specific contexts of historically shifting relations, penetrations and departures of and from local, national and global sites and spheres, bringing into question (the question of) just what is 'Okinawan music'. He focuses in particular on the emergence, especially since the late 1960s, of a series of performers in and (from) outside Okinawa whose music requires more complex understandings of 'Okinawan music' and of 'Okinawa'.

Through these case studies it will become apparent that the notion of globalization as homogenization (and in particular as Americanization) is untenable. What we are witnessing, and participating in, is not a homogeneous 'global culture', but various globalized local cultures, where the boundary between the original and copy, or the origin and destination, is constantly negotiated, reinvented and blurred. We thus propose a new framework of engagement with the topic of globalization and popular culture. It is clear that the local is not simply a counterforce to globalization, but a complex set of relations, some of which are, in fact, 'global'. More than hybridity, which in Homi Bhabha's terminology relates to the Fanon-inspired approach to the hierarchy of colonial power (Bhabha 1994), we propose to frame understanding popular culture associated with Japan within the context of a complex matrix of relations that include multiple power relations such as race or ethnicity, gender, class, ageism, popularity of popular culture, and the impacts of outside influences on producers and consumers of popular culture.

In particular, we hope that the authors in this volume are able to argue convincingly that contemporary 'Japanese popular culture' is far more complex and variegated than it is often represented. Indeed, the flows of influence both to and from Japan and the dynamics of this production and consumption of popular culture strongly indicate that there is considerable potential for much more research in this fascinating and rewarding field of study.

Notes

1 For the purposes of this book, we have employed a very broad definition of popular culture, which includes notions that move beyond simply 'the popular'. At its most elemental level, it can be said that popular culture is simply culture that is well liked by a lot of people. But this is reductionist and needs further explication. We need also to consider *how* it is that popular culture can appeal to so many people in so many nations and *what* it is that is so appealing about the artefacts that we are examining in this volume. Moreover, for our authors the desire to engage the global dimension of popular culture in the context of either the production or reception of artefacts in Japan is of central importance. Moreover, while some authors in this volume discuss, for example, phenomena that involve a mass audience, we are more interested in the processes that contribute to the flows of ideas as they move across borders.

2 *Otaku* refers to a group of usually young men who spend much of their time interacting with computers and other likeminded individuals in the quest to develop computer gaming skills, animation drawing skills and other effectively solitary activities. Computers provide these people with a communicative outlet for their singular lifestyles.

Bibliography

Abe, C. (2001) *Seikai sabukaruchâ kôgi* (Notes on lectures on subculture), Tokyo: Kawadeshobô Shinsha.

Aoki, T. (2004) 'Kûru pawâ kokka nihon no sôzô o! (Creating Japan as a cool power state)', *Chûôkôron*, October: 198–209.

Appadurai, A. (1996) *Modernity at Large: cultural dimensions of globalization*, Minneapolis, MN: University of Minnesota Press.

Axford, B. (1995) *The Global System: economics, politics and culture*, Cambridge: Polity Press.

Azuma, H. (2001) *Dôbutsuka suru posuto modan: oteku kara mita nihon-shakai* (Animalizing postmodern: Japanese society seen from *otaku*), Tokyo: Kôdansha Gendai Shinsho.

Bhabha, H. (1994) *The Location of Culture*, London: Routledge.

Chin, L. (2000) 'Globalizing the regional, regionalizing the global: mass culture and Asianism in the age of late capital', *Public Culture*, vol. 12, no. 1: 233–57.

Craig, T. (2000) *Japan Pop!*, Armonk, NY, and London: M. E. Sharpe.

Eades, J. S., Gill, T. and Befu, H. (eds) (2000) *Globalization and Social Change in Contemporary Japan*, Melbourne: Trans Pacific Press.

Fukuyama, F. (1992) *End of the History and the Last Man*, New York: Free Press.

Giddens, A. (1990) *The Consequences of Modernity*, London: Polity Press.

Hamano, Y. (1999) 'Nihon animêshon kôkoku-ron (Japanese animation empowers the country)', *Chûôkôron*, April: 138–53.

Igarashi, A. (1998) *Hen'yô suru ajia to nihon: ajia-shakai ni shintô suru nihon no popyurâ karuchâ* (Japan and Asia in transition: Japanese popular culture infiltrating into Asian societies), Tokyo: Seshiki Shobô.

Ishii, K. (ed.) (2001) *Higashi ajia no nihon taishu bunka* (Japanese popular culture in East Asia), Tokyo: Sôsôsha.

Iwabuchi, K. (2001) *Toransunashonaru Japan: ajia o tsunagu popyurâ bunka* (Transnational Japan: popular culture linking Asia), Tokyo: Iwanami Shoten.

——(2002) *Recentering Globalization: popular culture and Japanese transnationalism*, Durham, NC, and London: Duke University Press.

Jameson, F. (1998) 'Globalization as philosophical issue', in F. Jameson and M. Miyoshi (eds) *The Cultures of Globalization*, Durham, NC, and London: Duke University Press.

McGray, D. (2002) 'Japan's gross national cool', *Foreign Policy* 130: 44–54.

Martinez, D. P. (ed.) (1998) *The Worlds of Japanese Popular Culture: gender, shifting boundaries and global cultures*, Cambridge: Cambridge University Press.

Nye, J. (2004) *Soft Power: the means to success in world politics*, New York: Public Affairs.

Ogura K. (2004) 'Kokusai-zai no shin no kachi koso sekai ni hasshin shyô (Let's export the real value of international property)', *Chûôkôron*, October: 210–17.

Piaterse, J. N. (2004) *Globalization and Culture: global mélange*, Oxford: Rowman and Littlefield.

Schilling, M. (1997) *The Encyclopedia of Japanese Pop Culture*, New York: Weatherhill.

Shimizu, M. (2002) '*Manga-ron*' *e yôkoso* (Welcome to '*manga* studies')', Tokyo: D-bungaku Kenkyûkai.

Spybey, T. (1996) *Globalization and World Society*, Cambridge: Polity Press.

Thomlinson, J. (1991) *Cultural Imperialism: a critical introduction*, Baltimore, MD: Johns Hopkins University Press.

——(1999) *Globalization and Culture*, Chicago: University of Chicago Press.

Treat, J. (ed.) (1996) *Contemporary Japan and Popular Culture*, Honolulu: University of Hawaii Press.

Tsurumi, S. (2001) *Sengo nihon no taishûbunkashi* (History of mass culture in postwar Japan), Tokyo: Iwanami Gendai Bunko.

Ueno, T. and Mouri, Y. (2002) *Jissen karuchuraru sutadîzu* (Practising cultural studies), Tokyo: Chikuma Shinsho.

Yoshimoto, T. (1984) *Masu imêji-ron* (On mass image), Tokyo: Fukutake Shoten.

Part I
Reconfiguring Japan

2 Japanese popular culture and postcolonial desire for 'Asia'[1]

Koichi Iwabuchi

Introduction

> Cute Power! Asia is in love with Japan's pop culture . . . Everybody loves Japan! . . . Ask anybody in Asia: Western-style cool is out. Everything Japanese is in – and oh, so 'cute'!
>
> (*Newsweek Asia*, 8 November 1999)

> Pop passions – From animation to idols, Japanese youth culture building formidable army of devotees throughout the region (Asia).
>
> (*Nikkei Weekly*, 21 May 2001)

It has been widely recognized that any comprehensive analysis of cultural globalization needs to complicate the straightforward argument for the homogenization of the world based on Western Modernity. The rise of non-Western cultural centres of power such as Japan and Brazil, as well as lively local practices of cultural appropriation and hybridization, has often been pointed out to refute a straightforward view of Western cultural domination and to support an argument for decentralized Western cultural hegemony (e.g. Tomlinson 1997; Morley and Robins 1995). However, the arguments for transculturation, heterogenization, hybridization and creolization in the study of transnational flows of media and popular cultures still tend not to transcend the West/Rest paradigm in a satisfactory way. While there have been fascinating analyses of (non-Western) local consumption of Western media texts (e.g. Miller 1992, 1995) which go beyond a dichotomized perspective of the global and the local, 'global' still tends to be exclusively associated with the West and global–local interactions are mostly considered in terms of how the non-West responds to the West. It is based upon an assumption of the unbeatable Western (American) domination and the arguments are focused on how the non-West resists, imitates, or appropriates it. Dynamic interactions among non-Western cultural modernities have been seriously under-explored.

Since the mid-1990s, such an interaction has become more and more conspicuous in East Asian contexts. The development of digitalized communication

technologies has facilitated the simultaneous circulation of media information, images and texts on a global level. Various (national) markets are being
penetrated and integrated by powerful global media giants such as News
Corp., Sony and Disney. However, globalization does not just mean the
spread of the same (American) products all over the world through
American media giants. Technological convergence has also facilitated the
capitalization on regional cultural resonance. The recent rise of Asian
economic power which has given birth to various modes of vernacular
modernities in East Asia, together with globalization processes, shed light on
(dis)similar experience of urbanization, modernization and proliferation of
middle-class consumer culture in East Asia (Ang and Stratton 1996). In
these contexts, economic growth in Asia has not just given birth to affluent
youth-culture markets in the region to be penetrated by American popular
culture. Intra-regional cultural flows have simultaneously been activated in
many parts of the world with the emergence of several regional media
centres.

Here, new patterns of regional media consumption and collaboration
among local cultural industries have been generated. Cultural flows among
East Asian countries, particularly between Japan, Taiwan, Hong Kong,
China and South Korea are gradually becoming active and constant more
than ever. While the flows are becoming bilateral, and at times even multilateral, Japanese popular culture at the moment plays a central role in the flow.
As a former colonial power Japan has long been exerting cultural influence
on East and South East Asia. It is in the 1990s, however, that Japanese
cultural presence became much more conspicuous, when local industries of
East Asia found commercial value in promoting Japanese/Asian popular
culture with local markets increasingly capitalized (Iwabuchi 1998, 1999,
2001). From animation and comics to fashion, pop music and TV dramas,
Japanese popular culture has been so well received in East and Southeast
Asia that the above-quoted media coverage does not sound as remarkable as
it did just a few years ago.

Unlike conservative Asian-value discourses, the emerging resonance felt
among young people in East Asia is not based upon exclusive views of
primordial cultural traditions, because popular culture unavoidably
embodies heterogeneous origins and routes of cultural mixing. The image of
Asian youth, at least in marketing terms, might be defined as one of a
consuming hybrid; youth who have material power and passion for
consuming globally spread, fashionable cultural products and who do not
care about the origin of those consumer items or media products from a
political perspective. Nevertheless, preferred cultural products are not
without 'East Asian flavour'. Many young people in Taiwan and Hong
Kong, for example, might love *Titanic* and Mariah Carey, but are even more
addicted to the romance of Japanese TV dramas such as *Tokyo Love Story*
and *Love Generation* and the latest Asian pop music of Faye Wong or Utada
Hikaru. Those popular cultural forms made in East Asia are neither 'Asian'

in any essentialist meaning nor second-rate copies of 'American originals'. In these texts, the meaning of being modern is reworked in an Asian context, with various latest fads from all over the world intermingled. It is in this sense that I suggest that affluent youth in East and Southeast Asia are keen to consume things which are inescapably global and (East) Asian at the same time. Non-Western countries long tended to face the West to interpret their position and understand the distance from Modernity. The encounter has always been based upon the expectation of cultural difference and temporal lag. However, now some non-Western 'modern' countries are facing each other to find neighbours experiencing and feeling similar things and temporality of East Asian vernacular modernities via American-dominated cultural globalization. If Japanese popular culture tastes and smells like dim sum and kimchi by media industries and consumers in Hong Kong, Taiwan and South Korea, it might be because it lucidly represents an intertwined composition of global homogenization and heterogenization in an East Asian context.

However, it should be stressed that increasing intra-Asian cultural flows newly highlight uneven power relations in the region. It has been widely acknowledged that consumers are not cultural dupes manipulated by cultural industries but actively appropriate cultural products not of their own making and produce various meanings out of them. Nevertheless, the active construction of meanings takes place within the system of global capitalism, in which Japan has a major role. People's freedom of negotiation at the receiving end of the global cultural flow operates under unambiguously asymmetrical relations. The careful analysis of intra-Asian cultural flows will highlight the newly articulated time–space configurations and asymmetrical cultural power relations inflected with the recuperation of Japan's transnational desire for 'Asia', which is strongly shadowed by Japan's imperial legacy in the region.[2] In this paper, I scrutinize Japanese discourses to see how Japan's historically constituted Orientalist conception of 'Asia' and its desire for connecting (with) Asia resurfaced with the rise of Asian economies and the transnational reach of Japanese popular culture in the region in the 1990s. It was a time when Japan began reasserting its Asian identity after a long retreat following the defeat of World War II, when the cultural geography of 'Asia' reappeared in the Japanese national imaginary at the very time when Japan faced the challenge of (re)constructing its national/cultural identity in the era of globalization. While the Japanese popular cultural encounter with other Asian countries in the 1990s was more multiple, contradictory and ambivalent than a totalizing and cavalier Japanese Orientalist conception of 'Asia' would suggest, Japan's condescending sense of being the leader of Asia and the asymmetrical power relationship between Japan and (the rest of) Asia are still intact. Japan's cultural nationalist project has been reconfigured within a transnational and postcolonial framework, which increasingly capitalizes on the regional cultural resonance in Asia.

Trans/nationalism

Recently, the term 'transnational' or 'transnationalism' has come to be commonly used in academic discourses on globalization. The merit of the term 'transnational' in comparison with other related terms is various. As Hannerz argues, it is 'more humble, and often a more adequate label for phenomena which can be of quite variable scale and distribution' (1996: 6) than the term 'global', which sounds too all-inclusive and exhaustive. 'Transnational' also has a merit over 'international' that actors are not confined to the nation-state but range from individuals to various organizations and groups. While we should not underestimate the salience of the nation-state in the process of globalization, 'transnational' opens a new perspective on the flows, disregarding the boundaries set up and controlled by the nation-states, the most important of which are the those of capital, people and media/images (Appadurai 1996). Hence, transnationalism is first and foremost connected to the flows of diaspora as well as those of capital. In either case, the efficacy of the nation-state's boundary policing in the modern constitution of politics, economy and culture is deeply problematized.

However, it should be remembered that transnational connections do not fully displace national boundaries, thoughts and feelings. Rather, as Roger Rouse (1995: 380) argues, '[t]he transnational has not so much displaced the national as resituated it and thus reworked its meanings'.This point is particularly important when we look at Japan's widely observed reorientation towards 'Asia' in the 1990s (Iwabuchi 1999). With the emergence of an Asian capitalist sphere in which Japanese popular culture finds wider audiences, Japan's exploitative articulation of Asian cultural commonality has been reframed to accommodate itself to the disjunctive transnational flows of capital, cultural products and imagination (Appadurai 1996). Transnational popular cultural flows highlight the fact that it has become no longer tenable for Japan to contain its cultural orientation and agendas within clearly demarcated national boundaries. Yet, or perhaps precisely because of the impossibility of controlling the globalization process within a national framework, the transgressive tendency of popular culture and its boundary-violating impulse of cultural hybridization are never free from nationalizing forces, desperately seeking to re-demarcate cultural boundaries.

This is most markedly discerned in discourse developed by Japanese conservative thinkers, for whom capitalist modernizing Asia is a site where Japan's longstanding nationalist project for extending its cultural reach to a pan-Asian sphere has been reactivated. While, as Watson argues, '[t]ransnationalism describes a condition by which people, commodities, and ideas literally cross – transgress – national boundaries and are not identified with a single place of origin' (1997: 11), there has emerged in Japan a reactionary discourse of what can be called trans/nationalism, which is a claim for a distinctive Japanese cultural power against all the odds of transnational cultural flows. Any claim to universality is apt to be interconnected with the project of domination. As we see more closely below, the growing Japanese interest in its cultural export tends to be informed predominantly by the (unrealizable) impulse of containing intensified transnational flows within a nationalist framework; that is, to articulate a distinct 'Japaneseness' in popular cultural forms, to raise Japan's position in Asia, and to (re)assert Japan's cultural superiority. Here, the transnationalization of Japanese popular culture has not simply offered an emergent sense of nationalistic pride; it is strongly overdetermined by Japan's imperialist history and thus intertwined with its postcolonial desire for 'Asia'.

In the following, I will deal with how Japanese transnational cultural power is reasserted and newly articulated in terms of postcolonial imaginary. I will explore the ways in which the media globalization process generates Japan's nationalistic discourse on its transnational cultural power in Asia, the ways in which the transnational intersects with the postcolonial.

'In but above Asia': commonality and superiority

Many studies show that Japanese national/cultural identity has been constructed in an essentialist manner through its conscious self-Orientalizing discourse, a narrative which at once testifies to a firm incorporation into, and subtle exploitation of, Western Orientalist discourse (see Sakai 1989; Iwabuchi 1994). Japan is represented and represents itself as culturally exclusive, homogeneous and uniquely particularistic through the operation of a strategic binary opposition between two imaginary cultural entities, 'Japan' and 'the West'. This is not to say that 'Asia' has no cultural significance in the construction of Japanese national identity. Rather, the complicity between Western Orientalism and Japan's self-Orientalism effectively works only when Japanese cultural power in Asia is subsumed under Japan's cultural subordination to the West. While Japan's construction of its national identity through an unambiguous comparison of itself with 'the West' is a historically embedded project, Japan's modern national identity has always been imagined in an asymmetrical totalizing triad between 'Asia', 'the West' and 'Japan'.

It is widely observed that Japan and Asia tend to be discussed and perceived within Japan as two separate geographies, its inherent contradiction unquestioned. Japan is located in a geography called 'Asia', but it no less unambiguously exists outside a cultural imaginary of 'Asia' in Japanese mental maps. This points to the fact that 'Asia' has overtly or covertly played a constitutive part in Japan's construction of national identity. While 'the West' played the role of the modern Other to be emulated, 'Asia' was cast as the image of Japan's past, a negative picture which tells of the extent to which Japan has been successfully modernized according to the Western standard (Tanaka 1993; Kang 1996). As Takeuchi (1993: 103) points out, in the process of Japanese imperial expansion Japan came to be perceived to rise above other Asian countries, and 'Japan' and 'Asia' became two separate entities in Japanese discourse. The binary opposition between 'traditional' or 'underdeveloped' Asia and the 'developed' West has been necessary for Japan to be able to construct its national identity in a modern and West-dominated world order. Japan has constructed an oriental Orientalism against inferior Asia (Robertson 1998: 97–101).

However, the Japanese discursive construction of 'Asia' is marked by the impossibility of clear separation between Japan and Asia. As Stefan Tanaka commented when discussing Japanese Orientalism in the early twentieth century, Japan's 'Asia' poses an uneasy question of 'how to become modern while simultaneously shedding the objectivistic category of Oriental and yet not lose an identity' (1993: 3). While an essentialist pan-Asianism had been expressed along with de-Asianization since the late nineteenth century, the 1930s and 1940s particularly saw the passionate advocacy of pan-Asianist ideology by Japanese nationalistic thinkers, who understood the issue of 'commonality and difference' in Japan's relationship to other Asian nations mostly in terms such as 'similar but superior' or 'in but above Asia'. As the only non-Western imperial and colonial power which invaded geographically, racially and culturally contiguous Asian regions, Japan resorted to an ideology of pan-Asianism to camouflage its imperial ambitions. The idea of the Great East Asian Co-prosperity Sphere, promulgated at the time, was a claim for an Asian solidarity based in an inherent 'Asian' bond able to counter Western evil. The advocacy of cultural and racial commonality between Japan and other Asian nations naturally conferred upon Japan a mission to rid Asia of Western imperial domination and itself to civilize other Asians instead (Peattie 1984). Undoubtedly such a conception of its mission was highly motivated by Japanese anti-Western sentiment in response to the Western racist refusal to allow Japan to become a member of the Imperial club (Dower 1986).

The articulation of commonality and superiority still lingers as a source of ambivalence, which has long governed Japanese discourses on the recent spread of Japanese media and popular culture to other parts of Asia. For Japanese nationalists, the spread of Japanese popular culture to other Asian regions simply demonstrates Japanese cultural hegemony in the region, while also inferring a sameness between the Japanese and Asian populaces. Although Japan's prolonged economic recession in the late 1990s seems to have been detrimental to the legitimacy of the argument, the spread of Japanese popular culture in other parts of Asia easily led to the 'Asia-yearning-for-Japan' idea which confirms the shift of power from the United States to Japan around the 1990s. The eager reception of Japanese anima-tions and computer games among some Western fans as well as TV dramas and popular music among Asians, for example, arouses a nationalist claim that Japan has become the object of international yearning, as America once was for Japanese (see, e.g., Morita and Ishihara 1989: 151). This view reflected a belief that Asian people are now yearning for Japanese affluence, technology and popular culture in exactly the same way that the Japanese people once yearned for the American way of life in the postwar era.

This unambiguous claim of Japanese cultural superiority over other Asian countries is, again, camouflaged by apparent cultural commonality. This is clearly shown by Ishihara's subtle emphasis on observing the spread of Japanese popular culture in Asia from Japanese cultural superiority to that of Asian commonality. In a controversial book co-authored with Malaysian prime minister Mahathir, *The Voice of Asia* (1995), Ishihara refers to the spread of Japanese popular culture in Asia as a manifestation of the 'natural' commonality shared by Asians (Mahathir and Ishihara 1995: 87–9). Ishihara argues, referring to the spread of Japanese popular culture throughout Asia, that '[o]ur popular culture strikes a sympathetic chord across Asia. No hard sell is necessary: the audience is receptive' (Mahathir and Ishihara 1995: 88).

It can be argued that young people in Taiwan or Hong Kong actually perceive the sense of cultural similarity or proximity in positive ways in consuming Japanese popular cultural forms. Yet, even if this is the case, audience identification of cultural proximity should not be seen in any essentialist manner. It is a more complex and dynamic process of 'becoming', in which the perception of comfortable distance and cultural similarity is based upon a recognition that Taiwan, Hong Kong and Japan live in the same temporality, the recognition brought about by the narrowing gap of material conditions and the (globally) converging tendency in terms of the urban consumerism of an expanding middle class, the changing role of women in society and the development of transnational communication technologies and media industries. Hence, even if a craving for Japanese popular culture and consumer commodities is being generated among the youth in East Asia, it is not comparable to the yearning for 'America' evoked in 1960s or 1970s Japan, in which the people found pleasure in identifying with the materially and symbolically unambiguously superior centre (Iwabuchi 2001). However, as in the prewar era, the search for commonality between Japan and Asia and the articulation of Japan's leading role in Asia are effortlessly linked together as two sides of the same coin.

Hybridism

As Ching (2000) points out, while the object of such discourse has significantly shifted from aesthetics or high culture to commercialized popular culture, the similarity between prewar pan-Asianism exemplified by Okakura Tenshin's (1904) 'Asia is one' and the 1990s pan-Asianism uttered by Japanese nationalists is remarkable. With the turn of attention to modern consumerism and an affluent middle-class culture, the recent discourse finds the commonality between Japan and Asia less in Asian origin or values than in the common experience of absorption of Western modern civilization (see, e.g., Funabashi 1993; Yamazaki 1996). It is argued that the keen indigenization of Western modern civilization is giving birth to a shared (East) Asian civilization for the first time in history.

Notably, the emerging 'Asianness' is primarily articulated in the shared pursuit of urban consumption of Americanized (Westernized) popular culture. However, the spread of Japanese popular culture in Asia, like the prewar pan-Asianism discourse, does not simply generate an essentialized claim of Asian commonality but an ideological assertion that Japan's national identity should no longer be constructed simply in terms of its 'unique' receptiveness to Western Modernity. Rather, its capacity for producing attractive cultural products and disseminating them abroad, particularly to Asia, and its leading role in creating an Asian popular cultural sphere should feature in any such construction. Popular and consumer culture thus have become hot fields where Japanese commentators try to identify Japan's Asian identity and to newly assert Japan's position 'in and above' Asia through its sophisticated ability of indigenizing foreign cultures.

The argument that Japan and Asia share the common experience of 'hybrid' modernization is easily developed into the assertion that Japan's experience can be a model for other Asians' emulation – a position which presumes that Japan is a non-Western nation that has most sincerely and successfully absorbed Western civilization and culture (e.g. Kawakatsu 1991: 244–7; 1995: 81). Here, the Japanese mode of indigenized modernity is articulated as the model for other (East) Asian nations where Western civilization has been rapidly and eagerly indigenized. This is again reminiscent of the fact that Japan's imperialist claim of its superiority over other Asians was based upon its experience of quick, successful Westernization (Duus 1995). Only submission to Western cultural power made it at all possible for Japan to differentiate itself from other 'backward' Asians.

As indigenization refers to the local appropriation of foreign cultures and cultural products by mixing them up with local tradition and culture, it does not necessarily mean the incorporation of a new cultural form into pre-given, unchangeable indigenous cultural patterns but suggests 'a product of collective and spectacular experiments with modernity' (Appadurai 1996: 90). Although cultural indigenization is often accompanied by a substantial modern transformation of existing cultural forms and social structures, the discourse on indigenization tends to emphasize the immortality of local cultural patterns in the appropriation of the foreign (Buell 1994). An essentialist configuration of indigenization, what I call hybridism, is a key to understanding how Japanese national identity is re-imagined in the context of ever-increasing transnational cultural flows. Japan's response to globalization is producing less a straightforward exclusive national identity than a curiously inclusive imagining of its culture or civilization in the global cultural flow; the construction of a Japanese affirmative hybridism by which the putative Japanese national essence is imagined in terms of its exceptional capacity for cultural absorption of the foreign (see Iwabuchi 1998).

In the prewar era the Japanese capacity for assimilation was discussed from the perspective of the racially mixed origins of the Japanese people as well as the long history of importing foreign cultures. This point is particularly important when we consider how the image of the Japanese fusion of East and West was firmly incorporated into Japanese imperial ideology, which regarded the Japanese sovereignty over Asia as a national mission. In the first part of the twentieth century, Japan, as a colonizing centre, was concerned with the assimilation of non-Western (Asian) racial and cultural others into the empire as well as managing the absorption of Western ideas, technologies and culture. As Oguma Eiji (1995) shows in detail, there were competing arguments in prewar Japan, first evoked by Western scientific discourse, about the racial origin of the Japanese. Yet this discourse on the racially mixed origin of the Japanese was readily appropriated to justify Japanese colonial rule over other Asian nations: since Japan has long successfully assimilated foreign (Asian) races as well as culture, Japan is endowed with the capacity to harmoniously assimilate colonial subjects in Taiwan and Korea. Therefore, so the argument goes, Japanese colonial rule and assimilation policy, unlike those of its Western counterparts, is not based on racism (see, e.g., Peattie 1984; Oguma 1995; Duus 1995; Morris-Suzuki 1998). Needless to say, this ideology of Japanese racial hybridism sharply contradicted the reality of Japanese colonial rule and its harsh racial discrimination against people in Korea, Taiwan and China (Komagome 1996).

Ambivalence concerning the evaluation of Japan's assimilation of the foreign continued on after World War II into the second half of the twentieth century. However, there is a fundamental difference between prewar and postwar Japan. After the war, Japan no longer had to consider racial differences within the nation. Japan's defeat in World War II and its consequent occupation by the Allied Forces, led by the United States, allowed Japan to avoid seriously confronting the consequence of its imperialism/ colonialism. The postcolonial moment for Japan was articulated predominantly by its subordinate position to the United States: Japan was a victim, not an oppressor. While Japan as an imperial/colonial power had had to face seriously the cultural and ethnic difference within the empire of the prewar era, postwar Japan was free of this burden. It was allowed to forget its colonizing past and to become obsessed with claiming its racial purity and homogeneity through the binary opposition of two culturally organic entities, 'Japan' and 'the West'.

Here, the loss of Japanese imperial power in Asia was accompanied by an introverted shift of emphasis in discourse on Japan's hybridity from racial to symbolic/cultural mixing. After the war the usage of the term 'Japanization' suppressed its prewar meaning of assimilation of Asian others and focused on the Japanese indigenization or domestication of Western (primarily American) capitalist consumer cultures. The term used to express the process of indigenizing the foreign (the West) has changed from 'imitation', which connotes Japan's inferior status, to 'domestication' or 'appropriation', which emphasizes the active agency of the Japanese (see Tobin 1992). Japanese cultural capacity is conceived, if at all, as its introverted urge to counter external dominant Western cultures.

Hybridism has continued to retain its place in Japanese nationalistic discourse, but there was another significant shift in the 1990s. It was a time when discussions about civilizational divides gained momentum in many parts of the world, particularly as the ascendancy of 'Asia' became so politically and economically conspicuous. Under these circumstances, the Japanese discourse of hybridism changed from an introverted form where Japan's domestic culture was seen as characterized by its ability to absorb the foreign (the West) to an extroverted form where Japan is seen as having a special role in developing hybrid cultural forms suitable to other Asian societies. The latter can be most clearly discerned in Japanese civilization theories which reconfigure Japan's role in Asia as a translator or mediator between 'Asia' and 'the West', presenting Japan as a prototype of the fusion of global and local. Tsunoyama Sakae (1995), for example, interprets the spread of Japanese popular culture in Asia in terms of Japan's civilizational role in indigenizing Western material culture/civilization to suit Asian conditions.

Tsunoyama (1995: 98–114) contends that the significant role played by Japanese civilization is evident in its diffusion of Western material civilization in the production of affordable commodities for Asian markets. In his view, Japan has acted as a 'transformer sub-station' which successfully refashions original Western commodities to suit the taste and material conditions of consumers in Asia. Tsunoyama (1995: 102–4) further argues that the capacity of Japanese indigenization of things Western has elevated Japan to the status of a new power plant in the world, a major exporter of many kinds of commodities, even to Western markets. Nevertheless, in articulating Japan's civilizational role he puts a particular emphasis on the Asian context, where Japan is looked at as 'a familiar but yearned-for nation' that proves to be a prototype of industrialization for other Asians to emulate (Tsunoyama 1995: 189). Tsunoyama further applies this metaphor to the spread of Japanese popular culture in Asia:

> It is obvious that the origin of Japanese popular culture can be found in American popular culture. The Japanese indigenised American popular culture into something that suited Japanese tastes. Filtration through a Japanese prism has made American popular culture something more familiar to people in Asia . . . the universal appeal of Japanese popular culture in Asia is based upon its erasure of any nationality ('*mukokuseki*') from popular culture of American origin.
>
> (Tsunoyama 1995: 191)

Tsunoyama (1995: 191) stresses that Japanese popular culture is not appreciated in Asia for its 'authentic' cultural appeal and contends that it is Japan's skill of indigenizing Western culture in Asian contexts that articulates the transnational appeal of Japanese popular culture.

The claim of Japanese cultural superiority is still accompanied by a self-praising assertion of supposed cultural commonality between Japan and 'Asia'. A significant problem with Tsunoyama's argument is, as with other hybridism discourses, a failure to appreciate the existence of other modes of cultural mixing. Conferring a distinctive 'Japaneseness' on *mukokuseki* Japanese cultural products, Tsunoyama assumes that Japan is the first and final stop in the indigenization process in global cultural flows. In this kind of celebratory discourse the main thread is not so much concerned with the way in which recipient countries creatively and subversively consume, appropriate and indigenize Japanese products as with a narcissistic obsession with retaining a sense of superiority as a cultural exporter by disregarding the dynamic worldwide process of cultural indigenization. Uninterested in how Japanese media texts are actually watched and listened to in other parts of Asia, hybridism discourse can hold good only so far as it can defer acknowledgment and appreciation of the multifarious and contradictory ways of endless indigenization, appropriation and mixing all over the world.

Popular culture and postcoloniality: South Korea and Taiwan

The increase in the export of Japanese TV programs to Asian markets has demonstrated that Japan's colonial past does not prevent Japanese TV programs and pop idols from being accepted in East and Southeast Asia. Accordingly, a strong interest has emerged within Japan in the potential for Japanese popular culture to improve Japan's reputation in Asia. By disseminating Japanese contemporary culture, particularly among younger people who did not experience Japanese imperialism in the first half of the twentieth century, some hope to overcome and even suppress the history of Japanese imperialism in East and Southeast Asia. In other words, the spread of Japanese popular culture in East and Southeast Asia excited Japanese journalists, industry people, government officials and academics, as they found Japanese popular culture useful in the mission to enhance Japan's cultural diplomacy.

In this context, the Japanese government has been interested in promoting the export of TV programs and popular culture to other Asian regions. *Oshin*, the Japanese soap opera about the eventful life of a woman in the early twentieth century, was the primary example of this. It was distributed to many Asian countries as well as other non-Western countries for free under the cultural exchange program of the Japan Foundation, an extra-departmental organization of the Japanese Ministry of Foreign Affairs. It has been stressed that the popularity of *Oshin* in other Asian countries is important, because those people who had so far known Japan only through 'culturally odourless' products such as cars, consumer technologies and animation (Iwabuchi 1998) have come to see the 'real' lives of Japanese people through TV dramas (e.g. NHK International 1991).

Needless to say, what the 'real' Japan is, whether it is possible to represent Japan's 'real' faces, and how images of Japan are (in contradictory ways) consumed and received by audiences are highly contested questions. These questions are not taken seriously by those who stress the importance of exporting Japanese TV programs. What concerns them is the fact that a Japanese TV program, *Oshin*, has improved the image of Japan in other Asian countries. The usefulness of the TV program in this respect, then, lies in how observers view the 'real' and 'humane' faces of Japan.

Beneficial facets of Japanese popular culture in Japan's reconciliation with its neighbouring countries are not simply found in the common historical experience of the non-West and in traditional values. Other TV dramas which feature contemporary urban life in Japan and popular music are also thought to present a new possibility of promoting cultural dialogue between young Japanese and other Asians. Nevertheless, the crucial question left unanswered here is what sort of dialogue transnational mass-mediated consumption of popular culture could facilitate. How is the dialogue shaped by continuing unequal power relations between Japan and the rest of Asia? What sorts of images of 'Asia' are being imagined and where is 'Japan' positioned in them? The disregard for the complexity inherent in transnational cultural flows and consumption is still intact in the optimistic view that the spread of Japanese popular culture will facilitate cultural dialogue with Asia.

Political and diplomatic reference to the spread of Japanese popular culture has become even more visible in the last few years. Particularly evident is the increase in Japanese media coverage of Korean and Taiwanese reception of Japanese popular culture. Here, the transnationalization of Japanese popular culture to Japan's former colonies – one of which has most strictly regulated the inflow of Japanese popular culture and the other most eagerly imported and consumed it – generates further postcolonial curves in Japanese discourses in contrastive ways. On one hand, the deployment of popular culture for cultural diplomacy is most conspicuously seen in the case of South Korea. South Korea had long banned the import of Japanese popular cultural forms, because the exposure to the culture of the brutal colonizer was thought to adversely affect people in de-colonizing South Korea. However, in late 1998 the South Korean president, Kim, publicly announced on his visit to Tokyo that the government would progressively abolish its regulation policies. The abolition incorporated four steps and was significantly furthered by mid-2002 when South Korea and Japan co-hosted the soccer World Cup. The opening of the South Korean market to Japanese popular culture led to a rush of Japanese media products into the nation and there was massive Japanese media coverage of it (e.g. *Asahi Shinbun*, 28 June 2000, 17 December 2000; *Aera*, 5 June 2000). The overall tone is undoubtedly welcoming, as it apparently testifies to the belated historical reconciliation between Japan and South Korea, the end of longstanding Korean antagonism and suffering caused by Japanese colonialism.

The media coverage of the concert of a Japanese pop duo, Chage & Aska, in Seoul in 2000 is a case in point. The duo has actively entered other Asian markets. They had had concerts in Taipei, Singapore, Hong Kong, Beijing and Shanghai since 1994, but could not enter South Korea due to the cultural regulation policy. Their inroads to East Asian markets have been no doubt motivated by commercial reasons, but they are quite conscious of their role in overcoming Japanese imperial history (see, e.g., *Views*, July 1996: 78). In August 2000 Chage & Aska finally held a concert in Seoul. Japanese media enthusiastically covered it, reporting that this was an historic concert, because as the first performance by Japanese pop musicians in Japanese language this clearly marked the cultural thaw between Japan and South Korea. Chage and Aska expressed their sense of accomplishment: 'We younger generation, let's make a future together!' (*Asahi Shinbun*, 28 August 2000). Japanese media welcomed their comments, saying that the concert signified the coming of a new era of reconciliation with neighbours (e.g. *Asahi Shinbun*, 5 November 2000).

This excessively flattering narrative of the acceptance of Japanese popular culture in South Korea can be read symptomatically. It is engendered by the need to counter the uncomfortable recognition that positive consumption of Japanese popular culture does not guarantee Korea's acceptance of the history of Japanese colonial rule. Many Korean fans of Japanese popular music tend to refuse to conflate their craze for Japanese pop with their frustration towards insincere Japanese attitudes about its war responsibilities (Kanno 2000). Being the nation that has most strongly and constantly reminded Japan of its colonial violence, the Korean case ambivalently suppresses and exposes the fallacy that popular cultural flows will happily erase the historical memory of suffering caused by Japanese imperialism.

Taiwan's enthusiastic consumption of Japanese popular culture arouses Japan's postcolonial desire rather differently. Here, a celebratory tone of cultural diplomacy or historical reconciliation is absent, as there is no necessity for this in relation to Taiwan. This is because Japanese media assume it has an undying love for Japanese pop culture. For example, in 1994, when Chage & Aska performed successive concerts in Taiwan, Hong Kong and Singapore, Japanese media did not show as much interest in their concerts as in their debut in Seoul. Most newspapers even did not report on them. Some popular monthly magazines covered the story about their successful concerts in Taiwan, but interestingly the tone is rather different. A popular monthly magazine, *Views*', report on Chage & Aska's concert in Taiwan was part of the feature story entitled '*Taiwan ga Nippon ni koi o shita*' (Taiwan falls in love with Japan; February 1996: 36–47). This title is not just outrageously insensitive to and disregardful of the violence of Japanese colonialism and its aftermath, but also suggests the confirmation of lingering Japanese cultural authority in Taiwan.[3] However, in the article the emphasis is also put nostalgically on the changing nature of the Taiwanese craze for 'Japan' in the postcolonial era: if the recent popularity of Japanese popular culture in Taiwan rests on a much broader consumer base than before, the affection Taiwanese consumers feel towards 'Japan' is in decline. Taiwan's adoration of Japanese popular culture also signifies postcolonial loss of its master status.

As a former Japanese colony, in Taiwan the recent surge of Japanese cultural influence is also discussed in relation to that rule. A leading weekly news magazine in Taiwan had feature articles on Japanese popular culture in Taiwan titled 'Watch out! Your kids are becoming Japanese'. The journal coined a new Taiwanese word to describe young people who adore things Japanese (*Journalist*, 13–19 April 1997). The spread of Japanese popular culture is unavoidably associated with the colonial habit of mimicking, which has become sedimented deeply in Taiwanese society (see also *China Times*, 17 March 1997). From food and housing to language, examples can easily be found of a lingering Japanese cultural influence in Taiwan. The number of people speaking Japanese is second only to that in Korea, and many Japanese words and cultural meanings have become indigenized. Older people who were educated during the Japanese colonial rule still speak fluent Japanese and enjoy Japanese-language books, songs and TV programs. While many people have never forgotten Japanese colonial violence, a large number of the older generation tend to regard their former colonizers in a relatively positive light, the bitter memories of their rule having been diminished by contrast with the repressive and authoritarian rule of the Kuomintang (KMT) government which moved from mainland China to the island after World War II (P. Liao 1996). These conditions surely make Japanese TV programs much more accessible here than in other parts of Asia.

However, those who were educated after World War II hold quite different views of Japan. This generational divide is elucidated in Wu Nianzhen's film *Dosan: A Borrowed Life* (1994), which deals with the nostalgia of older Taiwanese for the Japanese period. This nostalgia was fuelled by their intense disappointment over the KMT's repressiveness (see C. Liao 1997). In brief, the film is about a Taiwanese man who has long harboured a dream to visit Japan. His dream can be seen as a wish on his part to affirm an identity and history which were forged during the Japanese period but which he was later forced to deny or repress under a KMT-governed Taiwan. Wu (quoted in *Views*, February 1996: 40–2) has recollected how, as a student who was taught negatively about Japanese colonial rule at school, he hated his father's longing for that period – a longing which was betrayed by the indifference Japan displayed to Taiwan after the war.

This generational divide has been exacerbated by the emergence of a youth audience for Japanese popular culture. In May 1997 I witnessed the occurrence of two incidents in Taiwan which, when juxtaposed, nicely illustrate that country's complicated relationship with Japan. The first was an anti-Japanese demonstration over the issue of Japan's possession of the Diaoyu Islands. The other was a popular music concert by Japanese artists which attracted much media attention as well as a young audience (see also the *Journalist*, 1-7 June 1997). This juxtaposition of 'anti-' and 'pro-'Japanese sentiment articulates a new generational divide. The meaning 'Japan' possesses for young Taiwanese is undoubtedly different from that which it holds for their forebears. The former, most of whom do not understand Japanese, make up the main audience for Japanese TV dramas, which they enjoy through dubbing or subtitles. The above-mentioned article of *Views* quotes Wu's comments on the recent popularity of Japanese culture among the younger generation in Taiwan:

> My generation and my father's generation have a deep love-and-hate feeling towards Japan, though in quite different ways. But the younger generation has no special affection for Japanese culture, as there is no difference between Japan, America and Europe for them. Japan is just one option among many. I think the relationship between Taiwan and Japan will be more superficial in terms of affective feelings while deepened materially.
>
> (*Views*, February 1996: 42)

The shift in the Taiwanese reception of Japanese popular culture, from an enthusiastic embrace to a more detached, superficial consumption, is often observed with reference to a general feature of the postmodern consumption of global culture (e.g. Chô 1998).[4] Although hinting at a significant change in the transnational consumption of globalized popular culture, this kind of perspective does not adequately address the issue of why Japanese popular culture is preferred to that from other parts of the world. Suffice it to say here that it tends to underestimate the symbolic appeal Taiwanese audiences find in a particular Japanese popular culture (see Iwabuchi 2001). More relevant for my argument is that the same observation of Taiwanese consumption of Japanese popular culture is exploited by Japanese nationalists in a reactionary way, in which a sense of colonial loss is provoked.

The recent increase in Japanese media attention to favourable consumption of Japanese popular culture in Taiwan apparently has something to do with the rise of a reactionary movement to revise secondary-school history textbooks. Condemning the hitherto common accounts contained in the history textbooks about Japanese imperial and colonial violence in Asian regions as too self-critical, self-torturing and derogatory to nurture Japanese national pride among youth, a group called Atarashii Rekisikyôkasho o Tsukuru Kai (Society for the Creation of a New History Textbook) have published a new history textbook, in which Japanese imperialism and colonialism are narrated in a self-justifying manner. After some revisions, the new history textbook has successfully passed screening by the Japanese Ministry of Education since 2001, and this has infuriated China and South Korea.

With the development of the textbook controversy, Taiwan has also gradually attracted wider attention in Japan, as it is regarded as a nation that cherishes the Japanese colonial legacy and thus is living testimony of the good of Japanese colonialism. Among various publications on Taiwan in the last few years, particularly well sold was a comic book, *Taiwanron* (On Taiwan; 2000), authored by a notoriously xenophobic cartoonist, Kobayashi Yoshinori, who is an active member of the association mentioned above. Observing colonial remnants and hearing pro-Japan compliments from some people in Taiwan, including new and old presidents, Kobayashi jingoistically romanticizes Japanese colonial rule of Taiwan, arguing that 'good old' Japanese spirits and values are still alive in Taiwan in even more sophisticated ways. In this outrageously self-justifying view of Japanese colonial rule of Taiwan, the current passionate reception of Japanese popular culture in Taiwan is perceived ambivalently. For Kobayashi, the intervention of 'evil China' – in the form of both the KMT and the Chinese Communist Party – is to blame for having imperilled the loving relationship between Japan and Taiwan in the postcolonial era. At the same time, while observing narcissistically, Kobayashi regards the recent craze for Japanese popular culture among Taiwanese youth as too trivial to match Taiwan's historically constituted affectionate relationship with Japan (though Kobayashi strangely ignores the fact that his cartoon is also part of such 'trivial' cultural forms). Yet 'superficial' consumption of Japanese popular culture in Taiwan is not so much denounced as taken advantage of in reinforcing his point that young people in Taiwan as well as in Japan should learn the modern history underlying the Taiwanese 'crush' on Japan:

> It is a pity that while there are so many Japanophiles in Taiwan, neither young people in Japan or in Taiwan know the history that the two nations were quite closely attached to each other and lived together. Sound national culture is engendered on the soil of sound historical perspective. The history [of Japanese colonial rule] should not be forgotten in order for Taiwan to produce its own culture of a higher degree of originality.
>
> (Kobayashi 2000: 12)[5]

Here, the spread of Japanese popular culture in Taiwan serves at once to destabilize and generate Kobayashi's postcolonial nostalgia for a 'Japanese spirit' found in the form of Taiwan's nostalgia. If the exclusive association of the consumption of Japanese popular culture with historical reconciliation is generated by the deep-seated anxiety about its real efficacy in the case of South Korea, Japanese nationalists take it as an opportunity to expose the positive side of Japanese colonial rule in Taiwan. If nationalist sentiment is projected into the future by way of suppressing the past in the South Korean case, the past is chauvinistically recuperated in the Taiwanese case. While the passionate consumption of Japanese popular culture by Taiwanese youth shows how 'Japan' is contradictorily consumed in Taiwan, it works for Kobayashi in the last instance only to intensify Japanese nostalgic desire to legitimize Japanese supremacy as colonial master.

Taking popular cultural flows seriously

In this chapter I have explored how the recent spread of Japanese popular culture in East and Southeast Asia is nationalistically discussed in Japan. The discourses are strongly haunted by the history of Japanese imperialism in Asian regions, hence the embrace of Japan's postcolonial desire. One thing that is certain is that those discourses fail to do justice to the contradictory, uneven and disjunctive transnational cultural flows, which make the assertion of the unambiguous centre and the expectation of equal cultural dialogues implausible. Put differently, such nationalistic discourses can only be foregrounded by not attending to or refusing to confront the complexity of transnational popular cultural flows. If we are to avoid harbouring too excessive – pessimistic or optimistic – expectations of transnational popular cultural flows, any discussion needs to take popular culture more seriously; that is, to analyse rigorously the complications of transnational production, distribution and consumption of popular culture against the background of wider socio-historical contexts.

However, Japan's engagement with Asian capitalist modernity cannot be entirely contained by the nationalist imaginary and desire. With the accelerating popular cultural flows within East/Southeast Asia under globalizing forces, transnational encounters and imaginations are newly hatched in ways that generate the (partial) demise of the Japanese nationalist project. The rise of Korean popular culture in East Asia, a phenomenon called Korean Waves, has significantly decentred Japan's position in the regional cultural flow. As the phenomenal popularity of Korean TV dramas, and particularly 'Winter Sonata' in Japan in 2003, demonstrate, more media texts produced in other parts of Asia have attracted people in Japan. Such mediated transnational encounters might promote more dialogical and self-critical views (cf. Thompson 1995; Appadurai 1996; Gillespie 1995). In the mediated encounter with a concretized Asia (e.g. appreciating 'Winter Sonata' or Faye Wong, not 'Asian' drama or music in general), Japanese (mostly female) audiences overtly or covertly reject the singular notion of 'Asia', which occupies the dominant discourse in Japan, to appreciate the cultural specificity of particular Asian cultural productions and the different modes of Asian cultural modernity articulated in them.[6] Furthermore, media consumption also encourages audiences to contact actual Asian neighbours. For example, in the case of 'Winter Sonata', the engaged consumption of the media narrative further urges many audiences to actively contact Korea by learning language, visiting South Korea and re-studying history of Japanese colonialism. Here, the idea of Japanese cultural superiority to other Asian nations is displaced, facilitating a more dialogic engagement with other Asian cultural modernities; dialogic in the sense that it involves self-transformation and a redefinition of one's own culture through a developed consciousness of a shared temporality with different Asian modernities (Iwabuchi 2003).

Yet, we also need to remember that this dialogic development accompanies a regressive counterpart. The celebration of Korean Wave occurred nearly spontaneously with the demonizing of North Korea and the attack of resident Koreans in Japan due to the abduction issue. The worsening relationship between Japan, China and South Korea over Prime Minister Koizumi's persistent visit to Yasukuni Shrine and the account of Japanese colonialism in history textbooks is another unfortunate development in the last several years. Political disputes over historical issues have made anti-Japanese movements surface especially in China and this has regressively caused anti-Chinese and anti-Korean discourses within Japan too. While Japanese leaders are even keener to use Japanese popular culture to improve the images of Japan in East Asia, what has become apparent is the urgency to discuss historical issues and memories among populaces of countries concerned. Popular cultural connections could be used as a starting point for promoting this dialogue but would never be an end in themselves for historical reconciliation.

Popular cultural encounter will keep on feeding new modes of transnational asymmetry and imagination among people in Japan and other Asian nations. Nothing guarantees any promising future. Nevertheless, no clear-cut armchair speculation would be able to fully capture the contradictory and unforeseeable processes of intra-regional dynamics of popular cultural flows in East Asia. We need to continue to critically attend to what is going on in the real world and to how the transnational intersects with the postcolonial under globalizing forces. While the consumption of Japanese popular culture and the historical memory of Japanese imperialism do not easily or directly link together in the minds of young people in East Asia, we as researchers need to make analytical efforts to forge the link between the two. Especially in the current situation, in which the uncertainty that has grown with the advent of globalization and the lingering economic recession has led to a rise of jingoistic sentiments in Japan, this seems more imperative than before.

Notes

1   An earlier version of this paper was first published in *Emergences: Journal of Media and Composite Culture 2000*, vol. 11, no. 2: 197–220.
2   For more details, see Iwabuchi, 2002.
3   Another feature article in the popular monthly magazine *Marco Polo* was also stolidly titled 'Bullied Taiwan's crush on Japan' (April 1991: 35–45).
4   The same observation that the widespread interest in Japanese popular culture in Asia has paradoxically been accompanied by a waning of the region's affection for 'Japan' in the 1990s is also made in Hong Kong and Singapore (see, e.g., *Hong Kong Tsûshin*, July 1996).

5   Kobayashi also exploits the 'native' view uttered by Taiwan nationals living in
    Japan. One of Kobayashi's favourite is Hsieh Yamei (who is nostalgically
    described by Kobayashi as more Japanese than Japanese women, most of whom
    have lost refinement and grace!). In her book *Nihon hi koishita Taiwanjin* (A
    Taiwanese who fell in love with Japan), which also uses the word 'love' in the
    title, Hsieh makes a similar comment on how the recent Taiwanese youth fad for
    Japanese popular culture is frivolous: 'The more Taiwanese young people follow
    the latest Japanese fashion, the more I tend to have a mixed feeling . . . I learn
    more about Japanese cultural virtues such as group solidarity and delicateness'
    (2000: 27). It should also be noted that *Taiwanron* was quickly translated into
    Chinese and the book became so polemical in Taiwan that there was a dispute
    about whether Kobayashi's entry to Taiwan should be officially banned or not.
    Here Kobayashi's narrative that self-justifies Japanese colonial rule and is full of
    anti-China sentiments was opportunistically exploited both by the anti- and pro-
    independence camps in Taiwan.
6   Young women also seem to take the lead in the consumption of Japanese
    popular culture in Taiwan and Hong Kong, but the Japanese case more clearly
    testifies to the gendered consumption of popular culture from other parts of
    East Asia. The gendered transnational desire apparent in the intra-East Asian
    cultural flows is a significant issue for further investigation, though this is beyond
    the scope of this chapter.

Bibliography

Ang, I. and Stratton, J. (1996) 'Asianizing Australia: notes toward a critical transna-
    tionalism in cultural studies', *Cultural Studies*, vol. 10, no. 1: 16–36.
Appadurai, A. (1996) *Modernity at Large: cultural dimensions of globalization*,
    Minneapolis, MN: University of Minnesota Press.
Buell, F. (1994) *National Culture and the New Global System,* Baltimore, MD, and
    London: John Hopkins University Press.
Ching, L. (2000) 'Aesthetic and mass culture: Asianism in the age of global capital',
    Public Culture, vol. 12, no. 1: 233–57.
Chô, K. (1998) 'Bunka ga jôhô ni natta toki (Consumption of foreign cultures as
    information)', *Sekai*, April: 82–107.
Dower, J. W. (1986) *War Without Mercy: race and power in the Pacific War*, New
    York: Panthenon Books.
Duus, P. (1995) *The Abacus and the Sword: the Japanese penetration of Korea
    1895–1910*, Berkeley, CA: University of California Press.
Funabashi, Y. (1993) 'The Asianization of Asia', *Foreign Affairs*, vol. 72, no. 5: 75–85.
Gillespie, M. (1995) *Television, Ethnicity and Cultural Change*, London: Routledge.
Hannerz, U. (1996) *Transnational Connections: culture, people, places*, London: Rout-
    ledge.
Hsieh, Yamei (2000) *Nihon hi koishita Taiwanjin* (A Taiwanese who fell in love with
    Japan), Tokyo: Sôgôhôrei-shuppan.
Iwabuchi, K. (1994) 'Complicit exoticism: Japan and its Other', *Continuum*, vol. 8,
    no. 2: 49–82.
——(1998) 'Pure Impurity: Japan's genius for hybridism', *Communal/Plural: Journal
    of Transnational and Cross-cultural Studies*, vol. 6, no. 1: 71–86.
——(1999) 'Return to Asia? Japan in the Asian audiovisual market', in K. Yoshino (ed.)
    Consuming Ethnicity and Nationalism: Asian experiences, London: Curzon Press.

——(2001) 'Becoming culturally proximate: a/scent of Japanese idol dramas in Taiwan', in B. Moeran (ed.) *Asian Media Productions*, London: Curzon.

——(2002) *Recentering Globalization: popular culture and Japanese transnationalism*, Durham, NC: Duke University Press.

——(2003) 'Nostalgia for (different) Asian modernities: Japanese consumption of Asia', *positions*, vol. 10, no. 3: 543–73.

Kang, S. (1996) *Orientarisumu no kanata e* (Beyond Orientalism), Tokyo: Iwanami Shoten.

Kanno, T. (2000) *Sukininattewa ikenai kuni: kankoku J-Pop sedai ga mita nihon* (A country you should not come to like: Japan in the eyes of Korean J-Pop generation), Tokyo: Bungeishunjû.

Kawakatsu, H. (1991) *Nihon bunmei to kindai seiyô* (Japanese civilization and the modern West), Tokyo: NHK Shuppan.

——(1995) *Fukoku utokuron* (On enriching the nation by cultivating virtues), Tokyo: Kinokuniya Shoten.

Kobayashi, Y. (2000) *Taiwanron* (On Taiwan), Tokyo: Shôgakkan.

Komagome, T. (1996) *Shokuminchi teikoku nihon no bunka tôgô* (Cultural integration in the Japanese colonial empire), Tokyo: Iwanami Shoten.

Liao, C. (1997) 'Borrowed modernity: history and the subject in "A Borrowed Life"', *boundary 2*, vol. 24, no. 3: 225–45.

Liao, P. (1996) 'Chinese nationalism or Taiwanese localism?', *Culture and Policy*, vol. 7, no. 2: 74–92.

Mahathir, M. and Ishihara, S. (1995) *The Voice of Asia*, Tokyo: Kôdansha International.

Miller, D. (1992) 'The young and restless in Trinidad: a case of the local and global in mass consumption', in R. Silverstone and E. Hirsch (eds) *Consuming Technologies: media and information in domestic spaces*, London: Routledge.

——(ed.) (1995) *Worlds Apart: modernity through the prism of the local*, London: Routledge.

Morita, A. and Ishihara, S. (1989) *'No'! to ieru nihon* (The Japan that can say 'No'!), Tokyo: Kôbunsha.

Morley, D. and Robins, K. (1995) *Spaces of Identity: global media, electronic landscapes and cultural boundaries*, London: Routledge.

Morris-Suzuki, T. (1998) *Re-inventing Japan: time, space, nation*, New York and London: M. E. Sharpe.

NHK International (ed.) (1991) *Sekai wa Oshin o dô mitaka* (How Oshin has been watched in the world), Tokyo: NHK Shuppan.

Oguma, E. (1995) *Tan'itsu minzoku shinwa no kigen* (The origin of the myth of Japanese Racial homogeneity), Tokyo: Shinyôsha.

Okakura, T. (1904) *The Ideal of the East with Special Reference to the Art of Japan*, 2nd edition, New York: E. P. Dutton & Co.

Peattie, M. (1984) 'Japanese attitudes toward colonialism', in R. Myers and M. Peattie (eds) *The Japanese Colonial Empire*, Princeton, NJ: Princeton University Press.

Robertson, J. (1998) *Takarazuka: sexual politics and popular culture in modern Japan*, Berkeley, CA: University of California Press.

Rouse, R. (1995) 'Thinking through transnationalism: notes on the cultural politics of class relations in the contemporary United States', *Public Culture*, 7: 353–402.

Sakai, N. (1989) 'Modernity and its critique', *South Atlantic Quarterly*, vol. 87, no. 3: 475–504.

Takeuchi, Y. [1961] (1993) *Nihon to ajia* (Japan and Asia), reprint, Tokyo: Chikuma Shobô.

Tanaka, S. (1993) *Japan's Orient: rendering pasts into history*, Berkeley, CA: University of California Press.

Thompson, J. B. (1995) *The Media and Modernity: a social theory of the media*, London: Polity Press.

Tobin, J. J. (1992) 'Introduction: domesticating the West', in J. Tobin (ed.) *Re-made in Japan: everyday life and consumer taste in a changing society*, New Haven, NJ: Yale University Press.

Tomlinson, J. (1997) 'Cultural globalization and cultural imperialism', in A. Mohammadi (ed.) *International Communication and Globalization: a critical introduction*, London: Sage.

Tsunoyama, S. (1995) *Ajia runessansu* (Asian renaissance), Tokyo: PHP Kenkyuaho.

Watson, J. L. (ed.) (1997) *Golden Arches East: McDonald's in East Asia*, Stanford, CA: Stanford University Press.

Yamazaki, M. (1996) 'Asia, a civilization in the making', *Foreign Affairs*, vol. 75, no. 4: 106-18.

3   *South Park* does Japan

Going global with Chimpokomon

Matthew Allen

Introduction

On 3 November 1999 Comedy Central screened 'Chimpokomon', an episode of the controversial *South Park* animated television series, on cable in the United States. It is ostensibly a parody of the *Pokemon* phenomenon, whose integrated merchandising and marketing strategy enabled it to become a popular, and often incomprehensible to adults, cultural icon of the 1990s in Japan, the United States and indeed in many nations. However, at a slightly deeper level, it also provides a rich vein of resources for understanding the cynical perceptions of series creators Trey Parker and Matt Stone, on the one hand, and the continued orientalized perspectives of Japan broadcast on US television, on the other. While *South Park* is a consciously parodying animation series, poking fun at US social conventions, here it extended its parody beyond US borders.[1] In going global, Parker and Stone's satirical representation of Japan, of the United States, of male obsession with sexuality and of conspicuous consumerism, aimed ruthlessly at children, is astute and funny. It also exposes the historical constructions of stereotypes and posits new forms of essentialism that inform a perceptional globalization.

While it is common for academics to look at Japanese animation (*anime*) as a culturally specific art form that has commercial and indeed sometimes cultural significance for US audiences,[2] few have examined how US animation represents Japan. Although it is important to understand how Japan is represented in sociology, anthropology, history, and geography texts, and in the cutting-edge cultural or critical media studies programmes hosted by tertiary institutions, *anime* surely influences far larger numbers of 'middle Americans', particularly, but by no means exclusively, youth. As Fishwick has observed about studying the *popular* popular culture: 'Why is this so important? Because popularity is what people's culture is about – and why studying and understanding it, with all its dubious qualities, is crucial and rewarding' (Fishwick 2001: 15).[3] And *South Park is* popular. It was the most watched cable programme *ever* on US television in its first season in 1997. Moreover, it was screened in the 10 p.m. slot, which made its popularity more startling. Although there was a decline in the teenaged audience in 2000, its ratings climbed again the next year; in 2001, 3 million households tuned in to the first episode of the new series (Kim 2001).

Another reason for looking at animation series flows from Dorfman and Mattelart's famous Marxist critique *How to Read Donald Duck*, published in 1989.[4] In this case, though, rather than attempting to read *South Park* as an example of US capitalism's attempts to marginalize and discursively maintain control over colonized peoples, I attempt to locate *South Park* in a number of contexts: as a marginal (in the sense that it remains out of the mainstream) but very popular series in the United States; as internationally successful in a commercial sense; and as a politically incorrect set of parodies of both US and overseas characteristics. Parody requires political awareness, and it is the conscious manipulation of symbols and historical motifs that underscores the humour in *South Park*; whether an audience would recognize the more subtle historical signifiers employed by Parker and Stone (for example President Hirohito's involvement in the planning of the revenge) is moot. There is little doubt, though, that their audience would be well aware of *Pokemon* and its incorporation into the American popular cultural milieu of the 1990s.

I will examine how the makers of *South Park* manipulated pre-existing stereotypes of Japan into slightly paranoid, orientalized, and ultimately emasculating images of Japan that place it in the role of the world's leader in the promotion of (immoral) global consumer ideology. The fact that the makers of an internationally popular animation series (itself an item of popular cultural consumption) would choose to lampoon merchandising of a pop cultural icon directly to children, and then label it a 'Japanese' process, when *South Park* merchandising to both children and adults itself is a marketing phenomenon, should not go unremarked upon. Indeed it is difficult to argue against the notion that integrated product development and marketing which directly targets children are products of a marketing philosophy which originated in the United States, Disney and its vast merchandising network often being seen as the archetypal form of such targeting production and development.[5] It could be said, therefore, that both *South Park* and the object of their humour, *Pokemon*, were founded on similar marketing strategies, although their target audiences were quite different.[6]

Big, long and uncut

The hype that has surrounded *South Park* since its inception has been informed by a commonly heard perception that it is vulgar, crass, objectionable, derides family values and is singularly unsuitable for consumption by children. The following review of the movie *South Park: Bigger, Longer, and Uncut* (1999) from a sympathetic critic expresses some of the reasons that the show has been both so popular and so offensive to some:

Added songs notwithstanding, not much has been changed from the formula that has made *South Park* a hit. The animation is still laughably poor, and much of the humor is still dredged from the gutter. There's lots of profanity, farts, more than a few dick jokes, and enough insensitive sexual and ethnic cracks to go around. In fact, the list of the groups who could be potentially offended from this film reads like a virtual Who's Who of vulnerable mainstream entities: small-town, middle class America, Christians, Celine Dion, Canadians, war, the President, homosexuals, African-Americans, Saddam Hussein, and the media, just to name a few. Luckily, *South Park* doesn't discriminate among those groups that are open to ridicule. It makes fun of them all, without fail.

(Dean 1999)

While this non-partisan political incorrectness is emblematic of the series as a whole, certain groups have taken offence publicly at representations of themselves. In particular, Christian groups have taken offence at the show. In 1998, Rosaline Bush in *Family Voice* had the following to say about it:

'*South Park*' – the latest 'cartoon' offered on cable – features crude renderings of foul-mouthed third-graders. The content is blatantly sacrilegious and offensive – [for example] a boxing match between Jesus and Satan. Episodes have shown kids poisoning their grandfather and conversing with a talking pile of feces. Each week they kill the same character in a new and gruesome way. One character's promiscuous mother is called a 'crack w[hore].'

(Bush 1998)

Such views were commonly expressed about *South Park* when it was first released. Today, it still produces some outrageous and very amusing, if overt, skits that cross the borders of what is 'general' and what is 'adult' entertainment. The incongruity of the characters' manipulative, politically incorrect and naïve antics, the originality and political incorrectness of their scripts and their highly evocative (and politically incorrect) swearing continue to pull viewers from around the world.[7] It is indeed the inappropriateness of the language and concepts ascribed to the children – particularly Eric Cartman – portrayed in the series that makes it both funny to many and offensive to others. It particularly appeals to its fourteen- to twenty-four-year-old male target audience (and others, both of the other sex and much older men). Its audience, therefore, is quite different to the object of its 'satire' in the episode I want to discuss.

The object of *South Park*'s disdain in the Chimpokomon episode is Japanese commodity fetishism and its influence in the United States, in this instance realized by the Chimpokomon Corporation. In a blatantly obvious, almost actionable parody of *Pokemon*, Matt Stone and Trey

Parker ridicule the cartoon series that has become one of the most prof-
itable animation lines ever. Aimed initially at a pre-teen and teen audience
in Japan, it was a phenomenon of market research, targeted sales strategies
and vertical integration of merchandise production and sales; it effectively
reproduced the same structures of production and distribution employed
by US animation studios and their representatives (Natsume 2002: 66).
From its very beginning, *Pokemon* was designed to become a 'success'. The
first *manga* (comics) sold in Japan were instantly popular and a Nintendo
game was soon released, followed by merchandised goods: dolls, Game
Boy controllers, badges, caps, clothing and accessories. The movie
Pokemon: The First Movie, when released by Warner Brothers in the
United States in 1999, hit 3000 theatres simultaneously, and occupied the
most-popular-film slot for a short while. It made more than $80 million at
the US box office and was backed up with the release of 10 million copies
of the video, generating further sales. Sales of merchandised goods,
branded clothing and trading cards exploded, and *Pokemon* became a
phenomenal marketing success in the United States. According to
Natsume, its success was all the more noticeable because so few Japanese
animation series had occupied the prominent status of *Pokemon* (Natsume
2002: 66).

The *Pokemon* craze continued in Japan and Asia through the late 1990s.
In the United States, however, the wholehearted public support for the cute
little critters evident in Japan and Asia was not so apparent, and an increasingly strident group of critics set about challenging the values that *Pokemon*
represented. These included religious leaders, who stated that *Pokemon*
educated children in ungodly ways and that it offered alien and subversive
messages to impressionable children.[8] Xenophobes, racists, neo-conservatives
and other right-wing organizations also criticized the ethics of *Pokemon*,
asserting that it portrayed foreign cultural values that would undermine the
otherwise Christian, American values portrayed on television (though
whether these were the violent police dramas, the reality shows or the quiz
shows is not clear).

Going global: us and them

The Chimpokomon episode marked a departure from the usual targets of
Stone and Parker's humour: it was aimed at Japan, a 'global' target; it was
informed by some sense of history; and it was a denunciation of Japanese
animation and marketing in a global market. Because both the *South Park*
and *Pokemon* series were being screened on Japanese television when the
episode was made, the televising of this particular episode was seen as
potentially politically explosive in Japan and was not put on the air,
although it was screened in other overseas destinations. The episode is an
astutely crafted parody of the *Pokemon* craze that was sweeping the countries of the OECD in the late 1990s. Its clever premise is somewhat undercut

by the playing out of cultural stereotypes of Japanese, which almost certainly would have caused offence in Japan.

Although Trey Parker majored in Japanese at the University of Colorado before dropping out to pursue a career in animation,[9] it is perhaps not surprising that, given the intention to shock and amuse, there was little cultural sensitivity in a show that was aimed at the US market. Certainly subtlety had not been a hallmark of the series to this point. However, to their credit, Parker and Stone did include colloquial and accurate Japanese-language sound bites in their show, in doing so paying some respect to the existence of a culture outside the United States. This is in contrast to their representations of Iraqis, Arabs and Chinese, where the characters utter unintelligible, stereotyped grunts and other incomprehensible (in any language) sounds. In terms of the Japanese language, it is clear that Parker and Stone are culturally aware that it generates meaning – even though the audience is not apprised of the meaning (there are no translations).[10]

The images and stereotypes of Japanese people and society in this episode of *South Park* could also be viewed at one level as a response to representations of 'Westerners' (referring to US citizens, most commonly) in Japanese and other Asian animation.[11] Given that the primary object of ridicule is the virtually incomprehensible to adults (and banal) *Pokemon* animation and its merchandising of related products, one of the more amusing aspects of this episode is the capacity to render competent, but very silly, parodies of the *Pokemon* characters and plots. In particular, the instantly recognizable, simplistic, two-dimensional animation style that is used when Chimpokomon characters appear on screen, when the boys start to speak Japanese in the classroom and when the children in Mr Garrison's classroom all laugh at a Japanese-language joke is a cruelly accurate parody of mainstream Japanese animation such as *Crayon Shin Chan*.

Exposed, cultural stereotypes of representation in animation lay bare certain tensions that underscore the Japan–US relationship, and which remain intact in the twenty-first century. These tensions are driven by essentialist representations of those who are perceived as Others and how this Otherness can be articulated in a way that enables observers to find it amusing. Edward Said, in *Orientalism*, observed in a well-quoted passage that interpretations of the Orient were driven by ideas of exoticized, fantastical worlds that were there to be 'discovered' by accidental occidental observers (Said 1979). In the desire to pacify and feminize the Orient, many occidental observers found what they sought: the Orient was a place that was gentile, undeveloped, passive, yielding, feminine and ultimately conquerable (Tanaka 1993). While such views were applied to Japan from the middle of the nineteenth century, following the rise of militarist Japan in the early twentieth century the images of Japan that were generated for popular consumption within the United States in particular became increasingly derogatory. These reflected the growing tensions between the two nations as they edged closer to war, driven by a plethora of factors including, quite specifically, racial and immigration antagonisms. John Dower has referred to the war that eventuated as 'total war' (Dower 1987). Indeed it is difficult to argue that the violence the two nations wrought against each other was anything other than total warfare. This included the absolute alienation and demonization of the Other, a mutual enterprise, which saw the transformation of both Japanese and American Others in each others' eyes. 'The Japanese' became an orientalized, despicable object, an image reinforced by US government policies enacted against Asian migration.[12] 'The American' was a barbarian with a long nose, hirsute (usually the men) and grossly proportioned, rapacious, evil and intent on dominating Asia.[13]

In the 1920s tensions between Japan and the US over immigration led to vicious, negative, jingoistic and chauvinistic representation of Japanese immigrants in the United States, while Americans living in Japan at the time were not so clearly discriminated against. The political relationship between the nations deteriorated following Japan's withdrawal from the League of Nations in 1932, largely over US and international condemnation of its actions in China, a nation in which the United States had considerable investment in capital and human resources. With Japan increasingly represented as the enemy, American parodying of Japanese continued.[14] By the time of the Pacific War, Japanese men were represented in US media (newspaper cartoons, popular magazines, political commentary, radio, movies) as short, untrustworthy, inscrutable, simian, cunning, deceitful, sexually impotent, violently treacherous and ultimately alien. Japanese women on the other hand retained their innocence; their child-like femininity and chasteness were dominant motifs in their representation.

Reading scripts

With this brief sketch of discriminatory representation in mind, I would like to turn to the Chimpokomon episode and examine how a self-reflexive attempt at self-parody (one of *South Park*'s distinguishing features) actually incorporates other parodies that extend beyond the usual targets for *South Park* humour; that is, groups *within* the United States.[15] It is striking that when parodying US institutions and values Stone and Parker often appear remarkably astute, observing society from the inside out. When they turn their gaze beyond the shores of the United States this informed, insider's view is transformed into the outsider's, orientalizing, view, for it is through treading on political correctness, one of the show's motifs, that its irreverent humour emerges.[16] The problem with such an approach is that, in order to reflect public opinion, the writers don't challenge ideas associated with truth and representation, as they are inclined to do with domestic issues, but rather focus on stereotypes as amusing *for their own sakes*. The level of sophistication of the humour are fairly basic at one level, because the basis of understanding is culturally driven and extends beyond the method of the four boys voicing the writers' opinions; that is, the humour reflects stereo-typed behaviours that are the object of ridicule.

But *South Park* also often carries deeper levels of engagement with stereo-types, and in Chimpokomon they continue this 'tradition'. The stereotypes in the episode are *developments* of the stereotypes generated by mainstream and more marginal media sources such as blogs, websites, discussion forums and other electronic communications media and hence are as extreme as the writers feel they can be. More importantly, they underscore and add meaning to the story, which certainly needs *some* meaning. In this episode of *South Park* the makers of Chimpokomon are planning to brainwash the children of America to overthrow 'the evil power [which] is the United States govern-ment' in revenge for World War II. To do this, they insert computer chips into the Chimpokomon dolls that insist children buy new products, at first, and then, through following this up with focused advertising on television and Game Boys, eventually insist that children all participate in the Chimpoko camps, which are referred to as 'Japanese military bases'. The irony of Japanese establishing military bases in the United States should not be (but presumably *is*) lost on most American viewers.[17] In the camps they are taught Japanese, which they use at school and at home. Eventually they are trained to fly jet fighters to attack Pearl Harbor, which they are prevented from doing at the last moment.

Below I focus on how certain scenes in *South Park* are produced to create the most potentially offensive, and hence amusing, stereotypes of characters. The humour revolves around perceptions of truth and acute observations. Effectively, indeed, humour incorporates ways of saying what others think in ways that make others laugh (Boskin 1997). At this juncture, I would like to emphasize that we need to resist the urge to deconstruct the humour in *South Park* in its entirety. In the reading I'm attempting, the icons of representation will be assessed, but I will not attempt to analyse all the humour in the script.

The new Chimpokomon dolls have arrived in *South Park* and three of the four boys who are the focus of the series have them. Kyle does not. He has a Cyborg Bill doll, which is labelled 'so yesterday' by his friends. Kyle is not able to keep up with the trends and is seen as 'uncool' by the others. The Chimpokomon dolls are named Furrycat (self-evident), Roostor (a rooster that can turn into a robotic stallion with a rooster crown), Chuchunezumi (a 'mouse' that does not really look like a mouse), Donkeytron (self-evident), Pengin (a purple penguin), Shu (a shoe) and Lambtron (the Pikachu-equivalent character – yellow, fuzzy and 'cute').[18] Children are encouraged to collect them by a woman announcer as they watch the Chimpokomon animation series on television.[19] The children are then encouraged to buy a PlayStation game console that enables them to become Chimpoko Masters and entitles them to admission to the Chimpokomon camp. At the camp the children are taught Japanese and are told that their duty is to destroy Pearl Harbor in revenge for World War II. The company president, Hirohito,[20] is dressed in full Tokugawan samurai regalia as he addresses the children, who all bow to his will, except Kyle, who doesn't really 'get it'.

The parents of *South Park* realize that their children are addicted to a fad but don't know how to counter it. The mayor and toy developers suggest other fads that could be developed and marketed to the children to compete with Chimpokomon, but they all predictably fail. Finally the parents realize that they need to convince the children that Chimpokomon is not cool, so, in a stroke of genius, they all arrive at the military base as the children are about to depart for Pearl Harbor, waving flags in support, telling them that they love Chimpokomon too (in Japanese). The children are disconcerted by their parents' interest in Chimpokomon and eventually decide that they no longer think Chimpokomon is cool.

The episode ends, as did most episodes in this season, with the death of Kenny, this time following an epileptic fit after watching one of the Chimpokomon episodes on television, a reference to the 1997 screening on Japanese prime time of an episode of *Pokemon* which saw 700 people admitted to hospital suffering from epileptic fits.[21]

There are some substantial themes that appear in this episode: one of these is about commodity fetishism and fads, their causes (apparently overseas) and solutions (apparently domestic); a second is about being an individual or being part of a group (the Self–Other distinction, in which the authors neatly mix the stereotypes of Japan and the United States); and a third is about the dangers of stereotyping others as harmless and inconsequential. All the themes are highly moral and profess secular, but presumably 'universal', values, the counter-sting that enables *South Park* to prosper in discursive territory where other animation series would never dare venture. In fact such themes are never raised in media for mainstream audiences, a point of departure and pride for the makers of the show.

The by-lines that appear as the plot unfolds in this episode reveal a number of fascinating cultural stereotypes that are parodies of parodies, and others that are simply designed for the most shocking effect. For starters, the use of language to make cultural points is insightfully and irreverently played out; indeed, the accuracy of the Japanese language employed in the script is quite refreshing. The authenticity of (most of) the language sets this particular episode aside from other, less culturally aware animation productions' representations of orientalism, such as Disney's *Mulan*, for example, which avoids any mention of Chinese language, or *Aladdin*, *Pocahontas*, *El Dorado*, *The Emperor's New Groove* – indeed, almost any recent Disney animation hit.[22]

Penis envy/complacency

A recurring motif, which relates to both the name of the actual episode and one of the major themes of the show, is the use of the word '*chimpo*', a colloquial Japanese reference to the 'penis'.[23] Indeed, when Red Harris, a

South Park toy-store owner, visits Chimpokomon headquarters in Tokyo, his complaints that the dolls are inciting children to overthrow the American capitalist government are met by obfuscation, apparently a commonly used ploy in Japanese corporate life, and by questions about the size of Mr Harris's penis.

President Hirohito: I'm President Hirohito. And this is Mr Ozeki. We understand you have big concern about our fine product.

Red Harris: Do you mind telling me what the hell this is all about? (He squeezes doll, which squeaks): 'The American government lies to you. Join the fight for Japanese supremacy of the world. More to come.'

President Hirohito: That is so strange. I do not know how this could have happened. But rest assured I shall make sure that it does not happen again.

Red Harris: Now come on. I don't think that quite satisfies me.

President Hirohito: You are American? You must have very big penis.

Red Harris: Excuse me. I was just asking what you were up to with these toys.

President Hirohito: Nothing. We are really simple people with very small penis. Mr Ozeki's penis is especially small

Ozeki: (simpers) So small.

President Hirohito: We cannot achieve much with so small penis. But you Americans, wow penis so big. So big penis.

Red Harris: Well I guess it is a pretty good size.

Ozeki: *Mina san, kite kite.* (Everyone, come here.) This man has a very big penis. (Many Japanese women applaud.) What an immense penis.

Red Harris: Well it certainly was nice meeting you folks. I just wanted to bring that little malfunction to your attention. Bye-bye now.

President Hirohito (to Red Harris): Good bye. Thank you for stopping by with your gargantuan penis. (To Ozeki) *Dame. Dame da. Naze konna chippu sotto ni detanda?* (This is no good. Why did that sort of chip get released to the outside world)?

Ozeki: *Wakarimasen. Mondai desu ne.* (I don't understand. It's a problem, isn't it?)

President Hirohito: *Sekininsha yobe.* (Bring me those responsible.)

This small excerpt plays out the stereotype that Japanese men have small penises while American men have large (gargantuan) penises, a source of pride (or really a source of sexual inadequacy?) to the archetypal American male. Moreover, the inference is clearly that with little penises the Japanese manufacturers are not a threat to the overriding masculinity and macho-ism of American males, and by extension (excuse the bad pun) American society.

This joke is played out again on three other occasions in the episode,[24] one time in a totally inappropriate context, when Ozeki uses the same line to deflect criticism of the dolls by a group of *South Park* adults, including the mayor, who is a woman, and many other women. By demonstrating how easily American males (and even females?) can be flattered and deceived into cooperating with, or at the very least losing focus on, what appears to be an evil plan to attack the United States, Parker and Stone are running with some potentially explosive themes, associating race and penis size, as well as innocence and penis size. But the controversial aspects of such essentialist perspectives would no doubt be lost on their teenaged and young adult, primarily male, audience.

In a quite literal interpretation of Freud's theory of the phallus as symbol of power, the writers highlight the popular perception that penis size equates with political power. President Bill Clinton, at the time reeling in the wake of Monica-gate, is presented as the ultimate phallocentric male – the leader of the free world, no less – in a less than subtle dig at the former president when he appears on television to placate the American people over the sudden appearance of many Japanese military bases on the continental United States:

President Clinton: My fellow Americans, I wish to address the concerns many of us have over the growing number of Japanese military bases forming in the United States. The new Japanese Emperor Hirohito has made our own children into fighter pilots who will soon fly to Hawaii and attack Pearl Harbor. I spoke with Mr Hirohito this morning and he assured me that I have a very large penis!
He said it was mastodonic, dinosauric, and absolutely dwarfed his penis, which he assured me was nearly microscopic in size. My penis, he said, was most likely one of the biggest on the planet. I applaud Mr Hirohito in his honesty. Thank you.

The scene then cuts to *South Park* airport. The kids, still holding their Chimpokomon dolls, are getting ready to fly to Hawaii and bomb Pearl Harbor, emphasizing the pointlessness and politically inconsequential status of the president. More importantly, perhaps, it reflects perception of Japan's international obsequiousness and untrustworthiness, in that the president of the United States is able to be taken in by the simple wiles of the inscrutable oriental toy-maker.[25]

Alienating globalization

Other markers and motifs employed by Parker and Stone refer to the former emperor Hirohito, who 'coincidentally' shares the same name with the president of the Chimpokomon company. While appearing fairly mild, in effect the overlap between the name of the company president and the emperor could be considered an insult to Japanese society and culture. Moreover, by inciting children in America to 'avenge' World War II, the use of the emperor's name has significance beyond the imagination of the creators of this episode. Until his death in 1989, discussion and criticism of the emperor was muted in Japan. Even today it is controversial, and in the major media taboo, to publicly criticize the emperor's role during the Pacific War within Japan; indeed, many criticisms of the emperor's actions both during and after the war have originated in the United States, the prerogative of the victors. In this sense, the Chimpokomon episode follows the trend of critiques of the emperor from the United States. But it is a silly critique, which relies on grossly exaggerated metaphor to make its point that Japanese toys and culture are penetrating the United States and altering the nature of the cultural landscape. While the latter may be true, it may also be indicative of increasing interpenetration of Japanese and American popular cultural capital and their products.

It is the engagement with globalization that is one of the more important elements of this episode. Unsettling for American audiences it may be, but there is little doubt that Japanese animation and Japanese merchandising based on this animation may well be becoming dominant commercial influences in the United States. While the 'synergy' approach to merchandising products and animation together was a Disney-developed concept, in practice Japanese companies increasingly are able to provide better integration, marketing and audience share than many US companies, including the leading lights (Natsume 2002). Moreover, as with *Pokemon*, more commonly Japanese companies are working with American entertainment companies, creating new 'synergies' that can potentially transform production and marketing practices.

This process, of replicating and modifying the structures of the most successful, and of then working to formulaic practices, is often seen to be an essentialized component of 'Japanese' popular cultural production. The result of such marketing strategies has been considerable inroads made into the American consumer marketplace by Japanese companies. Like the US fast-food franchises, animation marketers from Japan have targeted children as consumers, linking merchandised products and collectibles with fast food outlets, for example. Clearly this strategy has been successful. These attitudes are illustrated in the interaction between two mothers discussing the Chimpokomon dolls at the toy store:

Mother 1:   Honestly, I don't see what they find so amusing about those things.
Mother 2:   They're so strange. Where are they from?
Red Harris (store owner): Well, it's some new big thing from Japan. I tell ya, those Japanese really know how to market to kids.

This leads us to the issue of globalization and its impact on the spread of ideas across borders but within the same genre. In this episode, this is precisely the plot: the spread of ideas across borders, identifiably from Japan, which dramatically influences children, controlled by insidious and ubiquitous marketing campaigns aimed at children and supported by Japanese corporate and government interests. However, there are many other tropes that appear to cross borders, as I've intimated earlier in this chapter. I would like to assess the impact of these often subordinated themes within the contexts of both the episode that went to air and the historical representation of Japan in American popular culture.

The production and distribution of goods that fuel commodity fetishism are linked in interesting ways with Japan in this episode. The images of Japanese as industrious, two-faced, holding secret corporate and government agendas, being intent on global domination and using economic advantage to manipulate children and consumption patterns (not to mention having small penises) are both consistent with propaganda from World War II about Japanese and emblematic of contemporary US expansionary capitalism. It should be noted, too, that, while revenge for Pearl Harbor is presented as the motive for the action of Japanese corporate aggression, revenge for the atomic bombings of Hiroshima and Nagasaki or for the deaths of one-quarter of the entire Okinawan population is not articulated here. Is this a result of the politics of corporate American broadcasting or the authors' own self-censorship? Was it seen as too outrageous to highlight the United States' engineered violence as a reason for revenge?

The alien nature of the *Pokemon* fad and its demonstrable Japaneseness, from the animation style to the kinds of products that are being marketed, and from the means by which they are marketed to the philosophies that the stories promulgate, identify this as a totally outside concept. Yet clearly Michael Eisner, the former Chief Executive Officer (CEO) of Disney, and Ray Croc, the CEO of Macdonald's, built their empires on marketing to young people things that are not particularly good for their souls or stomachs. The issue here is the identity of the fad: it is clearly Japanese and as such is seen to carry with it its historical baggage, certainly as reconstructed by Parker and Stone.

Of the many historical images invoked, the president of the toy company in full samurai regalia, an improbable but symbolically evocative gesture of Japan's Eastern 'traditions'; the young children in their aircraft getting ready to depart on a suicide mission, reminiscent of the young kamikaze pilots – the cherry blossoms – who committed suicide in their often futile attempts to damage US ships and aircraft carriers during World War II; and the parade of *South Park* children marching down Main Street carrying a Japanese flag and a portrait of the emperor, an image symbolic of the militaristic Japanese state education system of World War II, are examples of the ease with which Parker and Stone manipulate historical markers. Entirely dependent on conservative American readings of Japanese history, these images, employed in the present to represent contemporary relations between Japanese nationalism, corporatism and the impact of this dual power on American children, could be simple reconstructions of the demonized Japanese 'Other' of the Pacific War.

From a plot perspective, perhaps the most interesting element of the episode is the morality of groupism that underscores it. That is, while cultism and fads are seen to be evil, and while such groups are associated with Japanese society and culture,[26] clearly in this episode it was the groupism of the *South Park* children that was represented as both manipulative and obsessive, *and* wrong. This is illustrated at the end of the script, when the children are sitting in their fighter jets wearing their khaki Chimpoko uniforms that bear an uncanny resemblance to World War II Japanese military clothing. The parents have just demonstrated to the kids that Chimpokomon is *not* cool by showing them how much *they* love the Chimpoko fad. The parents are drawn in symbolized 'Japanese-style' and talk in strong Japanese-English accents. They have rushed to the airport carrying Chimpokomon flags and toys:

Randy: We just came to support you! We love Chimpokomon too! It's super toy number one!
Stan: You like it?
Mr Garrison: You bet! I think Chimpokomon is Chimpoka-riffic! I've got Shoe. (He shows the boys his Chimpokomon Shoe.)
Mrs Cartman: C'mon, Eric. Let's try to battle your Roostor with my DonkeyTron.
Cartman: Uh, no. That's okay, mom.
Hirohito: What are they doing?
Ozeki: It's a trick!
Randy: Hey, Stan. Look at my new bumper sticker. Isn't that cool? (It reads 'My kid is a Chimpokokid!')
Stan: No! (All the grown-ups are laughing Japanese style.) Screw this, dude.
Cartman: Where're you going, Stan?
Stan: I don't know. Chimpokomon just doesn't seem that cool any more. I'm gonna go kill some ants or something.
Cartman: Wait for me. I wanna get out of these stupid clothes.
Everyone: Yeah! Me too!

The subtle plot reversal here is wonderfully perverse. Just as the children were manipulated by their desires to own Chimpokomon and become World Chimpoko Master, so their parents were able to manipulate them into despising the former object of their desire. In Marx's terminology, this illustrates commodity fetishism at its finest. With all the phallus-centric commentary going on in this episode, it's not inappropriate for the children to rebel against their authority figures in how they discursively frame the concept of 'cool' and at the same time empower themselves by rejecting the 'coolness' of the attack on Pearl Harbor. In one fell swoop, the children are able to reject the toys, their message and their mission – together, as a group. The commentary on the ephemerality of fads – fetishes – reinforces the liberal perspective that kids get over fads, that they (the fads) have a very short lifespan and that parents can be empowered to influence their children's behaviour.

The other children have climbed out of their jet fighters. Only Kyle is left in the aeroplane. Stan is talking with Kyle:

Stan: You see, we've learned something today. This whole Chimpokomon thing happened because we all followed the group. We only liked Chimpokomon because everyone else did. And look at the damage it cost!

Kyle: So now I should stop liking Chimpokomon because you all don't?

Stan: Yep.

Kyle: But if I stop now, I'd just be going with the group again. So to be an individual I have to bomb Pearl Harbor. See ya.

Stan: Oh wait. Actually I was wrong. You see, Kyle, I learned something just now. It is good to go with the group. A group mentality is healthy sometimes.

Kyle: Aw, screw it. I'm too confused.

Kyle then gets out of the airplane, and goes home with his parents. As the children leave the airport, they leave their Chimpokomon dolls behind. A shot of a Lambtron being trodden on punctuates the next set of comments about how the adults can put an end to children's interest in fads (or anything, probably):

Randy: Well, you were right, Sharon! The best way to make our kids not like something is to like it ourselves!

Sharon: That's right! Anything we like is instantly not cool! (To Mr Garrison) We know how to take 'em out, Mr Garrison! Spread the word! Get on the wire to every parent around the country and tell 'em how to bring those sons of bitches down!

Mr Garrison goes to send the telegraphs.

Conclusion

One moral of this moral tale is that ultimately if adults do what kids do there is no fun in it for the kids. The lesson is about the importance of being different – being an individual. Or is it about the importance of being part of the group? It is a conundrum: while Japan is represented as the antithesis to US individualism, Kyle remains confused in the scene described above. Indeed, by illustrating this conundrum Parker and Stone identify some of the problems with attempting to reify too tightly the idea that Americans are individuals above all else. Indeed, the comments above illustrate the problems associated with group-based commodity consumption and social pressures to conform within contemporary US society. Adorno cites Reisman's 1950 work to demonstrate that the transition from puritanical notions of being introverted to the more liberating extroverted behaviours that are expected of middle America today are driven by peer group pressures (Adorno 1991). Such pressures are clearly of interest to Parker and Stone, and their commentary about such things is conducted within the trope of contemporary popular cultural criticism. It becomes apparent that Parker and Stone acknowledge the difficulties of ascribing characteristics of behaviour to cultural stereotypes.

This is the pivotal concept around which this episode revolves. Exposing the hypocrisy of American popular memory and the desirability of 'good moral values', this episode of *South Park* engages some extremely controversial and arguably self-interested themes. When Stan's parents sit down to watch a videotape of Chimpokomon, they can't decide at first whether what they are watching is 'good moral values' because they can't understand the plot (a position, I suspect, in which many parents have found themselves after looking at any *Pokemon* episode). However, they come to a decision not to let their son watch the show:

Sharon: Randy, we can't allow our son to watch this stuff.
Randy: Well, it's not like it's vulgar or violent.
Sharon: No, but it's incredibly stupid, and that could be worse on a child's mind than any vulgarity or violence.

Vulgarity over stupidity is the claim, and it's hard to argue against it, though many conservative American commentators, themselves brought up under the guiding benevolence of Disney, may well disagree.

How is it that a children's animation series can cause so much offence to so many? I think that is in fact the point of most of the *South Park* episodes. By exposing people to the foolish delusions we hang on to about being upright, moral and in control, they also expose most of us as morally corruptible, immoral and out of control – simply put, hypocritical. This is in marked contrast to the *Pokemon* venture, which is so cruelly lampooned in this episode. *Pokemon* has crafted characters based on market research into what is 'cute' and what appeals to certain demographics in Japan.[27] *South Park* has employed an antithetical approach to this: its writers have consciously attempted to create characters and plots that are offensive, not at all cute, and which enable the authors to air politically incorrect, but astute and often very funny observations about the human condition. One of the constantly recurring strains is on fashion and ephemerality, the foundation of 'cool'.

The writers emphasize a cardinal point: that cool can *never* be attained by those outside the group – in this case parents. When the parents breach the code of what constitutes being cool and reproduce it, it is no longer cool. Cool must always, definitionally, be bounded by age and cultural constraints. At the end of this episode parents mercilessly exploited their access to this understanding of what constituted coolness, and in doing so rendered Chimpokomon 'uncool'. Finally, after being distracted by attempting to produce other, new, counter-*Pokemon* characters and products to tempt the children away from the evil impact of the banal *Pokemon*,[28] adults get a sense of how to beat the fad.

If we argue that humour is based on parodies of emblematic truths we find funny enough to laugh at, what does this tell us about the 'truth' of the jibes about penis size, Pearl Harbor and demonic Japanese plans to overrun the US? Do we really see enough truth in the parodies of peoples, history, cultures and indeed physical differences to find them funny? Is it the outrageousness of stating out loud what cannot be commonly voiced in public? Or is it the incongruity of the obvious role reversals that makes us giggle? How do we engage the repeated comments on the male obsession (Parker and Stone's obsession?) with penis size – either as a metaphor for power/powerlessness or as a symbol of obsessive but misguided notions of superiority/inferiority? Or is it a representation of a partial truth? Can these character assassinations, politically incorrect slurs and ethnocentric stereotypes collectively be seen as a parody of the ridiculous nature of American white middle-class male values? What of the choice of the name of the president of the toy company – Hirohito – and the ludicrous representation of him in samurai general's regalia? Is this an extreme representation of the 'corporate warrior' as described by Shintaro Ishihara, Tokyo's governor, and author of *The Japan that Can Say 'No'* (1989)? Is there not something terrifyingly astute about the observation that the parents' desperate struggle to come to terms with something like *Pokemon* – both alien and somehow appealing – is driven by their complete lack of comprehension? After watching an episode of Chimpokomon, Randy, Stan's dad, says, 'I don't know, but I suddenly want to own all the dolls.'

To return to the themes of globalization and representation of Japan in US popular culture, this particular episode of *South Park* reveals a complex set of understandings, stereotypes and misapprehensions. This episode, like many other *South Park* offerings, contains a plethora of messages about society, culture and prejudices. Parker and Stone use the children and the parents to make their big points about fads (that is, that commodity fetishism, as described by Marx, is a central part of the current middle class's obsession with objects of desire), about stupidity (in particular the shallowness of commodity fetishism), about foreign influences in the United States (whether the values incorporated in the Japanese *anime* are in fact congruent with US mainstream values), about the way products are marketed to children (a powerful backhander directed at the marketing campaigns of corporations like Disney, Warner Brothers, Macdonald's, Burger King and so on) and about slavish US attempts to produce alternatives to Chimpokomon. Underwriting these points is the assumption that popular culture is meaningful in our times, a reflection of, and inspiration for, people's hopes and futures, as Fishwick (2001) informs us.

The concluding message from this particular episode of *South Park* is a simple one really. Notwithstanding the banality of commodity fetishism, Parker and Stone conclude that, although it was (and remains) popular in the United States, *Pokemon* is not a threat to the youth of America. It's simply another fairly mindless fad designed to help alleviate the boredom of life among the great unwashed masses, and one that has a limited lifespan. Could the same be said of *South Park*? Which will have the greater cultural resilience over the years to come? Stay tuned.

Notes

1 *South Park* has routinely demonized, or at least portrayed as alien, a number of political figures and cultures. Unlike Disney's myopic reluctance to employ representative styles that differ from Main Street, USA, in their animation (*Pocahontas, Mulan, Aladdin*, etc.), *South Park's* representation of others is singularly parodic and often racially essentialist. The 'Starvin' Marvin' episode, where Ethiopians are portrayed as 'click'-making savages, is an example of *South Park's* representative style. Gays are exaggerated and derogated, women are demeaned, 'rednecks' are ruthlessly parodied, Saddam Hussein becomes Satan's gay lover, Canadians are made the enemy of the US and drawn in idiosyncratic fashion, Chinese are rendered incomprehensible and potentially evil, and so on. In fact, the series parodies any potential target. But it had not dealt with an invasion from overseas before.

2 See, for example, Napier 2000; Levi 2000; McCarthy 2002.

3 Fishwick (2001) discusses this concept in detail.

4 A more recent version is available (Dorfman and Mattelart 1991).

5 See Eric Schlosser's book *Fast Food Nation* (2002) for a scintillating account of the cross-industry marketing of products to children instituted by fast food chains in the United States, then adopted by entertainment industry representatives and tacitly supported by Congress.

6 As we see, while *South Park's* audience is mostly adolescent male, *Pokemon* has a much wider demographic of support in Japan, but a much narrower pre-teen market in the United States.

7 Epithets like 'Jew', 'Kike', 'bitch', 'crack-ho', 'gay', 'faggot', 'hippie', 'fat-ass', 'asshole', are used as insults or as ways of representing negative experience. There is also the standard range of 'fuck you'-type lines; for example 'Screw you guys', Hate you guys'.

8 A number of newspapers reported the backlash against *Pokemon* from among both the extreme political right and the self-consciously chic political left. Presumably this unlikely alliance of opinions was influenced by the alien nature of the series, its ideals and its representations. Susan Napier (2000) makes some interesting observations about such issues.

9 Stone and Parker dropped out of courses of study to concentrate on making the animation short feature *Cannibal! The Musical*.

10 Unlike the overtly hostile sentiments directed at Japan and expressed in the Chimpokomon episode of *South Park*, *The Simpsons* episode 'Thirty Minutes

over Tokyo', while incorporating some harshly critical and culturally savvy observations of Japanese life and culture, also incorporated many 'inside' perspectives, a dimension that Parker and Stone did not develop with much subtlety.

11 In many *manga* and Japanese animation series, Caucasian men are represented as large, often hirsute, usually evil and commonly sexually potent and sexually violent; Caucasian women, on the other hand, are represented commonly on the Madonna–whore spectrum as whores, with voluptuous figures, 'loose' sexual mores (commonly they are seen to have abandon and extreme sex with strangers), desirable and repulsive. (See Napier 2000 for discussions on stereotyping Europeans in erotic and business comics.)

12 In the early twentieth century increasingly draconian laws restricting Asian immigration to the United States and imposing land ownership and working restrictions on Asians were passed. By 1923 Japanese were specifically targeted, and tough anti-Japanese business and immigration policy was enacted.

13 For the purposes of this essay, I will concentrate on the US representation of Japanese, rather than on Japanese representations of the United States, though such representations were frequent during the years of the Pacific War.

14 This is a similar process to that which currently demonizes Osama Bin-Laden, Al Qaeda and, of course, Saddam Hussein.

15 The series routinely demonizes Canadians, but for the most part focuses on groups within the United States.

16 See, especially, Parker and Stone's treatment of Canada, Iraq (especially Saddam Hussein) and more recently China. They have also parodied Australians – the 'Crocodile Hunter' Steve Irwin, for example, whose job is to track down wild animals and 'stick me thumb up their arses', and Russell Crowe (a New Zealand 'Australian'), whose unsuccessful and often farcical fighting exploits have generated considerable media attention in recent years.

17 At the time of writing, there are more than 30,000 US troops stationed in Okinawa prefecture alone, and a further 15,000 in other parts of Japan.

18 These are cruel caricatures of the *Pokemon* dolls, the names of which are effectively incomprehensible to non-Japanese.

19 According to 'Wild Willy Westwood' (http://spscriptorium.com/Season3/E310 secrets.htm), the woman is Kumashiro Yumiko, a hardcore porn star, best known as one of the 'Ass-fuck Twins' in *Orgazmo*.

20 The name Hirohito refers to the former emperor of Japan, who reigned over the Empire during World War II.

21 In *The Simpsons* episode Thirty Minutes Over Tokyo they too played on the seizure event that accompanied the screening of an infamous *Pokemon* episode in which Pikachu – arguably the most popular *Pokemon* – flashed his eyes in a strobing pattern that caused epilepsy-like reactions in a sizeable number of people viewing it in its prime time 6.30 p.m. slot. About 700 people were seriously enough afflicted to warrant hospitalization. The news stations later that evening re-screened the footage which had caused the seizures and a further 300 people were hospitalized.

22 A good example is the following dialogue, when the children have returned from their Chimpokomon camp:

Mr Garrison:	Now we are going to try this again until we get it right. What's six times three.
Stan:	Juu hachi desu ka.
All:	Juu hachi desu nee.
Mr Garrison:	No goddammit it's eighteen.

Stan:	Juu hachi is eighteen, Garrison-san.
Mr Garrison:	For the last time. My name is not Garrison-san, and this is not Hat-san. Now you better start talking in a manner I can understand.

23 The word '*chin-chin*' is a word used by children for the penis. A more adult word, '*chimpo*', is also derived from this base.

24 This includes one memorable occasion when former president Bill Clinton's 'gargantuan, bulbous penis' is eulogized by Mr Ozeki.

25 There is little doubt that one of the more cynical interpretations of this process is to highlight the hypocrisy of US foreign policy and its establishment of US military bases in Japan, amongst other nations.

26 Nakane's famous *Japanese Society* (1970), originally published in Japanese as *Tateshakai* (1968), is the seminal work in this field.

27 See Kubo 2000.

28 One example is Alabama Man, who gets drunk, goes bowling, chews tobacco and beats his wife:

> Voiceover: (introducing a Ken-like male doll dressed in jeans, a checked flannel shirt, waistcoat, and Western-style hat) You can take Alabama Man to the bowling alley, where he drinks heavily and chews tobacco.
> Boy #1: (on TV) Wow! He can bowl!
> Commercial #2 Singer: (on TV) He bowls and drinks! He drinks and bowls! Alabama Man!
> Commercial #2 Announcer: (on TV) When wife asks him where he's been, just use the action button and Alabama Man busts her lip open!

> The kids are not impressed. Each of them pronounces in order that the new toy is 'gay' or 'totally gay'.

Bibliography

Adorno, T. (1991) *The Culture Industry: selected essays on mass culture*, London: Routledge.

Boskin, J. (1997) *Rebellious Laughter: people's humor in American culture*, Ithaca, NY: Syracuse University Press.

Bush, R. (1998) 'Family values under attack'. Online. Available HTTP: http://www.cwfa.org/library/music/1998-06_fv_light-your-world.shtml#southpark (accessed 15 January 2003).

Dean, M. (1999) 'Review'. Online. Available HTTP: http://www.jiminycritic.com/review.asp?ReviewID=7 (accessed 14 July 2004).

Dorfman, A. and Mattelart, A. (1991) *How to Read Donald Duck: imperialist ideology in the Disney comic*, trans. and updated introduction by D. Kunzle; appendix by J. S. Lawrence, New York: International General.

Dower, J. (1987) *War without Mercy: race and power in the Pacific War*, New York: Pantheon.

Fishwick, M. (2001) *Popular Culture in a New Age*, New York: The Haworth Press.

Ishihara, S. (1989) *The Japan that Can Say 'No'*, New York: Simon and Schuster.

Kim, C. (2001) '*South Park* S-Bombs', 23 June 2001, E! Online News. Online. Available HTTP: http://www.eonline.com/News/Items/0,1,8456,00.html (accessed 15 July 2004).

Kubo, M. (2000) 'Why Pokémon was successful in America', *Japan Echo*, vol. 27, no. 2, April: 24–7.

Levi, A. (2000) *Samurai from Outer Space: understanding Japanese animation*, Chicago: Open Court.

McCarthy, H. (2002) *Hayao Miyazaki: master of Japanese animation: films, themes, artistry*, Berkeley, CA.: Stone Bridge Press.

Nakane, C. (1970) *Japanese Society*, Middlesex: Penguin. Originally published as *Tateshakai* (1968) in Japanese.

Natsume, F. (2002) 'Japanese *manga* encounter the world', *Japan Echo*, vol. 29, no. 2: 61–7.

Napier, S. (2000) *Anime From Akira to Princess Mononoke: experiencing contemporary Japanese animation*, New York: Palgrave.

Said, E. (1979) *Orientalism*, New York: Vintage.

Schlosser, E. (2002) *Fast Food Nation*, London: Penguin.

Tanaka, S. (1993) *Japan's Orient: rendering pasts into history*, Berkeley, CA: University of California Press.

Westwood, W.W. (2001) 'Discussing *South Park*'. Online. Available HTTP: http://spscriptorium.com/Season3/E310secrets.htm (accessed 22 September 2003).

4 The film *Bishônen* and Queer(N)Asia through Japanese popular culture[1]

Romit Dasgupta

Introduction

The genesis for this chapter goes back to an evening in late 2000. A group of friends – both 'Anglo'-Australians and Asian-Australians – had gone to view a screening of a film from Hong Kong that was being screened as part of the Lesbian and Gay Pride film festival in Perth, Australia. I had gone along unaware of the name of the film and with no knowledge of the details of its plot. Consequently I was slightly surprised when the title came on during the opening credits. Despite the fact that the film was set in Hong Kong and that the dialogue in the movie was in a combination of Cantonese and Mandarin, the title, *Bishônen no Koi* (A Beautiful Youth's Love), was presented in Japanese, using a combination of *kanji* for the first and the third words in the title and *hiragana* for the connective particle '*no*'.[2] As is suggested by the name, the film, in terms of the storyline, the visuals and the almost angelic beauty of the two lead actors, came across quite explicitly as a cinematic rendition of a particular genre of *shôjo manga* (comics read by and targeting teenage girls and young women) in Japan, also known as YAOI or *shônen ai*, which revolve around homoerotic and/or homosexual attraction between adolescent males or young men (Sabucco 2003: 70–2; McLelland 2003: 54–8, 2000: 69–84; Aoyama 1988).[3] Despite the discernible Japanese influence running through the film, I assumed that the director, Yonfan, had adapted a pre-existing Japanese *manga* text and rendered it into a cinematic Chinese version. After all, this kind of inter-textual transference of Japanese popular culture texts is not uncommon. Examples include Yoshimoto Banana's debut novel, *Kitchen*, which was adapted into a Cantonese film, and Japanese *manga* which have been made into *anime* for an Asian audience, such as the *manga Hana Yori Dango*, re-packaged as a Taiwanese serialized television drama, *Meteor Garden* (see Chua 2004: 210; Iwabuchi 2004b: 17, 18). Most recently, Andy Lau's *Initial D* (starring Taiwanese star Jay Chou) was also adapted from a popular Japanese *manga* (see *Aera* 2005: 11). However, as I discuss below, in the case of *Bishônen* the situation was more complex than a simple case of cultural borrowing and adaptation.

The other aspect of the film that made an impression on me, and indeed contributed to my decision to explore and 'deconstruct' the film further, was the reaction of the friends with whom I had watched the film. The 'Anglo'-Australian friends I was with found the film frustratingly 'fuzzy' with respect to delineating a clear 'gay' identity, as well as melodramatic and sexually anti-climactic – the film ends without the relationship between the two 'beautiful' lead actors ever being sexually consummated. The Asians and Asian-Australians (myself included), on the other hand, found these very qualities of sexual reticence and indirectness actually added to the appeal of the film, a refreshing contrast to the 'in-your-face' directness of Anglo-American queer popular culture representations like the American television series *Queer as Folk* (and the British series it was based upon). While clearly it would be ridiculous to extend the observations of a few individuals to make culturally essentialist generalizations, nevertheless these differing responses to the film do bring to mind Audrey Yue's discussion of the ways a queer Asian-Australian – what she labels 'Queer(N)Asian' – audience read another queer themed Hong Kong film from the late 1990s, Wong Kar-Wai's *Happy Together* (Yue 2000). This reading, Yue points out, is situated within 'a transnational Asian queer connectedness [which] produces an identity that disrupts the post-Stonewall, Anglo-Saxon model of coming out as a narration of sexual identity' (2000: 253). Similarly, I would contend that the differing readings I encountered in relation to *Bishônen* may well point to a similar dynamic in operation, and this underscores the importance of the need to be reflexive about the nuances and complexities informing the production, circulation and consumption of popular culture texts.

This chapter uses the film *Bishônen* to draw attention to the ways in which dynamics of transnational and intra-regional popular culture flows intertwine with configurations of emergent 'Queer(N)Asian' sexualities. Specifically, the chapter situates the discussion within the context of cultural flows between Japan and other societies in the Asia-Pacific region. Much discussion of the dynamics of intra-regional popular cultural flows has focused on outward flows from what Eric Ma (2001) refers to as 'satellites of modernity'. Much less attention has been directed at the reverse – flows *into* these regional 'satellites of modernity'. Such vectors in the reverse direction may be less visible, but nevertheless do play a part in the shapings and artic-ulations of regional popular culture. One such example of the significance of reverse flows is the impact Korean popular culture has had on Japanese popular imaginings of Korea as a nation. I argue that *Bishônen* is also a good example of the ways in which common understandings of cultural flows and transfers may be disrupted.

Japan and popular culture flows

As has been pointed out by various writers (for instance Chua 2004; Morris 2004; Iwabuchi 2004b, 2002b; Moeran 2000), analyses of the dynamics associated with the phenomenon of 'globalization' still tend to be heavily slanted towards what Iwabuchi labels 'a West–Rest paradigm'(2004b: 3). However, the reality is one where intra-regional and even domestic flows of culture, capital, technology, ideas, images and people – the interfaces constituting what Arjun Appadurai refers to as 'scapes' – may be just as significant (see Appadurai 1996: 32–43).

This significance of intra-regional dynamics becomes evident if we consider the body of work that has emerged in recent years examining popular culture flows in East and Southeast Asia. In particular, a number of writers have addressed the role that Japan has played in shaping the contours of popular culture consumption and articulations of identity in the various societies in the region (see, for instance, Hu 2005; Chua 2004, 2000; Iwabuchi 2004a, 2002b, 2001; Ko 2004, 2003; D. Lee 2004; M. Lee 2004; L. Y. M. Leung 2004, 2002; Park 2004; Martin 2003c; Ben-Ari and Clammer 2000; Moeran 2000; Ching 1995). A common strand running through many of these works is the ways in which the consumption practices of Japanese popular culture texts are different from the ways in which products of Euro-American popular culture are consumed. One of the reasons often offered (frequently by consumers themselves) for this difference is a sense of 'cultural proximity' or 'cultural coevalness' (Iwabuchi 2002b, 2001; L. Y. M. Leung 2002). However, as Iwabuchi, Leung and others point out, while cultural similarities *may* well play some part, factors such as historical experiences of modernization, as well as the specific socio-cultural and economic conditions through which 'late modern temporality' (Iwabuchi 2004b: 12) is being experienced by (particularly) younger urban consumers in locations like Taipei, Hong Kong, Seoul and Singapore, are far more significant.

Intersecting with the above have been the perception of Japanese popular culture products as 'culturally odourless' (Iwabuchi 2002b: 24–8) and the 're-odourizing' of seemingly culturally neutral cultural texts as *Japanese*, precisely because of the cultural capital of the 'Japan as funky' type of association (see L. Y. M. Leung 2002: 74). These dynamics of distance/familiarity and cultural (re-)odour/odourlessness have played a part in the shaping of an emergent common urban, youth-focused popular culture that finds expression in texts (songs, television dramas, *manga*) and style (Japanese-influenced street fashions and hairstyles, layout of glossy magazines and boutiques) across the region (Chua 2004: 215–17). Moreover, it allows for manifold translations and transfigurations, leading to situations where the Japanese influence may well be invisible to some consumers of that particular text (Ching 1995: 281) but consciously apparent (or 're-odourized') for others. An example of this would be the recent *Hanryu* boom in Korean popular culture in large parts of East and Southeast Asia. At one level it may appear, from the popularity of Korean television dramas in the region, that Korean popular culture is replacing Japanese popular culture in defining what is 'funky' and 'cool' in the region (Chua 2004: 207, 208; Iwabuchi 2004b: 16, 17; also Yoon 2001). However, as Chua (2004: 207) and Lee Dong-Hoo

(2004) observe, underlying the emergence of Korean popular culture has been the (sometimes very deliberate) incorporation of elements of Japanese popular culture, which are then repackaged and disseminated through the region and consumed as products of Korean popular culture. A similar case could be made for the successful Taiwanese serial *Meteor Garden*, mentioned above, originally based on a Japanese *manga*, but which came to be associated with Taiwan, and in particular the Taiwanese boy band F4, in the minds of fans (Chua 2004: 210; Iwabuchi 2004b: 17, 18).[4] Such processes of translation and transfiguration then bring into question assumptions about 'authenticity' and 'origin', in the context of the shapings of popular culture in the region and the ways in which they intersect with articulations of identity.[5] This issue of 'origin' and 'authenticity' is something I will return to below, in the context of the popular culture text *Bishônen*.

Japanese popular culture flows and articulations of sexualities

While a substantial body of work dealing with aspects of Japanese popular culture's intersections with emergent East/Southeast Asian popular culture articulations has emerged in recent years, one area that has not been addressed directly is the role Japanese popular culture has played in influencing configurations and articulations of sexualities in the region. East and Southeast Asian political leaders and authority figures have often made links between processes of globalization, which they unquestioningly construct along a 'West/Rest' vector, and changing attitudes towards sexuality among youth in those countries (see, for instance, Tan 1999; Altman 2000; Drucker 2000).

However, what these 'gatekeepers' of public morality seem to be unaware of is that, given the *perceived* cultural 'proximity' coupled with the perception of Japan (or more recently South Korea or Taiwan) as culturally 'cool', popular culture texts emerging from within the region may well exert just as significant an influence in relation to articulations of sexuality and sexual practices. An example of this is the way in which the Japanese social phenomenon of *enjo kôsai* caught on among adolescent females in Taiwan (Ho 2003; Lam 2003). The literal translation of the term would be something like 'assisted socializing/compensated dating', but more generally it came to be associated in the Japanese media from the 1990s with the phenomenon of young teenage girls being paid by much older men to go on dates, which were sometimes platonic, but often involved (paid) sex. As both Ho (2003: 331) and Lam (2003: 355) point out, it was through a Japanese television drama, *Kami-sama, Mô Sukoshi Dake* (God, Please Give Me More Time), starring the popular part-Taiwanese, part-Japanese male actor Kaneshiro Takeshi, that the practice caught on in Taiwan. Significantly, it was not just the practice itself that caught on; rather, just as integral was the need to reproduce and embody the visual style associated with Japanese schoolgirls engaging in the practice – high tube-socks worn with very short school uniform skirts, *puri-kura* (print club) mini-stickers, lots of 'cute' accessories attached to mobile phones, for instance (see Lam 2003: 354, 355).

Similarly, for young female viewers in Singapore or Taipei or Hong Kong watching television dramas from Japan, identifying with the sexual and romantic relationships of a young, single female professional depicted in a Japanese television drama like *Love Generation* may well be far more imme- diate than identifying with the female characters in, say, *Sex and the City*. Indeed, as MacLachlan and Chua (2004), in their discussion of Singaporean women's readings of female characters in Japanese television dramas, note, the relatively liberated sexual behaviour and attitudes of the female charac- ters depicted in Japanese dramas represent a sort of ideal 'middle ground' between the (perceived) direct, confrontational portrayals of sex in Western popular culture and the 'frumpy' sexually conservative and patriarchal offi- cial public discourse in Singapore.

At the same time, depictions of sexuality in many of these representations also intersect with issues that bear far greater resonance for viewers' everyday reality than is the case for Euro-American texts. One such consideration is the way family and family relationships are often factored in. As Chua Beng- Huat points out, despite the focus on urban, young, single professionals, unlike American series like *Friends* and *Sex and the City*, which all but erase the family, 'in East Asian urban television dramas and films, the family still has a presence'. This is a presence which alternates between 'an obstacle and a refuge to romance in the city' (Chua 2004: 216) but nevertheless reflects the reality for a significant proportion of urban youth in these societies.

Shapings of an emergent 'Queer(N)Asian' identity

Such considerations would also translate across when considering emergent 'queer' identities across the region.[6] Much of the discourse on the increasing visibility of queer identities has focused on their intersections with flows of globalization along the West/Rest axis. The referent is invariably queer iden- tity as defined and articulated in Sydney, London, New York or Berlin. On one level, there is no denying that the powerful influence of Western-centric and -derived discourses of queer identity, intersecting with the socio- economic conditions of capitalist modernity in urban centres throughout the region, has resulted in increasingly standardized hegemonic ideals in terms of what defines queer – in particular gay male – identity. Thus, hegemonic gay male identity, whether in Jakarta, Bangkok, Singapore or Tokyo, may come across as being all about gyms, dance parties, upmarket designer boutiques or the latest episode of *Queer as Folk*, much the same as in Sydney or London (see Altman 2000: 138–40, 149–50).

However, as with the dynamics of globalization and popular culture flows, articulating queer identities may in fact be more complex and nuanced than initial impressions may suggest. First, as Peter Jackson notes, despite the powerful globalizing forces whereby the 'commercial gay scenes . . . in

Bangkok's Silom Road, Sydney's Oxford Street, Paris's Marai quarter, London's Soho, Greenwich Village . . . are . . . intimately related with each other as an interlocking global set of spaces', there *are* local specificities and indigenous discourses infusing these spaces. If we focus on these specificities and local articulations, 'materially and economically similar spaces are revealed as sites of remarkably diverse understandings of same-sex eroticism and equally diverse imaginings of gendered futures' (Jackson 2001: 13; also Berry *et al.* 2003). A variety of ethnographic and historical studies attest to the existence of locally specific articulations of queer sexualities, even in spaces and contexts that at first may come across as similar to those in the West (see McLelland 2005, 2000; Berry *et al.* 2003; Martin 2003b; Jackson 2001, 1999, 1995; Murray 2001; Boellstorff 2000; Chao 2001; Chou 2000; Rofel 1999).

Additionally, as with discussions of popular culture flows, the *intra-regional* flows within the East/Southeast Asian region have, in the context of queer sexualities, received very little scholarly attention. Anecdotal evidence would suggest that, in the same way that we can talk about an East/Southeast Asian popular culture in the collective, so too there may be shapings of an emergent East/Southeast Asian queer culture, which also links into diasporic Asian queer articulations in North America, Australia/New Zealand and Europe.[7] In a sense, this is the 'Queer(N)Asian' articulation that Yue (2000) refers to. Within the context of this 'Queer(N)Asian' regional/transnational identity, references to other urban centres in Asia feature alongside 'traditional' queer-associated urban centres in the West, such as Sydney, Paris or New York. Thus, for instance, *Fridae.com*, a popular queer cyber-community site based initially out of Singapore and subsequently Hong Kong but extending out throughout the region, concentrates on providing updates on events like dance parties, parades and queer film festivals, news, information and gossip from a range of East/Southeast Asian urban centres (*Fridae.com*, http://www.friday.com, accessed 12 October 2005).[8] What comes across is how articulations of queer in an urban centre like, say, Singapore feed off other centres – like Tokyo or Hong Kong – in the region as much as they use Sydney or New York as the point of reference. This is based, not just on the flow of information and images through the internet, but also on the physical movement of individuals travelling for events like regional dance parties such as 'Nation', which since it was first held in 2001 in Singapore has grown to become arguably Asia's premier queer dance party, with the venue shifting to Phuket in 2005.[9] Significantly, Japan comes across as being one of the premier nodes of this emergent regional queer culture.[10] For instance, a posting on 5 April 2004 in the public access 'Gossip' section of the site by 'greendragon' gave information about an upcoming 'Harajuku-style party' in Shanghai. A posting from Phuket on 2 September 2005 by 'xssx', reporting on the upcoming 'Nation' event in November, goes further in linking Japan with queer sexual capital, in reporting that 'Woof! There's going to be FIVE Japanese gogo boys performing at Nation . . . pant*pant*pant*' (http://www.fridae.com/gossip/index.php, accessed 17 November 2004 and 12 October 2005).[11]

From the above descriptions of dance parties and go-go boys, this 'Queer(N)Asian' identity may not come across as particularly different from dominant articulations of gay male identities in the West. However, there may also be significant points of departure from Anglo-American articulations. As Yue argues, these Queer(N)Asian articulations may challenge 'post-Stonewall, Anglo-Saxon' understandings and articulations of queer identity with respect to the 'model of 'coming out' and the social mapping of family and kinship' (Yue 2000: 253). Indeed, through these disruptions, Queer(N)Asian articulations may offer the possibility of deploying 'queer' in the original theoretical sense of the term – destabilizing binaries like hetero-sexual/homosexual, straight/gay, West/East, centre/periphery, among others. This disruptive potential is discernible in a number of queer (popular and sub-) cultural texts emerging out of the region. Japan, for instance, has seen a number of television dramas and movies over the past decade, emerging out of what McLelland refers to as a younger female consumer-driven 'gay boom', commodifying aspects of queer identities and lifestyles (McLelland 2000: 32–7). Many of these, such as the 1993/4 serial *Dôsôkai* and the 1999 *Romansu* (both aired on a mainstream commercial network) and movies like *Okoge* (1992), *Twinkle* (1992), *Hatachi no Binetsu* (1993) and *Hush* (2002), despite on the one hand sometimes appearing to conform to dominant soci-etal ideological expectations, also undermine and destabilize some of these very ideological underpinnings (like hegemonic definitions of marriage and fatherhood, for instance), in unexpected and sometimes quite profound ways (see Buckley 2000; McLelland 2000: 32, 98–102; Miller 2000).

Excluding Japan, arguably the greatest visibility of such cultural articula-tions has been in Taiwan and Hong Kong. Taiwan, for instance, has seen the emergence into the public domain of a rich discourse surrounding queer identities through popular culture channels (Liou 2003; Martin 2003a, 2003c; Wang and Parry 2000). In Hong Kong, too, a number of films have been produced that, as one authority notes, 'in various ways and to different degrees, challenge the heteronormative understandings of sexuality' (H. H. Leung 2001: 424). In particular, films such as Wong Kar-wai's 1997 *Happy Together* and Stanley Kwan's 1998 *Hold You Tight*, or even his 2001 film *Lan Yu*, as well as the film I focus on in this chapter, *Bishônen*, rather than being films about bounded *gay* identity, are situated along fluid, shifting, intersecting, colliding and diverging contours and faultlines; what Helen Hok-sze Leung, borrowing a term from Gordon Ingram, terms 'queer-scapes' (H. H. Leung 2001: 425).[12] Queerscapes, she argues, rather than being 'definitive habitats . . . [are] emergent sites of possibility, the potential of which cannot yet be properly articulated' (H. H. Leung 2001: 426). In this respect, it is not unlike the shapings and contours of the emergent (but as yet defying concise articulation) East Asian popular culture I discussed earlier, which calls into question many of the binary assumptions about transnational flows of culture. It is in this context that I discuss the film *Bishônen* below.

Bishônen, the film

As mentioned in the introductory pages of this chapter, *Bishônen* was directed by Yonfan, a Hong Kong-based director and photographer/cinematographer, who is also the creator of works like *Bugis Street* (1995) and *The Peony Pavilion* (2001), which featured the Japanese female actor Miyazawa Rie. Despite having a number of films to his credit, Yonfan and his films have not received the attention that other Hong Kong filmmakers like Stanley Kwan or Wong Kar-Wai have.[13] Most of the discussion of *Bishônen*, for instance, appears to have been limited to the popular (and queer) press and to online review, shopping and fan sites.[14]

The film was released in 1998 and was featured at a number of film festivals on the international circuit. It won the Best Picture at the thirteenth Milan and Bologna International Gay and Lesbian Film Festival, was featured at the 1999 Berlin Film Festival as an Official Invitation and was Official Selection at a number of other festivals on the circuit (including the Tokyo International Lesbian and Gay Film Festival). Despite these achievements, and despite its visual slickness and use of (even by Hong Kong standards) two exquisitely attractive lead actors, the film was not received with much enthusiasm by audiences and critics. Yonfan himself, in an interview with *Time Asia*, admitted that, 'financially, the movie was a total flop' (Short 2001, *Time Asia Online*, http://www.time.com/asoa/arts/column/0.9754. 180353.00.html, accessed 21 November 2004).

At one level, the negative reaction of audiences and critics does make sense. The good-looking actors and slick settings notwithstanding, the film *is* cheesy and sentimental, with a storyline and plot that are difficult to envisage in real life. In all of these elements, as well as in the choice of title, the film is suggestive of the genre of teenage/schoolgirl romance literature, particularly along the lines of Japanese *shôjo manga* (see, for instance, Aoyama 1988; McLelland 2000: 70, 71; ôgi 2001: 180–2).

The story is set almost entirely in central Hong Kong (Mizuta 2000: 112, 113).[15] It revolves around the intersecting and intertwined relationships between a set of young, attractive urban singles – Sam (played by Chinese-American actor Daniel Wu), a handsome, extremely upright young officer with the Hong Kong police force, Jet (Stephen Fung), a strikingly attractive male hustler working out of an upscale male callboy establishment, Ah Ching (Jason Tsang), Jet's colleague and housemate, K. S. (Terence Yin), a popular music idol who has curious links with the lives of the other three characters, and Kana (Shu Qi), a mysterious female figure who weaves in and out of the narrative, linking Jet and Sam together. With the exception of Sam's mother, Kana is the only significant female character in the film to have a *visual* role. There is, however, a voiceover of an (apparently) older woman (done through the voice of Brigitte Lin) narrating the story in the past tense. In contrast to the dialogue between the characters in the film, most of which is in Cantonese, this voiceover narration is in Mandarin.

The film opens with Jet encountering Sam and Kana at an upscale central city art gallery and becoming infatuated with the beauty of both. He subsequently bumps into Sam again, during the latter's late-night police rounds. The two become friends, and soon Jet is invited to dinner with Sam and his parents. In the family dinner scene, Sam comes across quite unambiguously as the 'ideal' Confucian man/son/husband – morally principled, respectful and filial towards his parents, and considerate towards his friend (for instance, cooking a fish dish he knew Jet liked).[16] This invitation to dinner appears to seal Jet's position as Sam's best friend and confidant, a development indicated by Sam's parents' relief that their normally introverted son has found a friend, and by the fact that the taciturn Sam opens up slightly to Jet. Jet starts falling in love with Sam in an unarticulated, disarming schoolboy infatuation kind of way, something quite different to his normal monetary-based relationships with his clients, an aspect of Jet's life Sam continues to be unaware of. In contrast to Jet's strengthening feelings for him, Sam does not display any concrete sign of reciprocating. Indeed, Sam seems quite distant and uninterested. However, whatever Sam's true feelings might be, what does come across is a strong 'homoemotional' relationship developing between Sam and Jet. The only people in whom Jet is able to confide his feelings (including his frustrations) for Sam are his two housemates and fellow rent boys, Ah Ching and Cindy.

Ah Ching one day encounters Sam on his police rounds. Ah Ching thinks he recognizes him as someone called Fai and calls out to him, only to be met with complete lack of recognition. The narrative then shifts to a flashback, where Ah Ching, in contrast to his present suave, hustler look, was a 'geeky' looking clerk in an office. A new clerk called Fai starts work at the same organization and is placed next to Ah Ching. The two, who share a common interest in comics, develop a close friendship and subsequently become lovers. However, their seemingly perfect love gets disrupted by the entry of the vain and narcissistic aspiring movie star K. S., with whom Fai becomes infatuated. Fai ends up asking for money from Ah Ching in order to help K. S. kick-start his career as an idol, but later discovers that the egotistical K. S. did not really need the money. In order to raise the sum Fai had asked him for, Ah Ching has sex for money, as a hustler – the beginning of his transformation from frumpy office clerk to sexy male prostitute. K. S. subsequently goes on to celebrity stardom.

Fai disappears from both Ah Ching's and K. S.'s lives; four years down the track he is Sam, the policeman, dutiful son and Jet's friend. The various past and present lives collide when Sam helps Jet back to his apartment after the latter sprains his ankle, and bumps into Ah Ching. Jet pursues Sam back to his apartment and confronts him with the knowledge of Sam's own past as Fai, and his own 'secret' life as a rent boy. This then leads to the first scene of physical intimacy between Jet and Sam, and as they grapple with and undress one another on Sam's bed it appears that the film is about to reach its final moment of cinematic and sexual resolution. However, before they can reach that point, someone appears to enter the apartment and leave before the two can find out who it was. A visibly shaken Sam asks Jet to leave. Later that evening, once his parents have returned home, Sam realizes it was his father who had accidentally walked in on Jet and himself earlier in the day. Although the father does not say anything, Sam works it out through the nuances of facial expression and body language. In keeping with the style of many Asian melodrama texts, Sam returns to his room, writes a letter and then throws himself off the balcony of the high-rise apartment in which he and his parents live.

The final scene of the film sees the reappearance of the enigmatic Kana delivering a letter to Jet, who cannot understand why Sam has so abruptly disappeared from his life. It turns out to be Sam's final letter, in which he explicitly states his feelings of love for Jet. The film ends with Jet being able to sleep soundly that night, secure in the knowledge that, even though he and Sam never had a sexual relationship, they truly loved each other. The closing credits come on to the accompaniment of a syrupy, sentimental love ballad.

There is no denying that, from the above sketch, *Bishônen* may well come across as being, at best, a superficial, vacuous, self-indulgent work that is little more than a cinematic *shôjo manga* pandering to the young female market. At worst, the film may come across as a retrograde, self-loathing cautionary tale about the unhappy end awaiting gay men. Yet, as the recognition at the various film festivals seems to indicate, the film *can* be read at a deeper level, and, like more 'serious' queer Hong Kong film texts such as *Happy Together* or *Hold You Tight*, it does destabilize binary understandings of sexual identity. For instance, the film is laced with what Helen Leung terms a '"post-gay" understanding of relationships . . . where the boundary between the sexual and the nonsexual never stays constant' (H. H. Leung 2001: 438). This 'ambivalent border zone' of the erotic allows for endless possibilities of various intersections and configurations. In the context of such a 'post-gay' framework of relationships between individuals is the understanding that 'eroticism overlaps with, but is not reducible to, sexuality'. In this regard, it permeates intimacies that do not necessarily find sexual expression. For instance, intense emotional bonds, casual physical contact or fantasies not acted on can all be erotic and still nonsexual:

> [Significantly,] [a]n honest recognition of this ambivalence jettisons the idea that all relational bonds can clearly be demarcated as either *sexual* or platonic, and that people can be categorized as either straight or gay, according to their sexual preference.
>
> (H. H. Leung 2001: 438)

In *Bishônen* the characters occupy these interstitial border zones. Jet has sex with men, but he does so for money, not out of pleasure. These interactions are portrayed as cold business transactions, or (in one case) ugly, sexual violence. He does fall in love with Sam, but their relationship is never sexually consummated. Indeed, until the very end of the story Sam and Jet do not engage in any *physical* intimacy either. Yet the very non-physicality and non-sexuality of their interactions is intensely charged with erotic possibilities which, as a consequence of Sam's death, remain open-ended. Jet is also attracted to the woman with whom he first sees Sam – the enigmatic and beautiful Kana, who weaves in and out of the narrative, appearing at random but nevertheless significant junctures in the story. In one scene, a drunken Jet propositions Kana for sex in a nightclub. Kana turns down Jet's offer, leaving instead with a woman with whom she had been making eye contact. At the same time, Kana's rejection is not conclusive and leaves open the possibility of a future relationship. Kana herself is never clearly defined in terms of her relationship with Sam. She is depicted as something of an intermediary between Sam and Jet, delivering Sam's farewell letter to Jet, for instance. Yet, apart from the opening scenes of the film, where they come across as an 'everyday' heterosexual couple on a date, she and Sam are never shown together, nor does Sam ever make reference to her. However, Kana's ambivalent position, and the cryptic quality to her interactions with Sam and Jet, actually heightens the erotic tension in the sets of relationships – between Kana and each of the two men and, indeed, between Jet and Sam. Similar shades of ambivalence inform many of the other relationships in the film – between Fai and Ah Ching, for instance, or between Ah Ching, Jet and Cindy.

In discussing the ambivalent sexual/erotic relationships in *Happy Together*, Leung notes that these open up possibilities not just for 'reinventing the boundaries of (sexual) identity . . . [but also] for configurations of political borders and identities that are not reducible to existing discourses of nationalism' (H. H. Leung 2001: 439). There has been discussion, for instance, of the ways in which texts such as *Hold You Tight* and *Happy Together*, produced in the mid- to late 1990s, were attempts at articulating some of the anxieties and possibilities surrounding Hong Kong's reversion to China in 1997, as well as the cross-border identities between China, Hong Kong and Taiwan (H. H. Leung 2001; Siegel 2001; Yue 2000; Stokes and Hoover 1999: 268–79). *Bishônen*, also made during these years, allows for such readings. For instance, the shifting between Cantonese and Mandarin is one way in which the intermeshing of the 'three Chinas' is given expression in the film.[17]

Moreover, in the case of *Bishônen* these 'new configurations of political borders and identities' (H. H. Leung 2001: 439) extend out to incorporate Japanese influences. By incorporating thematic and stylistic elements from Japanese *shôjo manga* the film provides an example not just of inter-textual transference, but also of intercultural and intra-regional creolization, in the context of the emergent Queer(N)Asian popular culture referred to earlier in the chapter. Apart from the visual parallels between the *bishônen* depicted in the *manga*, and their cinematic counterparts like Jet, K. S. and Sam, the film allows the viewer to read in attempts to present a deliberate 'odourless' Japanese gloss, which works to deterritorialize and 'de-odourize' the 'Hong Kong-ness' of the film. The names of most of the characters (Sam, Jet, K. S., a very Japanese-sounding Kana) are ambiguous enough for them to belong just about anywhere in the region, including Japan. Significantly, this distancing and delinking from everyday cultural and historic specificities is a common strategy in *shôjo manga* representations (see McLelland 2000: 71). In a similar vein, as noted earlier, the urban land-scape that acts as the setting and backdrop to the characters' lives – the art gallery in which Jet first spies Sam, the café-bar where K. S. first dazzles Fai, the antique gallery Kana runs, the apartment Jet shares with Ah Ching, the nightclub where Jet tries to proposition Kana – can be read as *anywhere* and *everywhere* in urban Asia, including urban Japan.

The *manga Bishônen* and Queer(N)Asian cultural flows

The above would suggest that the film *Bishônen* was modelled on an existing Japanese *shôjo manga*. There is, in fact, a Japanese *manga* version of *Bishônen*, written by Kido Sakura, the storyline of which is almost identical to that of the film (see Figure 4.1). However, interestingly the Japanese *shôjo manga* version came *after* the film had been produced, released and shown in Japan (where it did comparatively well within specific audiences). There was, in fact, no *shôjo manga*-style text upon which the film was based. The original writer of *Bishônen* was in fact Yonfan himself. Kido Sakura's inter-textual adaptation was about adapting a Chinese cinematic text into a Japanese *manga* version.

This is significant for a number of reasons. First, it calls into questions common understandings about the vectors of popular culture flows with the region. Much of the literature to date has been about the influence of popular culture from what Eric Ma (2001) refers to as 'satellites of moder-nity' to (in comparison) less 'modern' locales.

In this argument, discussions about the movement of Japanese popular culture replicate the global West/Rest dynamic on a regional scale and tend to be concerned with the ways in which Japanese popular culture texts and styles are consumed, resisted, appropriated and variously engaged with in different parts of Asia. The *manga* version of the Hong Kong film *Bishônen* is an example of the growing visibility of the flows in the reverse direction – from the periphery to the centre. Specifically, it is an example of the way in which *Hong Kong* popular culture, like Korean popular culture, and to a lesser extent popular culture from other Asian centres, is starting to have a discernible influence on the shaping of popular culture consumption within Japan, particularly among certain sections of the population like women in their twenties and thirties (see Carruthers 2004; Iwabuchi 2002a).

ASUKA COMICS CL-DX

原作／ヨン・ファン
監修／水田菜穂

木戸サクラ
Sakura Kido

美少年の恋

Figure 4.1   Kido Sakura's Bishônen no koi. © Sakura KIDO 2000
© Naho MIZUTA/Kaseieisha Yugenkoshi 2000.

Significantly, the Japanese *manga* adaptation of *Bishônen* does not just reproduce the story in the film. Rather, it quite firmly situates the *manga* within the framework of Hong Kong films and male sex symbols associated with Hong Kong films. Thus, accompanying the *manga* text are two appendices. The first is an essay by Mizuta Naho which situates the film within the spatial locations of Hong Kong, where it was shot. It then provides background information on the actors themselves, including their reactions to playing non-heterosexual roles. The second appendix is a catalogue of the male actors who appeared in the film, as well as a selection of male 'heartthrobs' (such as Nicholas Tse) of the Hong Kong screen. The afterword exhorts readers to read the novel based on the film (and the *manga*) and leaves them with the promise of the soundtrack to be released. What comes across is the selling and packaging of *Bishônen* not just as a standalone product, but rather as part of an overall strategy highlighting the consumption of a both slick queer *and* slick Asian identity.

While this in itself warrants looking at the film as an example of a text which destabilizes assumptions about the direction of the popular culture flows in the region, I believe that this inter-textual transference of *Bishônen* is also of significance because it challenges our assumptions about cultural/national origin of ideas, styles, concepts and images. At the end of the day, is the *manga Bishônen* an instance of a Japanese adaptation of a Hong Kong film that in turn drew upon Japanese popular culture and queer articulations in Japan? Or should we just treat *Bishônen* (the film, the *manga* and even the term '*bishônen*' itself) as an example of not just an emergent East/Southeast Asian popular culture but a Queer(N)Asian popular culture?

Notes

1   I would like to thank Dr Fran Martin and James Welker for their very encouraging and constructive feedback on the chapter. Also, my appreciation to the following people for their input: Darwis, Russell Harwood, C. Y. Hoon, Chris Tan.
2   The film also has an English alternative or subtitle, *Beauty*. The Chinese title of the film is *Meishaonian zhi lian*.
3   The lead roles were played by Stephen Fung and Daniel Wu. At the time both were relatively unknown names within Hong Kong cinema. Both of them (but especially Stephen Fung) have since gone on to become high-profile 'stars' in the Hong Kong movie world. At the time of writing, their most recent co-starring appearance was in the martial arts film *House of Fury*, which was directed by Fung and which debuted at the Hong Kong International Film Festival in March 2005 (see Scott 2005: C7).
4   Chua, citing a Singapore *Straits Times* report from 2002, points out that not only was *Meteor Garden* the first popular Chinese language serial to be screened after the ban on Chinese-language materials was rescinded following the fall of the Suharto New Order regime, but it also generated an interest in things Chinese among non-Chinese background *pribumi* Indonesians too. This was confirmed to me separately by friends during a recent visit to Indonesia.
5   This was brought home to me during a trip to Luang Prabang in Laos in mid-2005. When my travelling companion and I walked into the reception of the

accommodation we were booked into, the young men at the desk were engrossed in a Korean television drama, dubbed in Mandarin, subtitled in Thai (a language close enough to Lao to be widely comprehended) and broadcast over a Thai television network. While at one level this image does feed into much of the clichéd hype surrounding notions of the 'global village', at another level it did convey to us in a very immediate first-hand way the nuances and complexities of intra-regional flows.

6　I use the term 'queer' here in both senses of the term's common applications. The first is as a signifier for identities pivoted around sexual preferences that are often lumped together under the rather unwieldy collective umbrella term LGBTI (lesbian, gay, bisexual, transgender/transsexual, intersex). The second usage of the term is in the sense of 'queer''s project of destabilizing and interrogating some of the very same identity categories included within LGBTI, as well as challenging and destabilizing the heterosexual/non-heterosexual binary.

7　See, for instance, a special report ('Gay Asia') in the 28 October 2004 issue of *Far Eastern Economic Review*.

8　Another popular regional queer website, pre-dating *fridae.com*, is *Utopia-Asia.com* (see http://www.utopia-asia.com, accessed 15 October 2005).

9　The reasons for the change in host location (as well as the decision to relocate *fridae.com* to Hong Kong) lay with the Singapore government's increasingly condemnatory attitude towards a 'public' assertion of celebratory queer identity through events like dance parties and parades and its refusal to issue public permits for the holding of 'Snowball' in 2004 and 'Nation' in 2005 (for background, see *fridae.com*, 'News/Features', 7 June 2005: http://www.fridae.com/newsfeatures, accessed 12 October 2005).

10　For instance, Ageha, a venue for major queer dance parties in Tokyo since the early 2000s, is one of the regional dance party organizers involved in the planning of 'Nation 5' in Phuket.

11　Harajuku is one of the numerous youth-culture/street-fashion hubs in Tokyo. Although it has largely lost any kind of avant-garde cutting edge it might have initially had, it (along with Shibuya) continues to signify Japanese youth culture and street fashions outside Japan, particularly in Asia.

12　Another recent Hong Kong film which to an extent also challenges conventional understandings of sexuality is *Butterfly*, the story of a sexual and romantic relationship that develops between a respectable married middle-class teacher and a younger woman.

13　Yonfan himself appears to relish in this outsider status. A *Time Asia* feature on his work contains the following self-reflection: 'I love Hong Kong films . . . but does Hong Kong film love me?' Part of his reputation stems from his association with kitsch movies that are financial failures. As he almost brags in the same feature: 'If a Hong Kong actor says he's going to work on a Yonfan film, I think that would be like someone in the West saying, "I'm doing a Barbara Cartland novel"' (Corliss 2001, *Time Asia Online*, http://www.time.com/asia/arts/magazine/0,9754,180571,00.html, accessed 21 November 2004).

14　A sample of such sites includes Hong Kong sites such as *Love HK FILM.co* (http://www.lovehkfilm.com/reviews/bishonen.htm, accessed 9 November 2004), *Hong Kong Movie Database* (http://www.hkmdb.com/db/movies/reviews.mhtml, accessed 13 November 2004), *HKFlix.com* (http://www.hkflix.com/asq/, accessed 13 November 2004), *Another Hong Kong Movie Page* (http://www.kowloonside.com/movies/bishonen.html, accessed 21 November 2004), as well as sites in North America like *John Robert Brown's MyGayFilms* (http://www.johnrobert-brown.com/mgf/pgbeauty.html, accessed 21 November 2004) and in the UK, like *the Zreview.co.uk* (http://www.thezreview.co.uk/reviews/b/bishonen.htm, accessed 13 November 2004).

15 For viewers familiar with the city and its urbanscape there is no mistaking that the setting is Hong Kong. However, for viewers not particularly familiar with Hong Kong's landmarks the setting could easily be one of several interchangeable urban settings in East and Southeast Asia. As Chua observes, this increasingly standardized, familiar look to the central business districts of many cities in the region is a recognizable aspect of an emergent common East/Southeast Asian popular culture (Chua 2004: 216).

16 As the depiction of Sam, rather than his mother, preparing dinner seems to signal, he also incorporates attributes of the 'ideal' Confucian woman/daughter/daughter-in-law. During the dinner-table scene, for instance, Sam's father points out that his cooking is better than his mother's, and his mother notes that Sam always knows where everything is kept in the kitchen.

17 In addition, as pointed out in a number of online reviews, Daniel Wu (who plays the part of Sam), as a Chinese-American, had to be coached in Cantonese. Similarly, a friend I watched the film with on one occasion commented on the Hong Kong accents of actors like Stephen Fung (Jet) when they spoke Mandarin. This use of two Chinese languages is also evident in the 2004 Taiwanese queer-themed teen-romance comedy *Formula 17*, where one of the lead actors speaks Cantonese rather than Mandarin.

Bibliography

Aera (2005) '*Hyôshi no hito: Jay Chow* (Cover person: Jay Chow)', 17 October: 11.

Altman, D. (2000) 'The emergence of gay identities in southeast Asia', in P. Drucker (ed.) *Different Rainbows*, London: Gay Men's Press.

Aoyama, T. (1988) 'Male homosexuality as treated by Japanese women writers', in G. McCormack and Y. Sugimoto (eds) *The Japanese Trajectory: modernization and beyond*, Cambridge: Cambridge University Press.

Appadurai, A. (1996) *Modernity at Large: cultural dimensions of globalization*, Minneapolis, MN: University of Minnesota Press.

Ben-Ari, E. and Clammer, J. (eds) (2000) *Japan in Singapore: cultural occurrences and cultural flows*, Richmond, Surrey: Curzon.

Berry, C., Martin, F. and Yue, A. (2003) 'Introduction: beep-click-link', in C. Berry, F. Martin and A. Yue (eds) *Mobile Cultures: new media in queer Asia*, Durham, NC: Duke University Press.

Boellstorff, T. D. (2000) 'The Gay Archipelago: postcolonial sexual subjectivities in Indonesia', unpublished Ph.D. thesis, Stanford University.

Buckley, S. (2000) 'Sexing the kitchen: *Okoge* and other tales', in C. Patton and B. Sánchez-Eppler (eds) *Queer Diasporas*, Durham, NC: Duke University Press.

Carruthers, A. (2004) 'Cute logics of the multicultural and the consumption of the Vietnamese exotic in Japan', *Positions*, vol. 12, no. 2: 401–29.

Chao, Y. A. (2001) 'Drink, stories, penis, and breasts: lesbian tomboys in Taiwan from the 1960s to the 1990s', in G. Sullivan and P. A. Jackson (eds) *Gay and Lesbian Asia: culture, identity, community*, Binghamton, NY: Harrington Park Press.

Ching, L. (1995) 'Imaginings in the empires of the sun: Japanese mass culture in Asia', in R. Wilson and A. Dirlik (eds) *Asia/Pacific as Space of Cultural Production*, Durham, NC: Duke University Press.

Chou, W. (2000) *Tongzhi: politics of same-sex eroticism in Chinese societies*, New York: Haworth Press.

Chua, B. H. (2000) 'Where got Japanese influence in Singapore!', in E. Ben-Ari and J. Clammer (eds) *Japan in Singapore: cultural occurrences and cultural flows*, Richmond, Surrey: Curzon.

——(2004) 'Conceptualizing an East Asian popular culture', *Inter-Asia Cultural Studies*, vol. 5, no. 2: 200–21.

Drucker, P. (2000) 'Remapping sexualities', in P. Drucker (ed.) *Different Rainbows*, London: Gay Men's Press.

Far Eastern Economic Review (2004) 'Special report: gay Asia', 28 October: 52–63.

Fridae: Asia Gay and Lesbian Network. Online. Available HTTP:http://www.fridae.com (accessed 13 November 2004, 17 November 2004, 12 October 2005, 15 October 2005).

Ho, J. (2003) 'From spice girls to *enjo kôsai*: formations of teenage girls' sexualities in Taiwan', *Inter-Asia Cultural Studies*, vol. 4, no. 2: 325–36.

Hu, K. (2005) 'The power of circulation: digital technologies and the online Chinese fans of Japanese TV drama', *Inter-Asia Cultural Studies*, vol. 6, no. 2: 171–86.

Iwabuchi, K. (2001) 'Becoming "culturally proximate": the a/scent of Japanese idol dramas in Taiwan', in B. Moeran (ed.) *Asian Media Productions*, Richmond, Surrey: Curzon.

——(2002a) 'Nostalgia for a (different) Asian modernity: media consumption of "Asia" in Japan', *Positions*, vol. 10, no. 3: 547–69.

——(2002b) *Recentering Globalization: popular culture and Japanese transnationalism*, Durham, NC: Duke University Press.

——(ed.) (2004a) *Feeling Asian Modernities: transnational consumption of Japanese TV dramas*, Hong Kong: Hong Kong University Press.

——(2004b) 'Introduction: cultural globalization and Asian media connections', in K. Iwabuchi (ed.) *Feeling Asian Modernities: transnational consumption of Japanese TV dramas*, Hong Kong: Hong Kong University Press.

Jackson, P. A. (1995) *Dear Uncle Go: male homosexuality in Thailand*, Bangkok: Bua Luang Books.

——(1999) 'Tolerant but unaccepting: the myth of a Thai "gay paradise"', in P. A. Jackson and N. M. Cook (eds) *Genders and Sexualities in Modern Thailand*, Chiang Mai: Silkworm Press.

——(2001) 'Pre-gay, post-queer: Thai perspectives on proliferating gender/sex diversity in Asia', in G. Sullivan and P. A. Jackson (eds) *Gay and Lesbian Asia: culture, identity, community*, Binghamton, NY: Harrington Park Press.

Kido, S. (2000) *Bishônen no Koi*, Tokyo: Asuka Comics CL-DX (based on original by Yonfan, and editorial supervision by Mizuta Naho).

Ko, Y. (2004) 'The desired form: Japanese idol dramas in Taiwan', in K. Iwabuchi (ed.) *Feeling Asian Modernities: transnational consumption of Japanese TV dramas*, Hong Kong: Hong Kong University Press.

Lam, O. (2003) 'Why did enjo kosai anchor in Taiwan but not in Hong Kong? Or the convergences of 'enjo' and 'kosai' in teenage sex work', *Inter-Asia Cultural Studies*, vol. 4, no. 2: 353–63.

Lee, D. (2004) 'Cultural contact with Japanese TV dramas: modes of reception and narrative transparency', in K. Iwabuchi (ed.) *Feeling Asian Modernities: transnational consumption of Japanese TV dramas*, Hong Kong: Hong Kong University Press.

Lee, M. (2004) 'Travelling with Japanese TV dramas: cross-cultural orientation and flowing identification of contemporary Taiwanese youth', in K. Iwabuchi (ed.)

Feeling Asian Modernities: transnational consumption of Japanese TV dramas, Hong Kong: Hong Kong University Press.

Leung, H. H. (2001) 'Queerscapes in contemporary Hong Kong cinema', *positions*, vol. 9, no. 2: 423–47.

Leung, L. Y. M. (2002) 'Romancing the everyday: Hong Kong women watching Japanese *dorama*', *Japanese Studies*, vol. 22, no. 1: 65–75.

——(2004) '*Ganbaru* and its transcultural audience: imaginary and reality of Japanese TV dramas in Hong Kong', in K. Iwabuchi (ed.) *Feeling Asian Modernities: transnational consumption of Japanese TV dramas*, Hong Kong: Hong Kong University Press.

Liou, L. (2003) 'At the intersection of the global and the local: representations of male homosexuality in fictions by Pai Hsien-yung, Li Ang, Chu Tien-wen and Chi Ta-wei', *Postcolonial Studies*, vol. 6, no. 2: 191–206.

Ma, E. K. (2001) 'Consuming satellite modernities', *Cultural Studies*, vol.15 nos. 3/4: 444–63.

MacLachlan, E. and Chua, G. (2004) 'Defining Asian femininity: Chinese viewers of Japanese TV dramas in Singapore', in K. Iwabuchi (ed.) *Feeling Asian Modernities: transnational consumption of Japanese TV dramas*, Hong Kong: Hong Kong University Press.

McLelland, M. (2000) *Male Homosexuality in Modern Japan: cultural myths and social realities*, Richmond, Surrey: Curzon.

——(2003) 'Japanese queerscapes: global/local intersections on the internet', in C. Berry, F. Martin and A. Yue (eds) *Mobile Cultures: new media in queer Asia*, Durham, NC: Duke University Press.

——(2005) *Queer Japan from the Pacific War to the Internet Age*, Lanham, MD: Rowman & Littlefield.

Martin, F. (2003a) 'The perfect lie: Sandee Chan and lesbian representability in Mandarin pop music', *Inter-Asia Cultural Studies*, vol. 4, no. 2: 264–80.

——(2003b) *Situating Sexualities: queer representation in Taiwanese fiction, film and public culture*, Hong Kong: Hong Kong University Press.

——(2003c) 'Trans-Asian traces: watching schoolgirl romances on Taiwan television', paper presented at 'Mobile Genre: Asian Screen Culture Conference', Korean National University of Arts, Seoul, 8–9 November 2003.

Miller, S. D. (2000) 'The (temporary?) queering of Japanese TV', in A. Grossman (ed.) *Queer Asian Cinema: shadows in the shade*, Binghamton, NY: Harrington Park Press.

Mizuta, N. (2000) 'Atogaki (Afterword)', in S. Kido *Bishônen no Koi*, Tokyo: Asuka Comics CL-DX.

——(2000) '"Bishônen no Koi" mûbii gaido' (*Bishônen no Koi* movie guide), in S. Kido *Bishônen no Koi*, Tokyo: Asuka Comics CL-DX.

——(2000) 'Hong Kong yangu sutâ meikan (Directory of Young Hong Kong Stars)', in S. Kido *Bishônen no Koi*, Tokyo: Asuka Comics CL-DX.

Moeran, B. (2000) 'Commodities, culture and Japan's corollanization of Asia', in M. Söderberg and I. Reader (eds) *Japanese Influences and Presences in Asia*, Richmond, Surrey: Curzon.

Morris, M. (2004) 'Transnational imagination in action cinema: Hong Kong and the making of a global popular culture', *Inter-Asia Cultural Studies*, vol. 5, no. 2: 181–99.

Murray, A. J. (2001) 'Let them take ecstasy: class and Jakarta lesbians', in G. Sullivan and P. A. Jackson (eds) *Gay and Lesbian Asia: culture, identity, community*, Binghamton, NY: Harrington Park Press.

Ôgi, F. (2001) 'Gender insubordination in Japanese comics (*manga*) for girls', in J. A. Lent (ed.) *Illustrating Asia: comics, humour magazines and picture books*, Richmond, Surrey: Curzon.

Park, J. (2004) 'Korean American youths' consumption of Korean and Japanese TV dramas and its implications', in K. Iwabuchi (ed.) *Feeling Asian Modernities: transnational consumption of Japanese TV dramas*, Hong Kong: Hong Kong University Press.

Rofel, L. (1999) 'Qualities of desire: imagining gay identities in China', *GLQ: Journal of Lesbian and Gay Studies*, vol. 5, no. 4: 451–74.

Sabucco, V. (2003) 'Guided fan fiction: Western "readings" of Japanese homosexual-themed texts', in C. Berry, F. Martin and A. Yue (eds) *Mobile Cultures: new media in queer Asia*, Durham, NC: Duke University Press.

Scott, M. (2005) 'I get a kick out of Woo', *South China Morning Post*, Features: Screen, Thursday 24 March: C7.

Siegel, M. (2001) 'The intimate spaces of Wong Kar-wai', in E. C. M. Yau (ed.) *At Full Speed: Hong Kong cinema in a borderless world*, Minneapolis, MN: University of Minnesota Press.

Stokes, L. O. and Hoover, M. (1999) *City on Fire: Hong Kong cinema*, London: Verso.

Tan, B. H. (1999) 'Women's sexuality and the discourse on Asian values: cross-dressing in Malaysia', in E. Blackwood and S. E. Wieringa (eds) *Female Desires: same-sex relations and transgender practices across cultures*, New York: Columbia University Press.

Wang, P. and Parry, A. (2000) 'Documenting a beautiful youth: *Boys for Beauty* and *2,1*', *Inter-Asia Cultural Studies*, vol. 1, no. 1: 181–4.

Yonfan, M. (dir./writer) (1998) *Bishônen no Koi* (Chinese Title: *Meishaonian Zhi Lian*; alternative English title, *Beauty*).

Yoon, S. (2001) 'Swept up on a wave', *Far Eastern Economic Review*, 18 October: 92–4.

Yue, A. (2000) 'What's so queer about *Happy Together*? a.k.a queer(n)Asian: interface, community, belonging', *Inter-Asia Cultural Studies*, vol. 1, no. 2: 251–64.

5 Japan beating

The making and marketing of professional *taiko* music in Australia

Hugh de Ferranti

Introduction

In 2001 I wrote an article on Japanese popular music in which I drew attention to ways in which pop that is apparently mimetic of Euro-American styles – not aurally marked as music that 'sounds like' the non-Western people who make it – is nonetheless indigenously constituted and culturally determined.[1] In thinking about musical performance by Australians that sounds and looks Japanese, one can analyse this kind of apparently mimetic activity from the other side, as an instance of the processes whereby musical styles and traditions are invested with new meanings in terms of cultural and individual identities 'inside' and 'outside' Japan.

A group of Australians dressed in partially Japanese attire, virtuosically beating huge wooden drums and occasionally emitting shouts of joyous mutual encouragement reminiscent of the *kakegoe* calls of Japanese festival musicians – all carefully illuminated on stage before a well-heeled audience at a concert hall in the heart of Australia's largest city. This spectacle brings to mind an assertion Michael Taussig makes in *Mimesis and Alterity*: 'the making and existence of the artefact that portrays something gives one power over that which is portrayed' (1993: 13).

TaikOz has risen to fame as an Australian *taiko* ensemble during the era of Howard conservatism, and the group's beginnings are coterminous with the heyday of Hansonist anti-Asian rhetoric and the public support it evoked. An interpretation in terms of Taussig's claim, informed by the worldview of such rightist politics, might see the group's performances as a meticulous mimicking and appropriation that exorcizes the spiritual disturbance and threat to 'old Australia' posed by Japanese cultural encroachment. Could TaikOz be an instance of 'the Macarthur effect', whereby in the 1940s Cuna shamans sought to dispel evil by making carvings of white men, including a seven-foot tall image of none other than General Douglas Macarthur (Taussig 1993: 10)?

Hardly – that is a perverse reading of TaikOz's music, for it is wholly at odds with the group's declared intentions of honouring the spirit of a Japanese drumming tradition, 'drawing people together by means of music,

Figure 5.1 TaikOz. Photo: Greg Barrett. Courtesy of Ian Cleworth.

and fostering a greater sense of community' and 'developing a distinctively Australian form of Taiko while keeping the essential elements and philosophies of the Japanese original' (Cleworth 2002). Yet inherent in the production and reception of this, Australia's most publicized 'Japanese' music ensemble, are Australian responses to images of Japan mediated in popular culture of global reach. If fashion brands, sushi, *anime*, PlayStation software, Zen, martial arts and now *taiko* music are rarely portrayed as symbols of a malevolent cultural power,[2] they are nonetheless widely recognized throughout the developed world as bearers of Japanese cultural identity. As *wadaiko*[3] is of comparatively recent Japanese origin, in each of the cultural settings in which *taiko* is now played, its practitioners have acted as conduits for 'Japan'; whether they wished it or not, they have been received and represented as performers of Japanese music.

The analysis herein is purposefully not an ethnographic one – it contains no interview or field data – but is based on resources available to the Australian public: TaikOz recordings and stage performances, website information, publicity and informative materials, newspaper, television and radio coverage. My intent is neither to critique nor promote the group as an advocate, but to problematize why this music is presented in the manner that it is, why it has been so successful, and in what senses it is a hybrid entity in which images of Japanese and Australian culture are embedded.

Wadaiko in the world

What makes *wadaiko* ensemble music an important topic for the themes of this anthology is that its short history epitomizes the process of a two-directional cultural flow, from 'outside' into Japanese historical cultural traditions and from 'inside' Japanese practice to new practices elsewhere. All of this is in evidence in the events of a few decades, from the 1950s to the 1980s, and the dense flow of influences has since continued. When musicians who learnt from Japanese practitioners established groups outside Japan, they chose to maintain select elements of the Japanese repertory, presentational style and philosophy of practice as they had acquired it, while deliberately transforming other elements and introducing new ones in response to the music's new settings. Accordingly one can now speak of a thirty-five-year-old *taiko* tradition in the United States that bears many different characteristics to *wadaiko* in Japan. One can also see diverse *wadaiko* networks and repertories in Europe, and a developing practice in Australia that is markedly different again.

Among all genres of Japanese traditional music, only in *taiko* ensembles do people under forty typically make up the majority membership. At the same time, in amateur *taiko* groups one sees substantial numbers of players of *all* age groups, instead of the smattering of young people among a predominantly middle-aged and elderly membership which characterizes the membership of groups for most other forms of traditional music. And *wadaiko* is the only Japanese ensemble genre that has been taken up broadly in other societies. Reasons for *taiko* music's appeal and continued success both in Japan and elsewhere are many and complex, but there is no doubt that it constitutes the sole form of Japanese traditional music that experienced rapid growth in the last decades of the twentieth century and shows potential for continued strong popularity in the early twenty-first century.[4]

It is often said that *wadaiko* has a history of just a few decades. This is true when the word is used as a general term for the modern *ensemble* drumming genre (*kumidaiko*) initiated by the amateur jazz drummer Oguchi Daihachi in the 1950s and professionalized by Ô-Edo Sukeroku Daiko and others in the 1960s. That is the most common contemporary usage of the word, but because *wadaiko* means both 'Japanese drums' and 'Japanese drumming', many far older performance traditions are often located within the umbrella term's range of meaning. Drumming repertories associated with community festivals whose historical locus was local shrine rites, styles of drumming played for local Obon festivals celebrated in conjunction with mid-summer Buddhist rites for the dead, as well as various drumming traditions for dances and rituals unique to single locales, have all been subsumed within *wadaiko*, as both scholars and performers concerned to construct a unitary national tradition have revised and promulgated terminology for discussion of these musics.[5] As a result, the sphere of *wadaiko* today is an extremely complex one composed of various genres, but its two principal kinds of musical group are as follows:

Matsuri-bayashi: These are *hayashi* (groups made up of two or more types of drums and a transverse flute; one or more handheld gongs is added in *matsuri-bayashi*) for performing *matsuri* (festival) music. Their repertories are solely made up of items performed for the duration of community festivals organized around a shrine. In most cases this music is played for hours on end (usually by rotating teams of performers), with a certain degree of flexibility and improvisation in response to events in the festival space and programme. Many *matsuri-bayashi* traditions now have a 'concert *hayashi*' subsidiary repertory, in which festival items are arranged for stage performances and commercial recordings.

Kumidaiko: These are the ensembles of many kinds of drums, generally played by larger numbers of musicians than typical *matsuri-bayashi*, first devised in the 1950s by the jazz drummer Oguchi Daihachi as a way of combining his love of kit-drumming's array of tones and layered rhythms with concern for the music and *kagura* traditions of his local shrine.[6]

The chief conceptual term of difference between these two kinds of groups is that *matsuri-bayashi* are categorized by both researchers and governmental arts policy as a form of *minzoku geinô*, or 'folk' performing art associated with ceremony and communal events in specified locales. *Kumidaiko* ensembles, on the other hand, are considered to be constructed practices (*sôsaku geinô*) that have no grounding in 'folk' performance tradition; that is, localized, historically documented festivals and their affiliated music and dance. These terms of differentiation do reflect the fact that *kumidaiko* began in the 1950s, and by the 1980s yielded a profession for the best drummers, while most *matsuri-bayashi* performers are amateurs who play *taiko* after work hours and take pride in their repertory's association with a local festival for centuries (even if the documentation for such claims is sometimes doubtful). Yet, like most such categories, those of *kumidaiko* and *matsuri-bayashi* tend to weaken in the face of ever-changing actual practice. Questions of professionalism and ties to folk tradition in the practice of modern-day *wadaiko* are complicated by the above-mentioned existence of 'concert *hayashi*' which adapt the music and visual presentation of renowned *matsuri-bayashi* traditions such as that of the Chichibu *yatai-bayashi* for shorter, staged performances (Alaszewska 1999: 27–30), as well as a tendency since the 1980s for towns and new suburban districts which had never had a shrine-based festival tradition to devise new municipal festivals, replete with *matsuri-bayashi* repertories adopted from elsewhere. During the 1990s, moreover, a blurring of distinction between 'folk' (*minzoku*) and 'constructed' (*sôsaku geinô*) forms resulted as the latter kind of new *taiko* groups came to be presented as performance traditions representative of towns or villages (*furusato geinô*) in diverse contexts.

Also significant for interpreting the development of *taiko* practice in Australia is the thirty-five-year-old practice of *wadaiko* in North America. There are at present more than 150 groups active in the United States and Canada (Terada 2001: 37), several of which include professional players. Initiated in 1968 by a single immigrant martial arts teacher, Tanaka Seiichi, the North American *kumidaiko* tradition[7] was at first shaped by Tanaka's training with the Japanese groups O Suwa Daiko and Ô-Edo Sukeroku Taiko, but then developed many strands; it is characterized by a richness of innovation that has produced repertories and styles distinct from Japanese *wadaiko*. Importantly, the early groups were exclusively formed by Japanese-Americans and the music has developed in close relation with the growth of Japanese- and Asian-American minority rights activism. In the late 1990s many groups continued to stress socio-political engagement as central to their performance, training and community recruitment activities:

> Although acknowledging its Japanese and Japanese-American roots, they see in *taiko* a potential for constructing a collective culture and seek to redefine *taiko* as a representative venue for a uniquely Asian American expression based on their shared history and experiences in North America as a cultural minority.
>
> (Terada 2001: 46)

This is a defining characteristic of American and Canadian *wadaiko* that reflects both the scale of Japanese emigration to North America in the early twentieth century and the flagrant injustice of incarceration of citizens of Japanese ethnicity during World War II. In the case of the United States, moreover, it reflects the continuing centrality of racially constituted identity politics to civil society.

TaikOz

Since the late 1990s *wadaiko* ensemble performance has been one of the most publicly conspicuous genres among a range of Asian performance traditions that have come to occupy a far less marginal place in Australian musical culture than they had in the past. The music of professional performers of *ud, sarod, shakuhachi* and *koto*, as well as dance-theatre performances by Australians trained in Indian, Javanese and Japanese dance traditions, can be heard and seen frequently in the major cities and on national media. *Wadaiko* is performed by as many as ten groups around the country, among which the Sydney-based ensemble TaikOz has achieved national renown and popularity since its formation in 1997.[8]

TaikOz (a compound formed from *taiko* and Oz, Australians' nickname for their homeland) was founded by two professional musicians already well known throughout Australia in their own fields, the percussionist Ian Cleworth and *shakuhachi* player Riley Lee. Cleworth, the principal founder of TaikOz,[9] is one of Australia's finest concert-hall percussionists. As a professional performer of 'classical' percussion, he has a unique profile in that he had the opportunity to take lessons in *wadaiko* with a leading Japanese performer, Amano Sen, when he received a grant for *taiko* study in the early 1980s. By maintaining this student–teacher relationship through occasional visits to Japan over several years, Cleworth acquired a high degree of skill in *taiko* playing and was able to perform in Sen's ensemble, both in Japan and on two Australian tours. From the late 1980s he sought ways of incorporating this skill into his work with Synergy Percussion. In addition to occasional performances of pieces he had learned in Japan, arranged for the few Japanese drums then available to Synergy, his efforts led to a number of new works for the ensemble that included *taiko* (in most cases one or more *shimedaiko*) in combination with non-Japanese percussion. After some years Cleworth also began to seek a means of establishing a *kumidaiko* group in Sydney, and conferred with the American *shakuhachi* player and one-time member of Ondekoza, Riley Lee, who had taken up residence in Sydney to undertake a research degree. Lee participated in a number of Synergy productions – most notably the 1991 dance and music-theatre work entitled *Matsuri*,[10] in which Sawai-school *koto* professional Odamura Satsuki and *nihon buyô* practitioner Chin Kham Yoke also performed. It took until 1997 for the collaborative efforts of Cleworth and Lee to yield both a full set of instruments and a group of musicians who would form the core of an ensemble.

TaikOz has produced several CDs and a concert-footage DVD, made performances in all of Australia's metropolises and appeared in a number of concerts in Japan. The BBC chose a January 2000 concert to represent both Australia and 'the East' in its Millennium Broadcast series. In 2004 TaikOz's performances drew full houses in both the capital cities and regional centres, and by offering workshops and apprenticeship programmes the group members are nurturing a new pool of *taiko* players through which the ensemble will renew itself in time.

While it is Australia's best-known 'non-Western' musical ensemble, TaikOz is also acclaimed – and marketed – as a professional percussion group that has created a fusion of Japanese and Australian elements, thereby making a style of Japanese music available for both appreciation and *participation* by Australians of diverse heritage. This implies that TaikOz is an agent actively engaged in indigenizing *wadaiko* in an alien setting. I take the view that for expressive culture the process of indigenization entails the emergence of hybrid art forms, but that hybridity or 'in-betweenness' itself varies in different cultures and historical circumstances. In Australia today, hybrid musical practices appear to allow the musical and cultural boundaries 'between' which they exist to remain audible and visible; in other words, some Australian musicians are practising and adapting Asian musical traditions in a socio-cultural space that continues to frame their performances as Other.

How, then, is TaikOz going about trying to make a Japanese percussion tradition Australian?

Wadaiko and the performing arts traditions inside-out Japan

To understand TaikOz's appropriation of *taiko* music 'outside' Japan, something must first be said about ideas and approaches to tradition in the *wadaiko* world, and more broadly in Japanese performing arts today.

In English-language writings on *wadaiko*, the term 'neo-traditional' has been employed to characterize the way in which member musicians have drawn upon strands of historical practice to construct a modern-day musical genre that allows for composition and innovation on a broad scale, but bears the trappings of a traditional – that is, a historical – performing art (*dentô geinô*).[11] This term is also apt in that it conveys the fact that, thirty or more years after their formation, *wadaiko* practices of representative groups such as Osuwa Daiko, Ô-Edo Sukeroku Daiko, Ondekoza and others have come to be seen as traditions in their own right by group members and students. Yet *kumidaiko* stands in a relation to historical tradition that is quite unlike that of the great majority of Japanese performing arts classed as traditional. Among the latter there are in fact many schools of practice which came into being through an individual founder's radical or otherwise innovative activities in the modern era – for example Miyagi-school and Sawai-school *koto*, and Tsuruta-school *satsumabiwa* – but in all cases an extant and widely acknowledged body of orthodox repertory, some or most of which is regarded as of pre-modern provenance, was acquired through direct transmission from authorized teachers and carried on as the core repertory of the new practice. New schools were regarded as divergent practices within a pre-existent framework of a *koto* instrumental-and-vocal or a *biwa* recitation tradition. *Kumidaiko*, however, is a genre that came about through individuals reworking elements from localized historical traditions *of which they were not successors*. Because *kumidaiko* music's founders in the 1950s and 1960s were not part of any single pre-existent performance tradition in which skill is legitimate in the course of transmission, it is not regarded as a 'traditional performing art'. Unlike the repertory of groups who are recognized both by local custom and national bureaucracy as bearers of Edo-*bayashi*, Gion-*bayashi* and the Chichibu *yatai-bayashi* traditions,[12] moreover, for most *kumidaiko* groups pieces classed as 'traditional' do not comprise the bulk of repertory.

Can these be called 'neo-traditional' ensembles nonetheless? A link to historical tradition, emphasized and reinforced through repertory, terminology, modes of transmission, discourse about training and performance, and material and visual codings in performance, seems still to be fundamental to the identity of most – if not all[13] – Japanese *taiko* players. At the same time, staged concert music performances and engagement in contemporary artistic innovations that involve combinations of *taiko* with other instruments and media have characterized the public activities of many neo-traditional *wadaiko* ensembles.[14] In this regard, *wadaiko* can be usefully contrasted to another modern Japanese performing art which has evoked interest from large audiences and a considerable number of performers internationally, but which is certainly not a neo-traditional practice: *butô*.

As a dance form, *butô* (often transliterated as *butoh*) rarely employs costuming or visual props that are identifiably historical or traditional. Leading dancers and choreographers such as Amagatsu, Marô and Ôno have occasionally made deliberate reference to images and figures from Noh, kabuki and other forms of traditional theatre, but such references have been conscious gestures embedded in larger dance narratives, not presentations of any norm for *butô* performance. The movement vocabulary of Hijikata and his successors undoubtedly incorporates techniques and elements from the *kata* of Noh and kabuki actors, and at times even those of *nihon buyô*, but the vocabulary as a whole is not grounded or centred on such techniques, and the characteristic aesthetic of early *butô* was, if anything, a rebuttal of values associated with both elite and metropolitan dance traditions of Japanese history. Music employed by celebrated *butô* troupes has rarely included any of the styles or formats of Japan's traditional dance- and music-theatres. Finally, although Hijikata in public statements identified with expressive traditions of the rural poor of northern Japan, neither he nor later *butô* artists have foregrounded links between their practice and traditional performing arts.

While there is no emphatic 'traditionalism' in the public identity of most *butô* performers, in the case of modern *wadaiko* representative groups from the first have emphasized *both* a continuity with traditions of various regional festival drumming styles and their efforts to develop a new, contemporary repertory and public profile. This (neo-)traditionalism of *wadaiko* has been important for both its practitioners and audiences.

Continuity with Japanese tradition

Cleworth's and Lee's relations with leading *taiko* performer-composers in Japan have meant that they continue to draw upon Japanese resources as they nurture the group's activities and develop its repertory. No one who is interested in TaikOz's music can remain unaware of the names Ondekoza, Hayashi Eitetsu and Amano Sen, for references to these sources of training and transmission, as well as to some traditions of *matsuri-bayashi*, abound. Representation of these various Japanese resources as both 'roots' and vital points of reference for TaikOz's music is an important part of the group's identity, and Cleworth, in particular, has emphatically stated that their activity is in no way a radical departure from Japanese *wadaiko*:

> What we do is we use the language of the Japanese drums but the way we put it together is slightly different. I'm not saying radically different, but just enough that [Japanese audiences] could hear that it was slightly different.
>
> (*Courier Mail* 2001)

In this and other public statements, there is a concern to emphasize continuity with Japanese tradition, as the foundations of TaikOz's musical identity, while also voicing recognition that that identity is intrinsically hybrid.

Repertory and onstage presentation

TaikOz's recorded and concert repertory as listed on the group's website includes works described as traditional and works attributed to individual composers. The list shows that TaikOz emphasizes ties to two kinds of *wadaiko* practice in Japan: 'traditional' *matsuri-bayashi* drumming for festivals such as the Chichibu, Gion and Asakusa Sanja *matsuri*; and the *kumidaiko* ensemble practice that has been built around the styles and compositional activities of Osuwa Daiko, Ô-Edo Sukeroku Daiko, Ondekoza, Kodo and other leading *wadaiko* groups and composers since the 1950s:

1 Traditional
 '*Yataibayashi*'
 '*Hachijo*'
 '*Miyake*'
 '*O Daiko*'
 (one *shakuhachi* piece is also listed here)

2 Compositions by Japanese composers for *kumidaiko*
 'Reflections' (Amano Sen)
 '*Nebuta*' (Hayashi Eitetsu)
 '*Sanzetsu*' (Hayashi Eitetsu)
 '*Umi*' (Hayashi Eitetsu)
 '*Dyu-Ha*' (Ishii Maki)
 'Monochrome' (Ishii Maki)
 'Monoprism' (Ishii Maki)

3   Original compositions by TaikOz members
    '*Asobibachi*' (Ian Cleworth)
    'Dedication' (Ian Cleworth)
    '*Kenjô*' (Ian Cleworth)
    '*O-TA-I-KO*' (Ian Cleworth)
    'Small Forest' (Ian Cleworth)
    '*Yuuraku*' (Ian Cleworth)
    'Knots' (David Hewitt)
    'Knots 2' (David Hewitt)
    '*Chi*' (Ben Walsh; listed in 2004, but removed from repertory thereafter)
    '*Chi*' (Graham Hilgendorf)

There are four pieces included in the category of traditional repertory: '*Yataibayashi*', '*Hachijo*', '*Miyake*' and '*O Daiko*'. The first three of these are items from regional festival music which have come to be played in multiple versions and arrangements by many *kumidaiko* ensembles, while the origins of the fourth item are obscure.[15] The piece '*Yataibayashi*', while associated with festival ensembles of the Chichibu region, was first acquired by Lee during his Ondekoza training.[16] Documentation of the other traditional items is minimal. For example, the short text about '*Hachijo*' was written by Ikegawa Masae, a Japanese female member of TaikOz since 2001 who had learned *taiko* for three years in Japan. In addition to a brief description of the form of the piece, Ikegawa's notes tell us only that '[i]t has a long tradition and is played by women in traditional kimono. The rhythm is one of sorrow and softness' (TaikOz website, 'Repertoire' section). No source is given for this expressive interpretation of the rhythm, nor is there an explanation of how TaikOz learned the traditional item. Performance in this drumming style today is mostly by men on Hachijo Island itself,[17] but the older practice of performance by women has been adopted by many *wadaiko* groups who play the piece; it is performed by two women, Ikegawa and Kelly Staines, on a CD-ROM section of TaikOz 2001. It may be that Ikegawa acquired this version of the piece before coming to Australia, then taught it to TaikOz. Similarly, for the pieces '*Miyake*' and '*O Daiko*', there are no explanations of sources and transmission (we are told that Cleworth arranged the latter piece, but not the source for that arrangement), nor of whether there is a diversity of versions and performance practice for the piece in Japan.

These 'traditional' items, however, are far outnumbered by modern compositions for *kumidaiko*. Among the compositions that comprise the bulk of TaikOz's repertory are works by Hayashi Eitetsu and Amano Sen – two renowned players who have served as occasional teachers and collaborators in TaikOz performances – and by the late Maki Ishii, a concert-hall avant-gardist composer who in the 1970s became interested in *taiko*'s potential as a sonic resource, then wrote works for Ondekoza and in turn Kodo.

Modern compositions of Japanese origin in turn are slightly outnumbered by TaikOz members' original compositions, the majority of which are by the group's founder, Ian Cleworth. Many of his works have Japanese titles, the meanings of which are explained for listeners in varying degrees of detail.[18] The title of another original work, '*Chi*', by former TaikOz member Ben Walsh, is explained as a reference to spirit or energy (as in Tai Chi), but one of the Sino-Japanese words for ground or earth is also implied. Although these are not listed on the website as established repertory, TaikOz also performs occasional pieces, including a commissioned work for the group by the Adelaide-based composer Graham Koehne; Koehne chose to title the work 'Gojiro' in the understanding that this was 'the original name for Godzilla'.[19]

CD liner notes to *Kenjô* tell us about Cleworth's view of fidelity to a Japanese musical tradition: he took 'several *taiko* instrumental forms and styles and fused them in a way that is true to the spirit of each tradition, but extends them rhythmically and contrapuntally' (TaikOz 2001). Listening to the piece itself, one hears a sequence of distinct styles in the first half and elements from each combined thereafter, as rhythmic figures that are more complex or far more syncopated than is typical of each of the source styles occur with increasing frequency. By truth 'to the spirit' of the source traditions, then, Cleworth may mean the way in which particular sounds and musical figures are taken 'whole' as elements in a composition, but deployed and modified so as to create non-traditional structures.

TaikOz's highly effective stage presentation reflects the long experience of Cleworth and Lee as professional performers. In particular, Cleworth's experience with Synergy presenting percussion music to a diverse audience of both elite followers of contemporary concert-hall composition and percussion enthusiasts of many kinds may have shaped much of TaikOz's approach to building a following and polished stage display.

At a performance the first thing that strikes the eye – before a single drumstroke is heard – is the drums themselves, carefully positioned and lighted so as to emphasize their bulk and construction, with large metal studs and intricate wood grains fully visible. When performers enter, the eye is drawn to their costuming and bodily display; unlike the low-key attire adopted by most instrumental performers of concert-hall music, TaikOz's costuming makes a deliberate physical display.

The group's stage attire has varied since 1997, but in all the costuming there are elements of Japanese historical dress, ranging from full women's kimono with *obi* sashes for performances of '*Hachijo*'[20] to what appear to be light-fitting singlets[21] and trousers worn with white *tabi* socks. Since the group's formation the lack of shoes has been a conspicuous presentational element; instead, *tabi* socks are worn in most pieces (the exception is '*Hachijo*', played barefoot when performed by women in *kimono*). While to some extent this results from the need to sit cross-legged on the floor when playing *shimedaiko* in some pieces, it is also a marker of Japanese traditional performance practice, where shoes are not worn on stages except as conspicuous theatrical devices.

From 2001 TaikOz members also took to wearing light blue *haori*; that is, short coats cut off at the shoulders and open at the front.

The overt display of physicality and fitness among members of a 'team' that is a fundamental characteristic of any TaikOz performance is important for the ensemble's strong appeal to young people. Despite the fact that, as the national media tells us in 2004, Australia has the highest rate of obesity per capita after the USA, fitness, a love of invigorating outdoor activity and an ease with physical teamwork continue to figure importantly in the national self-image. TaikOz appeals strongly to all these images and values, both deliberately and implicitly; while the very nature of *wadaiko* performance elicits comparison with team sports and praise for physical achievement, the group has actively exploited Australian society's 'body fetish' in its choice of stagewear that exposes the shoulders and upper back muscles used so much in beating *taiko*. The success of this strategy is reflected in commentary on the physique and fitness of the musicians among audience members at TaikOz concerts, and in performance reviews that almost invariably include praise for physical display, for example:

> sinewy & muscular physicality . . . a winner, irresistible to all listening affiliations in its visceral engagement with the deep sources of mercilessly pounded sound.
>
> (*Sydney Morning Herald* review quoted on Biographies page of TaikOz website; date unknown).

> It is hard to know how to approach such a concert . . . The drums are played in a style closer to choreography than just drumming with an all over effect as much physical theatre as concert.
>
> (*Canberra Times* 2002b)

This also suggests that the bodily display afforded by TaikOz's costuming serves a dual purpose: the instruments and the music itself demand vigorous bodily movements that generate a great deal of perspiration, so exposure of the torso allows the musicians to be more comfortable. At the same time, the constant bodily motion, its resultant exhibition of physique and the co-ordination of such motion as an element of stage presentation ensure that the audience remains visually engaged with the performance even during longer, aurally challenging items.

Ritual associations

Unlike traditions of Balinese *gamelan*, Laotian ceremonial drumming and many other non-Western percussion traditions, there is no ritual obligation or particular religious practice associated with playing *wadaiko*. For forms of *taiko* that are used in certain Shinto and Buddhist rites, ritual context needs to be acknowledged when presenting the music in stage performances, but today even the typical 'festival music' group format of Edo-*bayashi* is usually played in Kanto region festivals that for most participants are vigorous celebrations of community and commerce; the content of formal ritual segments of such festivals is known to relatively few, and in some cases only to the shrine priests and attendants.

Despite this general lack of ritual context for Japanese drumming – and in particular for *kumidaiko* ensemble percussion – in TaikOz performance reviews aspects of onstage behaviour that contrast with most concert presentations in Australia have evoked responses such as the following:

> Indeed the very physicality of the performance, with its emphasis on power, force and the fanaticism of obsessive self-discipline would be disturbing were it not purified by the spiritual demeanour which gives this a selfless quality.
>
> (McCallum 2002)

Such writing reflects a commonly held view that Japanese arts (including martial arts) demand an intensity and gravity of manner of a kind associated with religious rites. That much is implicit in the following interpretation of one concert performance:

> By the end, though, we had all come to appreciate the ritual that Ian Cleworth and Riley Lee, co-founders of TaikOz, have made such a vital part of the group's performance . . . We learned too to internalize by the end of this surprisingly varied concert, leaving appropriate space for the ritual.
>
> (*Canberra Times* 2000)

This expresses a concept of 'ritual' that is close to Turner's idea of individual transformative experience through participation in formalized repeatable actions (Turner 1969). The description of audience members' acquisition of the ability to 'internalize' and 'leave space', however, suggests that elements of these performances are readily interpreted as 'ritual' in the language of New Age practices. The onstage actions of TaikOz that evoke such interpretations may be an integral part of *wadaiko* practice transmitted to Cleworth and Lee or a general reference to traditional practice of the Japanese stage arts (in which movement of properties is usually done calmly and unhurriedly), or they may have been choreographed for particular effect in an Australian context. Whichever the case, their reception has been in the context of extant ideas about the innately ritualistic nature of Japanese somatic arts – ideas that enhance the fascination of TaikOz performances for many.

Audience and marketing

As an ensemble formed by two established professional musicians, one of whom was already at the pinnacle of the Sydney 'classical' music world (Cleworth, a Sydney Symphony Orchestra percussionist), TaikOz had access to high-profile performance opportunities and effective media publicity from the very first. TaikOz's central role in the process of *wadaiko*'s introduction to Australia is in keeping with the pattern of 'top-down' appropriation of Asian musical elements established in the 1970s and 1980s by concert-hall composers such as Peter Sculthorpe, Anne Boyd and Ross Edwards. Yet at the same time as reaching the elite concert-hall audience used to regular infusions of 'Asian influence' in Australian contemporary music since the 1970s, TaikOz has reached well beyond the concert hall.

Performance by Australians of an Asian ensemble music in little-changed form was unprecedented beyond immigrant communities (an exception is performances by amateur *gamelan* groups based at university campuses since the 1970s). Such an ensemble bore an immediate appeal for people educated or interested in either or both non-Western musics and Japanese historical culture. But while such people are – together with elements of the contemporary 'art music' audience – an important component of TaikOz's audience, the group's marketing and presentational strategies have ensured access to a far larger audience: There is now a fan base for TaikOz composed, on the one hand, of people for whom it bears association with martial arts, sports and fashionable elements of Japanese contemporary culture and, on the other, of people for whom *wadaiko* performance is a ritualistic, spiritually charged experience because of its declared philosophy and practice of performance. By performing at events such as the reopening of Sydney's harbourside amusement centre, Luna Park, at the annual Mind–Body Festival and in select regional towns, and by running public workshops in *wadaiko* for school students and corporate 'team' employees, moreover, TaikOz has drawn in people who have little or no contact with the 'art music' world or elite contexts for presentation of Japanese traditional culture.

In its publicity texts, website materials and onstage behaviour TaikOz displays the consciously sought egalitarianism that is typical of most group undertakings in Australia. One aspect of Japanese tradition that has been modified to conform with Australian norms is the central role of hierarchy. In interviews Cleworth has shown recognition of social hierarchy as fundamental to Japanese culture, but also a desire to negate or downplay that reality by interpreting *taiko* playing for an Australian audience as a 'levelling' activity.[22] In performance, moreover, there is no attempt to highlight Cleworth and Lee; while the group's organization and continuing success are dependent on their skills and leadership, that is in no way visually underpinned on stage.

The TaikOz website, which in many respects resembles a pop group's fan site, is a further important element in this strategy. In his prolific 'News' notes, Cleworth writes accounts of the group's activities in training and on tour; by continually referring to 'we/us', he downplays the vast differences in levels of experience between, on the one hand, himself and Lee, and junior ensemble members. The language and degree of detail of material on the site avoid any hint of elitism, and the 'News' page is written in a style that addresses readers as members of a friendship circle or club. All visitors to the site are given the opportunity to contact group members, including Ian Cleworth, and fans who've made an effort to meet and talk with the group after concerts are sometimes acknowledged by name.

Ideology

No general study has been made of the overseas reception and active engagement of foreign musicians in Japanese traditional genres. Such a project would have to acknowledge and interpret the important role of ideology – as expressed in a philosophy of performance practice that stresses spiritual and ethical concerns – in drawing individuals to learn *wadaiko* and *shakuhachi*, the two genres that have flourished outside Japan. In the reception of these instrumental repertories one can see a fortunate conjunction of ideology concerning the purpose of training and performance, which is yielded by the music's history in Japan, with sets of ideas about personal spiritual development, human ecology and interpersonal relations embraced by many people in Western societies since the 1970s.[23]

This is a 'fortunate conjunction' for the obvious reason that it has helped some fine musicians make a living teaching and playing Japanese music in North America, Australia and elsewhere, but I am not being sarcastic: *wadaiko* and *shakuhachi* performers have been able to reinterpret Japanese tradition in the language of alternative lifestyle, therapy practices and eco-philosophy, and this has been tremendously useful for marketing purposes, yet in most cases there is little cause to doubt the sincerity of the performers' claims that their music-making constitutes a spiritual practice. For *shakuhachi* there is documentary evidence for the use of an important body of historical repertory in meditation exercises among some Zen Buddhist sects. For *wadaiko* there is no such historical link to an institutional or formal spiritual practice.[24] In writings by members of Japan's leading *kumidaiko* ensembles, however, one finds the purpose of training expressed in terms of mental discipline and spiritual development as much as the development of physical and musical skills. These are ideas familiar to anyone who has engaged in Japanese martial arts training, and indeed in any musical genre that originated during the medieval period when the ideals of the warrior class were pre-eminent; as such, the modern-day practice of *kumidaiko* is informed by an ideology about spiritual 'merit' that is basic to most traditional Japanese performing and martial arts.

At the same time, in the documentation and publicity texts produced by most leading groups there is an ideological framework that is as culturally hybrid and emblematic of its time as were the very origins of *kumidaiko* in the 1950s. This ideology has come down to TaikOz, too: in expressions such as '[the philosophy of *wadaiko*] focuses the whole body, mind and spirit on the creative act, with the aim of drawing people together by means of music and fostering a greater sense of community' (Cleworth 2002) there is a direct reflection of the anti-materialist, anti-capitalist ideology that lay behind the formation of the original Ondekoza in 1970 by the left-wing activist Den Tagayasu, and which in turn has informed the rural communal lifestyle of Kodo, the world's best-known *taiko* group. As a nativism that drew upon both indigenous Japanese practices regarded as elements of traditional village life and Euro-American counter-cultural ideology, this aspect of the modern *wadaiko* 'tradition' has sat well with subsequent manifestations of alternative lifestyle philosophy.

References to meditative states, spiritual connectedness with the earth and the environment, holism, elemental simplicity and the like occur not only in TaikOz's marketing texts; they are also common in statements by group members about the *wadaiko* and Japanese artistic traditions, and about the aesthetics of performance. There seems nothing cynical or calculating in these characterizations; it is clear that Cleworth and other members of the group identify with such elements of a 'philosophy' that inheres in *wadaiko* as it has been transmitted to them and as they now experience it. Indeed, Cleworth defines *wadaiko* as 'Japanese drumming and its philosophy', and it seems that he, in particular, sees presentation of that as a major responsibility he bears as a player and teacher of *wadaiko* in Australia. My point is that the conjunction between a transmitted ideology of Japanese *wadaiko* practice and the concerns of large numbers of people in contemporary Australia (where environmentalism, alternative lifestyle movements and New Age culture have blossomed since the 1980s to an extent rivalled perhaps only California) has been an important factor in generating the ensemble's popularity.

Conclusion

There may be many reasons why TaikOz has presented and continues to present its music and attendant ideology in ways that emphasize its Japanese origins and the ongoing importance for the group of transmission from Japanese teachers and experience of Japanese culture. It could be said that TaikOz's approach is rather conservative in its treatment of the elements of tradition received from its Japanese teachers. In contrast to the activities of many performers in North America, among whom *wadaiko* has long taken on a life independent of its Japanese origins, and indeed the current range of approaches to *wadaiko* performance worldwide, TaikOz's leader Ian Cleworth keeps coming back to Japanese sources and referring to the practice of Hayashi Eitetsu, in particular, as a touchstone for his ensemble. It is likely that he and most other group members see this self-declared mimetic approach as a way of showing due respect for a performance tradition that is not of their own culture.[25] Yet this has not inhibited media representation and acceptance of the group by audiences as a hybrid entity. Indeed, in the sense that I outlined at the start of this chapter, TaikOz has invested and continues to invest *wadaiko* with new meanings for group members, and for audience members or listeners who experience its performances and recordings as Japanese music imbued with characteristics of contemporary Australian identity.[26]

TaikOz has established a substantial following and generated a broad public interest in *taiko* playing. The success of the group is in part the result of its response, through marketing and presentation, to images of 'Asian' and Japanese traditional arts among various sectors of Australian society; yet it can also be said that in this case the public's preference for stereotypes has drawn it into contact with a more complex range of representations of past and present-day Japanese performance culture. Through a selective traditionalism and measured claims to authenticity, TaikOz has presented aspects of past and present-day Japanese performance culture to many Australians who otherwise might have neither means of access nor interest. They have done this by displays of outstanding musicianship and virtuosity, building repertory with original compositions that deploy musical materials from various Japanese drumming traditions, and actively marketing to an audience beyond musicologists, contemporary music enthusiasts and Japanophiles. These are people who find in TaikOz's music elements that speak to their own identities, including the sheer physicality of presentation (tremendously fit bodies creating a huge sound); a perceived egalitarian 'team sport' approach to training and performance; and a Japanese or more generally 'Asian' aesthetic and philosophy that connect strongly with their interests in spiritual experience and personal development. I expect that all these elements will continue to be important in shaping the hybrid identity of an emergent Australian *wadaiko* tradition.

Notes

1 See de Ferranti 2002. This is part of a project that deals, on the one hand, with the projection of Japanese modern and historical music beyond the Japanese market and, on the other, with ways in which Japanese actualize a musical habitus in their contemporary music-making.
2 One of the best-known exceptions is the 1993 film *Rising Sun*, in which the sound and images of *taiko* performance are blatantly used as an analogy for a perceived Japanese threat to American economic power.
3 Literally 'Japanese drumming'; see further explanation of meanings in the chapter.
4 Music-theatre traditions such as Noh and kabuki are vital at the start of the twenty-first century – contrary to expectations of a few decades ago – but their growth cannot compare with the proliferation of amateur and professional *taiko* groups since 1980.
5 Note that on TaikOz's website the term '*wadaiko*' is used variously in both the broader and narrower senses; it is also defined as 'Japanese drumming and its philosophy'.
6 See Oguchi 1987: 30ff.
7 This is distinct from a *taiko* ritual practice developed within and unique to North American Buddhist sects, *hôraku*.
8 Among the musicians in these ten groups, some members of TaikOz and the Melbourne-based performer and teacher Sakamoto Toshi make their living from *taiko* music.

9   Cleworth and Lee founded the group jointly, but Cleworth has also served as the group's artistic director.

10 The compact disc of the programme (Synergy *et al.* 1994) bears the subtitle text 'a festival of inter-cultural percussion celebrating nature and technology', inscribed on the CD itself.

11 See the discussion of terminology in Chapter 1 of Bender 2003.

12 Recognition at the local and national levels is not always in agreement. See Alaszewska 1999 for a description of the case of music of the Chichibu festival tradition and the disagreement among local practitioners with government designation of one group as bearer of an Intangible Cultural Asset.

13 A notable exception, for example, is the group Dak-t, in which three performers who have played *wadaiko* since childhood appear in much the same attire as rock musicians and often 'dance' around their drums in movements that reference popular dance styles.

14 Kodo, for example, stresses that its collaborations 'extend right across the musical spectrum and continue to produce startling new fusion and forms' (Kodo website).

15 A piece of the same name is performed by Kodo, and presumably was part of the repertory of its predecessor, Ondekoza. Documentation by Kodo describes the piece in such a way as to suggest that it is a 'traditional' item, but specific information about sources is not given.

16 In notes posted on the website it is stated that Lee taught it to TaikOz, but there is no reference to which of the multiple versions of '*Yataibayashi*' Lee himself had learned. In December 2002 Cleworth attended practice sessions prior to the Chichibu *Yo-Matsuri* festival 'under the watchful eye of the President of the Drummers Organisation for Preserving Intangible Cultural Property of Japan, Mr. Toshio Takahashi' (TaikOz website, 'News' section, vol. 3, no. 1, January 2003), but no mention is made of further instruction on the piece. As an introduction to Takahashi – the man documented as having taught the piece to members of Ondekoza – had been received, it is likely that the TaikOz–Ondekoza version is close to that of Takahashi's groups.

17 Jane Alaszewska; oral communication, 24 June 2004.

18 Two compositions have dedicatory titles ('*Kenjō*', or 'offering', to his first teacher, Amano Sen, and '*O-TA-I-KO*', after the *taiko* training facility where TaikOz members spent time in 2001), while the other two pieces' titles refer to performance technique ('*Asobibachi*', or 'stick play') and content associations ('*Yuuraku*', translated as 'Night Piece').

19 TaikOz website: 'Reviews and Press Quotes' section. The meaning of Koehne's claim is obscure, as Godzilla is a rendering of the Japanese name Gojira, which combines elements of *gorira* (gorilla) and *kujira* (whale).

20 See the excerpt from an August 2001 performance by Staines and Ikegawa on the CD-ROM included in TaikOz 2001.

21 These are *haragake*, Japanese workmens 'aprons' that nevertheless resemble, when viewed from the front, a style of dark-coloured singlet once commonly worn by males in the Australian summer.

22 For example, '[i]n a very hierarchical society, the drums were one activity which everyone could enjoy at the same level' (*Canberra Times* 2002a).

23 Keister 2004 is one recent text that 'surveys the shakuhachi phenomenon in the West' and ways in which the instrument's historical function as a 'tool for meditational practices (*hōki*) in some Zen sects 'has been foregrounded in the process of appropriation by many enthusiasts outside Japan' (Keister 2004: 123).

24 One might regard drumming for particular ceremonies of some Buddhist sects as a formal spiritual practice, but those drumming styles have had little to do with the development of modern *kumidaiko* repertory.

25 Unlike most *wadaiko* practice in North America, the lack of Asian ethnic heritage among most Australian *taiko* players means that they are easily accused of exploiting Asian cultural resources if they stray too far from the transmitted performance practices. Public displays of reverence for *wadaiko*'s cultural origins may serve a precautionary function in such circumstances.

26 Conversely, the group may also have contributed to the changing meanings of *wadaiko* in Japan; as TaikOz has performed in Japan several times, on most occasions in large-scale concerts organized with one or other of Hayashi Eitetsu's ensembles, their compositions and performance style have been exposed to considerable numbers of Japanese *taiko* enthusiasts.

Bibliography and Audiography

Alaszewska, J. (1999) 'Preservation as a force for innovation: recent developments in Japanese festival drumming', unpublished MA thesis, SOAS.

Bender, S. (2003) 'Drumming between tradition and modernity: *taiko* and neo-folk performance in contemporary Japan', unpublished PhD thesis, University of California at San Diego.

Cleworth, I. (2002) 'Under the spell of a demon drummer', *Australian Financial Review*, 19 July, weekend Review: 6.

Courier Mail (Brisbane) (2001) 'Watching Japanese drumming is as important as listening to it', 4 August, BAM: 8.

de Ferranti, H. (2002) '"Japanese music" can be popular', *Popular Music*, vol. 21, no. 2 (Spring): 195–208.

Keister, J. (2004) 'The *shakuhachi* as spiritual tool: a Japanese Buddhist instrument in the West', *Asian Music*, vol. 35, no. 2: 99–131.

Kodo Online. HTML: http://www.kodo.or.jp/frame.html (accessed 3 July 2004).

McCallum, P. (2002) 'Putting some muscle into the SSO', *Sydney Morning Herald*, 30 July. *Canberra Times* (2000) 'First night opera house: audiences faces a cultural learning curve', 11 January, Tuesday Edition.

——(2002a) 'Taiko trainees beating to a different drum', 15 July, Monday Final Edition.

——(2002b) 'More than just a drum show', 16 July, Tuesday Final Edition.

Oguchi, D. (1997) *Tenko*, Nagano: Ginga Shobô.

Synergy with associate performers (1994) *Matsuri*, Celestial Harmonies: 13081–2 (CD).

TaikOz (2001) *Taiko no sekai* (The world of *taiko*), TaikOz: 1 (CD).

TaikOz (2003) *TaikOz Live at Angel Place*, New World Music and Media. NWADVD100 (DVD).

TaikOz Website. Online. HTML: http://www.TaikOz.com (accessed July–October 2004 and July 2005).

Taussig, M. (1993) *Mimesis and Alterity: a particular history of the senses*, New York and London: Routledge.

Terada, Y. (2001) 'Shifting identities of *taiko* music', in Y. Terada (ed.) *Transcending Boundaries: Asian musics in North America*, Senri Ethnological Reports 22, Osaka: National Museum of Ethnology: 37–59.

Turner, V. (1969) *The Ritual Process: structure and anti-structure*, Ithaca, NY: Cornell University Press.

6 Who reads comics?

Manga readership among first-generation Asian immigrants in New Zealand[1]

Yukako Sunaoshi

Introduction

Manga (Japanese comics)[2] are everywhere. Even here in Auckland. One can find various titles in their original versions as well as in Chinese, Korean and English translations. Who reads *manga* in today's Auckland? How and why do they read them? What can we observe about a flow of Japanese popular culture in the midst of globalization in this context? And finally, what can we learn about the lives and identities of young Asian immigrants in Auckland by examining their lives through the 'window' of *manga*? These are the main questions I raise in this chapter, based on a case study conducted in Auckland, New Zealand.

One of the main purposes of this chapter is to present a concrete case study to illustrate what is termed ethnoscape (Appadurai 1996: 33), one of the dimensions of the disjunctive nature of cultural flow in this globalized world. The present study also leads to a reassessment of the notions of 'home' and 'community' (Robertson 1995: 30), because the simultaneous, multi-directional flows of people, materials and consumption patterns all indicate movements much more complex than simply 'something/somebody coming or leaving home'.

Why study *manga* consumption patterns by Asian immigrants in New Zealand? I'm interested in this topic because observing this particular activity (*manga* reading) by people broadly grouped as 'Asians in Auckland' concretely exemplifies non-isomorphic flows of various factors in globalization. The rather old-fashioned form of entertainment has not only been transported and translated into neighbouring countries' languages, but is also read and enjoyed away from both the country of origin and the countries where the translations were done, and from where the young immigrants originally hailed. The identities of new Asian immigrants as ethnic minorities in New Zealand are complex because, despite a common perception of Asians as wealthy with higher qualifications, they are also subject to types of racial discrimination common among Asian ethnic groups in European-dominant societies. There is also intra-Asian discrimination and discrimination by Maori and Pacific Islanders directed at Asians.

Manga in Japan is big business: approximately 35 per cent of all publications in Japan are *manga*, which include both serials and paperbacks.[3] The three companies with the largest market share of *manga* publications (printing approximately 70 per cent of all *manga*) each publish several weekly and monthly *manga* serials, some of whose single issues sell over a million copies (Yoshihiro 1993: 6–7; information at the time of writing). Themes appearing in *manga* stories are varied, and the genres have diversified to capture a much wider audience than just children (for example, see McLelland 2001 on women's *yaoi* 'boy love' genre). The popular *manga* artists generate a billion-dollar merchandizing industry, where their messages can be more influential than newspapers or TV (Yang et al. 1997: 46). Popularity of *manga* beyond Japan has reached not only other Asian countries (Ng 2002) but also Western countries such as the USA and France (Craig 2000: 4–17; Yamanaka 2004: 126; Yang et al. 1997: 47) and New Zealand.

Auckland is the business centre of New Zealand, with a population of over 1.1 million (Census of Population and Dwellings 2001). Currently in New Zealand popular parlance the term 'Asians' loosely refers to people from East Asia (Ip 2003: 1), and that is how I use the term 'Asians' in this chapter. Auckland has the most concentrated Asian[4] population, comprising 13 per cent[5] of the total city population (Ip 2003: 1).

A new and rapid flow of immigration from East Asia started in the early 1990s (Ip 2001: 46). The participants in this study more or less[6] belong to this newly emerging category. We can see evidence of deterritorialization (Appadurai 1996: 49) in the lives of these families, as they typically continue their ties with both New Zealand and their countries of origin, transcending traditional notions of both boundaries and loyalties. The first language of these young immigrants is typically their 'mother tongue' and they use English as a second or third language, using two or sometimes more codes in a diglossic manner (see Hudson 1992 for a review on Diglossia). Culturally, too, they lead multilayered lives. For example, one of the participants in this study describes his life as having different 'modes' depending on the context: 'It feels like [when] you walk out of your front door, you start just going into the English mode. (laughter) I see my overseas friends, *Chinese mode* . . . So it's like that . . . You don't really feel it [switching around]' (italic denotes spoken emphasis; John,[7] Taiwan origin). It is in this context that these young Asian immigrants lead their lives in Auckland. And it is in this context that we need to situate their *manga* consumption, as their interviews reveal their simultaneous multiple memberships in different communities.

Manga reading in Auckland (or New Zealand) is not a widespread phenomenon. Ien's observation on the invisibility of Japanese dramas in mainstream Australia, except within certain Japanese and Asian communities in Sydney, applies here (Ien 2003: 291).[8] Flows of *manga* consumption are visible partially through the increasing number of Korean and Chinese comic and video rental shops located in Auckland in areas in which there are substantial numbers of relocated Asian immigrants.

In the following, I first discuss the method used for the data gathering and analysis. I then analyse the data, focusing on the added values and meanings of *manga* for the Asian readers in Auckland in relation to the participants' identities. I conclude with further observations on disjunctive cultural flows and ethnoscapes.

Method

The data for this chapter are firstly drawn from open-ended interviews conducted with twenty-five participants of Asian origin. The interviews lasted from forty minutes to seventy-five minutes,[9] depending on the flow of the conversation. The profiles of the participants are listed in Table 6.1. The participants immigrated with their families to New Zealand[10] some time between their primary and high school years. Their countries of origin were mainly Korea, Taiwan and Hong Kong, and their ages ranged from 16 to 28. The major criteria used to select interviewees were: (1) the participant either reads or used to read *manga* regularly and (2) s/he is sixteen years or older.[11] Because I wanted to gain as many voices as possible from a relatively limited population pool (compared to, say, interviewing Koreans in Korea), the number of participants was not strictly controlled according to their age and gender. Also, depending on the participants' social networks, the interviews were conducted individually, in a pair or in a group (of four). Initially, questions regarding their *manga*-reading behaviours were used as starting points (for example when they started, what kind of stories they read, why they liked these stories), then interviewees elaborated on various aspects of their *manga*-reading activity. This interview data is supplemented with observation and brief interviews at several Korean and Chinese comic rental shops. Further, a single interview was conducted at a Japanese *manga* rental shop for comparison.

General themes to build the participants' profile

A large number of universal themes were found in the interviews, such as how interviewees encountered *manga* and how they internalized stories. However, as the focus of this chapter is aspects specific to Asian readers in Auckland, I only briefly introduce a few such themes, which are necessary to build the participants' profiles. These themes illustrate aspects of more 'hooked' or devoted readers among the participants.

The first theme is their re-reading of not only their favourite stories but also favourite scenes. An example is a scene where the main character in *Slam Dunk*[12] beats his rival in a basketball game. Miho describes her reason for re-reading certain scenes as an act of instantly re-experiencing certain emotional states such as *setsunai* (yearning, usually for romance), and this

Table 6.1 List of study participants

Name (age)/origin (age when left)	Gender/ Status	Individual or group?/ Language
Alex (20), Malaysia (6)	M, Univ student	Pair-1, English
Mick (22), HK (18)	M, Univ student	Pair-1, English
Jack (28), Taiwan (15)	M, Working	Individual, English
Matt (20), Taiwan (11)	M, Univ student	Group-1, English
John (20), Taiwan (5/6)	M, Univ student	Group-1, English
Shawn (20), Taiwan (14)	M, Univ student	Group-1, English
Tom (20), China (11)	M, Univ student	Group-1, English
Kitty (26), Taiwan (11)	F, Grad student	Individual, English
Sean (early 20s), Taiwan	M, Univ student	Individual, English
Ji Na (early 20s), Korea	F, Working	Individual, English
Jae Yong (early 20s), Korea	M, Shop attendant	Individual, English
Sang Mi (17), Korea	F, Univ student	Pair-3, Korean
Eun Hee (16), Korea	F, High school	Pair-3, Korean
Lisa, Taiwan	F, Univ student	Pair-2, Mandarin
Isaac, Taiwan	M, Univ student	Pair-2, Mandarin
Sheng Yen, Taiwan	M, Univ student	Group-2, Mandarin
Yu Shing, Taiwan	F, Univ student	Group-2, Mandarin
Ling Yi, Taiwan	M, Univ student	Group-2, Mandarin
I Wen, Taiwan	F, Univ student	Group-2, Mandarin
Kyu Min (16), Korea	M, High school	Group-3, Eng/Korean
Min Soo (16), Korea	M, High school	Group-3, Eng/Korean
Woo Min (16), Korea	M, High school	Group-3, Eng/Korean
Jin Chul (16), Korea	M, High school	Group-3, Eng/Korean
Jung Mi (22), Korea	F, Working	Individual, Korean
Min Hee, Korea	F, Studying	Individual, Korean
Miho, Japan	F, Shop attendant	Individual, Japanese

explanation seems to resonate with other, especially female, non-Japanese readers as well. By remembering which volume or page(s) of which story contains an appropriate scene to invoke the type of feeling she wishes to experience, she can instantly *hitaru*, or indulge herself, in the emotion whenever she wants (cf. *kyara-moe* by *otaku* in Azuma 2001: 58–77).

The second theme is the readers' intensive reading pattern. Sang Mi recalls her high school days (in Auckland) when she would read a whole series of forty volumes in one day. Eun Hee recalls that a circle of friends formed at a *manga* rental shop in Korea once checked the shop's computerized rental record and found out that most of them had rented over 3000 volumes each already.

Third, a couple of participants are absolute devotees of *manga*. For example, Kitty treats her *manga* collection (once as many as thousands) with such respect that she keeps it in her room and will not touch her favourites without washing her hands beforehand. In this way, she protects her *manga* from damage even after re-reading them 'countless times'. Such devotees are dissatisfied with the quality of translations. In Kitty's case, she has purchased both Mandarin and Japanese versions of some stories for this reason.

Some of the themes that emerged seem to be shared with other Asian readers 'back home'. First, many participants admit they started reading *manga* when they were young without thinking or noticing their origin, and only later did they realize where they had come from. *Manga*, to them, are both 'familiar' and 'foreign', creating in them various feelings such as excitement, ease, fun and intellectual stimulation. As M.-T. Lee (2003: 146–9) points out regarding the popularity of Japanese TV dramas in Hong Kong, there seems to be a comfortable distance between *manga* and the readers here: different but similar, similar but different.

According to some participants, while Hong Kong or Korean *manga* depicting their native historical events seem a lot like a review of school history class, a fictionalization of a Japanese historical event or even a Chinese historical event by Japanese *manga* artists produces a comfortable balance between intellectual stimulation, realism and fantasy. This is reminiscent of Ko's claim regarding the popularity of Japanese TV dramas in Taiwan (2003: 170–6): what is perceived as 'real' is what is imaginable to the audience, rather than their actual, everyday reality. The sense of 'real' also comes from *manga*'s less tamed nature compared to its Korean and Chinese equivalents.[13] Participants claim that, whether it is homosexuality, violence, naked bodies or using a toilet, everything seems to be drawn explicitly and vividly in Japanese *manga*. Further, *manga* is where the wildest imaginations are articulated. Being loyal to a messy or even grotesque form of 'reality', many *manga* stories avoid becoming a simple vehicle for delivering morals to the audience.[14] Consequently, these stories can offer the quality of being 'real'.

Added meanings and values of *manga* in the context of Auckland

What aspects of the participants' *manga*-reading habits are unique to their transnational identities? As stated in the previous section, for many participants reading Japanese *manga* in translation was a habit acquired in their childhood. Continuing this activity in New Zealand, therefore, was a natural carryover of their old habit. Jack articulates this situation: 'Although [*manga*]s are from Japan, because I was reading them in Taiwan, I treat them as part of my life. My childhood.'

In Taiwan's case, the atmosphere of appreciating anything Japanese (see, e.g., Ito 2004; Ko 2004a, 2004b; M.-T. Lee 2004 on this phenomenon called *hari*) was already present among youth before the participants came to New Zealand, making *manga*-reading activity quite 'natural' and 'matter of fact' (see Chapter 2). In this regard, like other familiar habits, it has provided young immigrants with a sense of comfort during their initial adjustment to New Zealand society and in their ongoing daily lives. Jack's story is particularly intriguing, illuminating the complex interplay of his individual life history, on the one hand, and emerging globalization and cosmopolitanism at the city and national level, on the other.

Coming to Auckland first to be a student of an English-language school at age fifteen in 1990, Jack encountered by accident several *manga* in their original version in a Japanese restaurant near the language school, which offered a cheap set lunch popular among English-learning students like himself.

> So I just looked at the pictures. But some of the *manga* like *Doraemon*[15] or *Dragon Ball*[16] are what I read previously in Taiwan. So I kind of knew the stories . . . It was only those stories I had already read that I picked up at the restaurant and read.

Lack of entertainment in Auckland (in Jack's mind) and his low level of proficiency in English both contributed to making *manga* his major form of entertainment as well as a 'comfort activity' in his initial days in Auckland. There were several forces at work simultaneously here. First, this was the beginning of the boom of the ESOL (English for speakers of other languages) industry in Auckland, which flourished from the early to mid-1990s (and is in decline at the time of writing). The ESOL boom marked one of Auckland's first steps towards becoming a cosmopolitan, multi-ethnic city. Anecdotally, in those days there were not nearly as many Asian restaurants as there are now. The Japanese restaurant's offering of a reasonably priced lunch then must have had a certain appeal to students from Asia, both economically and in terms of familiarity. There, the Taiwanese student, who grew up in the era of 'Japan fever' in Taiwan, happened to find familiar titles, and re-read them again and again, partly from curiosity to find out if the two versions were the same, but also prompted by his loneliness and isolation as a newcomer. In fact a common theme among participants is this sense of isolation; that is, while it is a fairly large city of over one million people, Auckland continues to struggle with issues about integration and tolerance toward Asian Others, whose sheer numbers and physical and cultural characteristics stand out.

Kitty's account illustrates a different yet equally intriguing partial picture of how *manga* are located and used in a young immigrant's life. Coming from a well-known doctor's family in Taiwan, her life since childhood had always been full of restrictions. All her time had been consumed by studying back in Taiwan, but once in New Zealand she had 'freedom' to be on her own, as her parents travelled back and forth.[17] The freedom allowed her to secure ample time for *manga*. Still deeply unhappy as a high school student, she tried committing suicide. In that context, she believes '*Dragon Ball* saved my life', literally, as wanting to know what would come in the next episode in the then ongoing story gave her hope to live (notice that the theme of *Dragon Ball* is a naive boy's physical and spiritual growth through challenges against bigger and stronger beings). Though she states that *manga* enable her to 'escape from reality', they still occupy a very special place in Kitty's mind. In her case, the combination of her family's wealth and New Zealand's relatively 'free' educational and living environment granted her an opportunity to enjoy *manga*.

Interest in Japanese culture or language hardly preceded the interviewees' growing fondness toward *manga*. Sheng Yen clearly says that the correlation between her reading *manga* and interest in Japan is minor at most; Yu Shing is quick to point out that *manga* is a weak source as a cultural text. The meaninglessness of an attempt to search for 'Japaneseness' in Japanese animation has been pointed out before (Iwabuchi 2001: 98–9, 124), and the argument supports the present finding as well. Some say, however, that after establishing their *manga* habit they developed a new interest in Japanese culture or language. Sang Mi and Eun Hee enthusiastically admit that their interests now extend to Japanese fashion and pop idols. Matt, who took Japanese in high school (in Auckland), suspects that most of his Chinese classmates back then wanted to study Japanese because they were *manga* fans. Kitty, after doing a short-term homestay in Japan, had her host family send *manga* serials to her for a few years. Reading these volumes together with taking Japanese at high school eventually made her quite a competent user of the language without living in Japan for an extended time.

When some participants mentioned reading the original versions, their non-understanding of Japanese did not seem crucial for a few reasons. As shown earlier, Jack's re-encounter with *Doraemon* at a Japanese restaurant turned out to be a curious and joyful experience due to his prior familiarity with the story. Alex says, 'Well some of them I really don't understand but I look at the pictures and get it from the context.' Out of the participants, Alex is the most 'Kiwi-ized' immigrant.[18] Recalling his high school days, he gives the following episode, which confirms how he positions himself in the ethno-cultural mapping of high school life in Auckland. The episode also gives a fascinating instance of how the language barrier can be dismissed in enjoying *manga*.

Alex: We did bring *manga*, but not with Asian kids, because I mostly hang around with interracial kids. I've got a friend who was born in New Zealand, but he (that is, his family) came from Lebanon, and [I have other friends who are] Korean, [from the] Gilbert Islands, America, France, all sorts. And we just, basically were all brought up in Kiwi culture, so we just bring *manga* or comics to school and we just read them. We just ask around and see what the book's about.

Researcher: But that's a Kiwi *manga* you are talking about.

Alex: No, it's Japanese.

Researcher: So how did they know [about *manga*]? Did you introduce those to them?

Alex: No, no. Actually my friend from Lebanon actually brought it to us. And he was talking about it with a friend who was Korean.

Researcher: Interesting, but it was in English, right? English translation.

Alex: No it was in Japanese. They just look at the pictures.

Researcher: Oh, okay, and that was entertaining enough?

Alex: For them. I could read better because I was taking Japanese at that time, but I just look at how they write, and what [the characters] looked like.

(Excerpt from interview with Pair 1, in answer to the researcher's question 'Did you share *manga* with other Asian friends back in high school?')

In New Zealand, access to ranges of familiar products from 'back home', be it food, books or any other cultural materials, can be difficult, and access to *manga* is no exception. Through interviews, however, it became evident that the participants create and maintain multiple channels through which they satisfy their appetite for *manga*. Their major access routes are: personal import through family members or acquaintances who are still in their places of origin or in Japan (see, for example, Jack's and Kitty's cases above), or when they themselves return 'home' for a visit; local (Auckland) connection and sharing; and (illegal) free downloading from the Internet. The second method varies from something sporadic to something more organized. Some say they use rental shops in town, but they turned out to be the minority. They complain about the high cost of renting, which is not much cheaper than the purchase price back in Taiwan, for example. By renting, they also have to read the stories with a time constraint of overnight or two days, which makes it difficult to enjoy repeated reading or appreciation of the details of drawings.

Some find it too troublesome to obtain regular access to *manga* here, though they all admit it has become much easier in the last five years or so. Matt and John, though they are clear about their preference for Japanese *manga*, mainly read Hong Kong *manga* now as they can download them much more easily from proper companies (whereas they say that Japanese *manga* occasionally available via Internet are pirated and scanned images, whose quality is not as high). Jack says he no longer reads *manga* and has shifted to Japanese TV dramas. Though the recent trend back in Taiwan is Korean anything (cf. Leung 2004), he cannot relate to this boom, as he did not spend time in Taiwan when it happened. This shift occurred as a result of a combination of finding access to *manga* too cumbersome, gaining independence by having his own place with a TV and a VCD (video compact disc)[19] player, having his own car and finding that VCD is more easily and cheaply accessible either by purchasing during his occasional trips back to Taiwan or by renting at local Chinese video rental shops.

Despite these challenges in accessing *manga*, Auckland is still a fertile place for *manga* reading. Some, especially those originally coming from big cities, say there is 'nothing to do here'. In addition, their initial linguistic limitations and different expectations toward socialization must have limited their integration. Furthermore, though New Zealand is an English-speaking 'Western' country, it is not a major centre of popular culture production or distribution. Jack's early days' experience as a rather lonely language-school student in Auckland encouraged his *manga* reading, while if he had been in Taiwan he might have found other entertainments. Like Kitty, Tom states that he has much less academic pressure here than in China, so he now has time to devote to reading *manga*.

Part of the enjoyment of reading *manga* for these Asian migrants comes from the nostalgic feelings that the activity invokes. Yu Shing feels as if she were in a comic store in Taiwan when she reads *manga* in Auckland. And while Sang Mi, who spent most of her time in school in New Zealand, does not feel nostalgic, Eun Hee's mind often diverts to the time when she used to chat over noodles with her friends and the owner of a *manga* rental shop after school, and that easily makes her homesick.

Manga reading can also inform a social group identity, as Alex's account of 'Chinatown' indicates:

> I was in an all-boys school. There we have groups, like 'Chinatown', 'Iraqi centre' [laughter] . . . and Chinatown is usually based around the basketball areas[20] and [the Chinese students] all go there. Sometimes they sit in a group . . . and read comics, and some guys just read them and then go play basketball and come back.

Alex's school is located in a neighbourhood with a high percentage of Asian residents. He adds that 'Chinatown' has been established for a long time now, and that new Chinese students can still join. Reading *manga* in their native language can be a meaningful part of their own local ethnic group formation.

Another set of responses reveals that *manga* can be used as a means to establish a new line of inter-ethnic relationships (though such relationships are usually limited within different Asian ethnic groups[21]). Auckland is an interestingly neutral place for readers from different backgrounds, where they can share their *manga*-reading experience. Alex's example of his international group is the most striking, but a number of the participants also say they have talked about *manga* with other Asians in high school. Such interactions can start by coincidence. For example, in one interview a Korean girl described how she saw a group of Taiwanese girls circulating the Chinese version of *Doraemon*. She was excited that she now knew they had something in common to talk about, and they compared Korean and Chinese versions and continued talking about other stories they both knew. The multi-lingual context of the discussion here is worth noting. The Korean and Taiwanese girls spoke in English, their lingua franca, while the texts discussed (which had been translated from Japanese) were written in their respective languages.

Similarly, Eun Hee recalls:

> When I was reading *Hana yori dango*[22] in school, my Japanese friends came and said excitedly, 'I like this story very much, too.' One of them brought the Japanese version to school the next day. We were both just so happy and excited . . . Pointing at different male characters in the story, we said to each other, 'I wish a guy like him would become my boyfriend.' This incident made us closer than before.

Boys seem to share *manga* stories orally in a similar manner to these two accounts, but some, like Jae Yong, also experienced a different type of sharing among boys. Being a big fan of *Slam Dunk*, he recalls playing basketball together with Korean, Taiwanese, Chinese and Japanese boys in high school. They started imitating the main characters' form, talked about the story, then they found out the protagonists had different names in respective languages.[23]

Because it is difficult to get hold of Japanese *manga*, for some of the study participants fewer than 10 per cent of the comics consumed were of Japanese origin. This percentage increases, as John reveals, when back in Taiwan, where *manga* can be purchased or rented cheaply. They enjoy *manga* as a form of entertainment in general; they would prefer Japanese ones if they had easy access, but, if not, alternatives would do. For some of those who categorize themselves as *manga* addicts, like Ji Na, the origin of *manga* is irrelevant compared to the quality of the product itself. Pair 3 say their favourite titles consist of a mixture of Japanese and Korean *manga*, and they also enjoy reading Internet novels these days. Like Jack, Group 1 mention watching Japanese dramas, as they can do a collaborative personal import easily and cheaply. That is, each of them buys one or two VCDs from Taiwan and then they share them when back in Auckland.

Consumers' attitudes

As Ji Na succinctly stated, 'you read [*manga*] as the market allows you'. She intuitively knew that in this globalized world consumers can at best be choosers but not actors (Appadurai 1996: 42). Consumers can access items globally by either direct or indirect means. In the present case, they can access products from 'back home', from Japan, from New Zealand or, in fact, from anywhere. By being physically away from their 'homelands', they may be (at least partially) detached from nationalistic discourse (see D.-H. Lee 2003: 254–5; 2004; Ko 2003: 152; Yoshihiro 1993: 51) which sometimes surrounds *manga* 'back home'. But products are readily available. Interviewees are globally informed, in the sense that their mobile life histories have given them knowledge of what *manga* are available and where they can obtain them. My participants were mainly either university students or students of well-regarded high schools in Auckland, which fits a stereotype of recent Asian immigrant families: financially affluent and living in 'good' school districts.[24] In short, the reasons they gave for reading *manga* were pleasure, the high quality of the products, easy access to *manga* and easy consumption.

In multiple ways, *manga* satisfies the criterion of being read 'for pleasure', as shown in the analysis above. As with any saturated industry, the second factor, 'quality', is important as well. Thousands of titles available from Japan (and others in translation) are subject to close scrutiny by regular readers. Some titles win instant popularity, which sometimes further progresses into the status of a long-running bestseller. *Slam Dunk* is an example of this category. As Jae Yong witnesses, in the rental shop where he works *Slam Dunk* remains a popular item, as older readers keep renting issues to re-read, while new readers discover the story.

In this fierce competition, *manga* by Taiwanese, Hong Kong and Korean authors are not given automatic approval just because they are of local origin. With heavy influence from Japanese *manga*, many writers still struggle to establish their unique styles (Kusaka 2000: 284–5; Ng 2002: 30–1). At the same time, I did not feel a sense of loyalty toward 'Japanese' *manga*[25] from the readers I interviewed, either. As John put it, 'Good's good' regardless of its origin or type. What this implies is that if there are *manga* artists from those regions who can produce excellent stories (and there are more and more), then they will have every chance to win the readers' hearts.[26] As much as participants enjoyed the blurred sense of 'familiar' and 'foreign', they would probably equally enjoy the feeling of (predominant) familiarity.

Korean *manga* were considered fairly favourably by some of the Korean interviewees. This change may be partially due to the politicized aspect of Korean versus Japanese *manga* (Yamanaka 2004); in any case, some of the Korean interviewees already hint at the potentially emerging preference toward Korean *manga*.[27] Jae Yong says that now 80 per cent of the *manga* stock at the rental shop are of Korean origin, whereas when it opened eight years ago virtually everything was of Japanese origin. Although a big fan of *Slam Dunk* who read the story '100 times', he admits that now he mostly reads Korean *manga* because they are easier to read and he can relate to them better. To Eun Hee, Korean *manga* is a cultural window through which she can learn about Korean high school life. Sang Mi and Eun Hee, looking back on their high school days in Auckland, sadly describe their days as having few friendships, unlike the formation of lifelong friendships often depicted in Korean *manga*. To satisfy their unfulfilled yearning for such friendships, and simply to learn how it would be to lead a (supposedly) more meaningful high school life, they enjoy reading Korean *manga*.

Concerning the accessibility of *manga*, consumers are also constantly weighing effort and resultant benefits: 'How can I get the latest, most interesting item with the least effort and expense?' This is the ultimate question of access.

To summarise, the participants of this study constantly swim in the middle of two contrasting currents: one is market forces, while the other is their transnational consumer identity. The former places the readers in a largely passive role, while the latter grants them power to choose based on their own criteria.

Shifting identities and *manga* reading

I start this final section by discussing how Appadurai's notion of disjunctive cultural flow can be observed in the present setting. There are at least several major factors at work here: the Asians' construction of (ethnic, consumer) identity, various patterns of *manga* consumption, flows of products (*manga*) via various channels and a shifting sense of 'home' and 'community'. These are all taking non-isomorphic paths, making it impossible to assume a preset correlation of any two factors. This complex picture of movements of people and the popular cultural product force an ongoing reorganization of these factors' interrelationships. Furthermore, this disjuncture is now the norm, rather than a process to form a more 'stable' situation. In other words, global patterns of *manga* consumption will probably never go back to the good old simple 'in–out' binary flow, where the consumption took place mostly within Japan, and later by simply importing from Japan into another country. The ethnoscape of Auckland and its constantly shifting nature are observed through the young Asian immigrants' transnational and transient stances. This dynamic ethnoscape has been illuminated through examining their *manga* reading. What follow are a few more detailed observations of the present setting, focusing on the young immigrants' identity formation *vis-à-vis* their *manga*-reading activity.

The first point to address is that readers attach different meanings to reading *manga*. Even within the narrowly defined group of readers, the diversity was evident. Indeed, for individuals, how *manga* were used could vary depending on the context. We are seeing here a tension (or what Ien 1996: 14 would call 'contradictions') among forces from different directions concurrently at work. Moreover, as Ien (1996: 1–15) argues, being an 'active' consumer does not allow one to escape from the influence of market forces. These factors make it impossible for us to simply characterize the readers as either active or passive. Even the narrowing down of the participants to a category roughly framed as 'young Asian immigrants' did not provide us with a neat picture. Instead, the diversity of their responses and the different ways they consume *manga* became underscored because the pool of participants was relatively narrowly defined. Conveying the diversity yet simultaneously making it a 'neat mess' has indeed been a challenging task (cf. Pieterse 1995: 55), though I am not certain if the quest for neatness should be the point of this project at all. Even when one studies local people's consumption behaviours in their homeland, the picture of what and how they consume is a *mélange* (see, e.g., M.-T. Lee 2004). It is then inevitable that this tendency is intensified and necessitated by my participants' mobility and transnational perspectives.

On one hand, based on how they articulated their lives and feelings, I think of them as *permanent transients* who feel they cannot fully belong to any one community or culture. On the other hand, they can also be described as *transnational citizens*, who move comfortably across linguistic and cultural borders by living in many ways beyond the borders of either 'imagined community' (that is, New Zealand or 'back home'; Anderson 1983) (cf. two contrastive views on Chinese business immigrants to New Zealand in Ip 2001: 45). At the macro level, several forces are at work. Auckland is a cosmopolitan city, and the recent increase in the Korean and Chinese populations has led to a mushrooming of various retail businesses, including video and comic rental shops. Easy access to an international airport, Internet connections and an ongoing inflow of new immigrants from East Asian countries all contribute to an environment in which young immigrants keep continual ties with multiple communities. At the national level, relevant factors include Asians' 'newness' as immigrants, New Zealand's small scale (thus small job market) and society's ambivalence toward immigrants, which results in challenging employment situations for many Asians. This in turn draws an insecure picture of long-term settlement. Hardly passive bearers of their destinies, however, the young immigrants themselves choose to live their lives as transnational citizens as well. Touching on their future career prospects, for example, Group 1 elaborated on various possibilities they naturally think of in New Zealand, Taiwan and maybe Japan. Good or bad, they are not tied down to one geographical area. This, however, may be a matter of degree rather than a unique characteristic among immigrants, as the same transnational career perspective may also be present among many Kiwi youth.

Here, the issue may not be whether or not (or how much) one wants to assimilate into the mainstream society. Rather, in the era of a fluid post-modern world, they are supported by capital and educational qualifications. And they can afford, and are willing, to stay in a highly mobile position, looking simultaneously at different directions, their multi-sensory antenna catching ever-increasing information and options to choose from. They naturally maintain ties with several communities as needed: for example back 'home' (Taiwan), New Zealand mainstream society, Taiwanese in Auckland, other 'Asians' in Auckland. The multifaceted nature of *manga* in turn seems to symbolize the fluid positioning of the participants: Japanese *manga* are popular cultural artefacts originating in Japan, translated into Chinese/ Korean, imported on an individual basis or as a small business, now some- times available in English translation and increasingly accessible (but not so much five years ago) in the city of Auckland. Note also that even this rather archaic form of entertainment (*manga* are printed, bound and cheap) owes a great debt to the Internet in its worldwide distribution.

Paradoxically but quite understandably, the participants articulated their ways of forming networks and eventually communities amidst their tran- sient positioning. As there is no one community to which they can wholly belong, they continually search for partial ties based on different kinds of commonalties. Simple variants such as their ethnic origin may not serve as a sufficient commonalty by themselves.

A case in point is how my participants (and in fact myself) understand and use the term 'Asian' to illustrate an example of manipulating popular notions with respect to who we are. Because 'Asian' is initially a label imposed by the mainstream society, the notion is never native to us, the objects of the labelling. From the mainstream's perspective the term can be used for easy stereotyping. From the perspective of those who are labelled as such, figuring out who fits in that category is to be negotiated and manipu- lated, as well as learned. This situation leads to a confusion at one level, making it tricky for me to decide how I use the term in this chapter, for example. At the same time, because of this fluid nature of the category 'Asian' one can observe how speakers situate themselves with respect to others in the society. For example, when Alex talked about 'Asian kids' back in high school, he himself was not included. From what he said, 'Asian kids' refers to certain demeanours, including lack of language and cultural competence, that 'interracial kids' (a self-referential term for Alex) like Alex himself do have. It was also observed that when Korean participants talked about interacting with 'Asians' the term included East Asians but not Koreans, expressing a distance between their own national/ethnic group and the rest of 'Asians'. Interaction requires language, which different Asian groups do not share. Thus, this is one instance where Koreans differentiated themselves from other 'similar faces' (notice in fact that all the examples above utilize the mainstream society's gross grouping here). Lastly, when some of the participants talked about positive aspects of sharing *manga* with other 'Asians', they pointed out that these experiences of *manga* can only be understood and shared by 'Asians'. In the last usage, the term refers to all of them, as the mainstream roughly defines us. This shifting sense of labelling and categorization is a reflection of their own multifaceted and dynamic sense of identity.

To reiterate my earlier points, considering hybridity (that is, the partici- pants' identification with popular cultural products from multiple origins) as something less than a whole, as has been assumed (and as has been pointed out by Pieterse 1995: 54–5), is a rather limited viewpoint. Rather, what I suggest is to record and observe the dynamism, where readers 'dance' in the continuums of relativity, such as 'passive' versus 'active' and 'insider' versus 'outsider'. Indeed, globalization, as seen through the window of *manga*, involves reconstruction of concepts of 'home' and 'community' (Robertson 1995: 30), though, as I discussed above, one person is likely to belong simultaneously to more than one 'home' and 'community'.

Lastly, there is one more layer of relativity that people like the participants in this study have to deal with. That is, not only do they step in and out of boxes of 'insider' and 'outsider' in New Zealand society, but also the sense of inequality is real. The relevant continuums here are 'peripheral' versus 'central/mainstream', and 'incompetent (= less than a whole)' versus 'competent (= normal)'. The young immigrants' *manga*-reading behaviour marks them as 'different'; that is, non-mainstream and not comprehensible.[28] Conversely, such behaviour creates new connections between immigrants from different (yet mainly Asian) backgrounds, concurrently creating a new community while confirming and reinforcing the mainstream labelling of 'Asians' in New Zealand.

Notes

1 My foremost appreciation goes to the participants of this study. Without their valuable input this project would not have been possible. I also thank my research assistants: Hae Sook Whang, Annie Mei-Yin Wu, Seunghee Lee, Shaw Cheng, Yi-Fang Chiang, and Li-Chia Yeh for their hard work and invaluable assistance in Korean and Mandarin, without which some of the interviews would not have been possible. This research was funded by the University of Auckland Staff Research Fund.

2 In this chapter, the term *manga* is used to refer to comics (with stories or *stoorii manga*, not short pieces as appearing in newspapers, for example) drawn by Japanese artists. However, when comparing those with similar products drawn by artists from Hong Kong, Taiwan and Korea, *manga* is further specified as 'Japanese *manga*', 'Korean, *manga*', etc.

3 Most commonly, *manga* stories first appear in print in one of the *manga* serials (commonly weekly or monthly), together with several other stories. When enough episodes of a story have appeared in this manner, they are bound and republished as a paperback.

4 Placing people in boxes always invokes a danger of stereotyping and oversimplification, despite its convenience. In the present (mainstream) New Zealand society, the distinction based on nationality or the degree of sociolinguistic competence has not yet been widely made when referring to those from these ethnic and geographical backgrounds. For example, an international student from China, a permanent resident who came to New Zealand from Taiwan as an elementary school pupil and a second-generation ethnic Chinese whose native language is English would all be categorized as 'Chinese' or 'Asian' in the eyes of mainstream society at present. This is partly due to the relatively short history of large-scale immigration from Asia.

5 Here, for statistical purposes, twelve groups, based on population size significance in migration flow, are included. They are the Chinese, Indians, Lao, Vietnamese,

Cambodians, Thai, Japanese, Filipinos, Malay, Sri Lankans, Iranians and Koreans (Statistics New Zealand 1995). Thus, when statistical information is cited in this chapter, this categorization of 'Asia' is used.

6 As Table 6.1 shows, some of the participants moved to New Zealand in the late 1980s.

7 All the individual names used in this chapter are pseudonyms. English pseudonyms are used when the individuals go by English names, while Chinese or Korean pseudonyms are used when they go by their original ethnic names. This is due to my belief that choosing one's name has to do with an expression of one's identity and/or one's stance on the mainstream Anglophone society, and it should be respected as such.

8 However, note that English translations of *manga* (though on a much smaller scale than Korean or Chinese translations) have become available in Auckland. To my knowledge, currently the largest book shop in central Auckland has a section of *manga*. There is also one *manga* café in town, which holds volumes translated into English.

9 An exception to this is the interview with Min Hee, which lasted approximately ten minutes. This was because she was recruited randomly at a rental shop and the interview took place right there.

10 Except for one: the Korean participant Min Hee was on a student visa.

11 This second criterion was set for ease of processing in the University of Auckland Human Subject Ethics approval process, and because I wanted participants who were old enough to articulate their ideas. This research was approved by the University of Auckland Human Subject Ethics Committee (Ref. 2002/350).

12 *Slam Dunk* (by Inoue Takehiko) is a mega hit in *shônen manga* (boys' comics) and is about high-school boys' growing up through playing basketball. No male participants failed to mention their love of this story. A few female participants mentioned they have read it, too.

13 Some Korean participants recall seeing edited parts in early Korean (pirated) versions they read. These parts were obviously noticeable, as if quickly having been smeared with correction liquid. Examples of such censorship include changing the Japanese flag to the Korean's on the chest of a judo costume, redrawing Korean costume over a kimono or a naked body and omitting certain language to make the story less sexually expressive, which risked making the story rather inconsistent.

14 This is not necessarily true in all *manga*, however. My impression is that the *manga* targeted at younger audience, especially when they are animated for a wider audience including parents, tend to have simpler (and safer) moral messages.

15 See Shiraishi (2000) for the global consumption of this much-admired classic *manga*.

16 *Dragon Ball* (42 vols, by Toriyama Akira; plus two successive series) is a modern (and highly original) version of the Monkey King from Chinese folklore. See Introduction in Craig (2000) for a brief analysis of the story.

17 This is a common profile of emigrant parents (mainly fathers) who have a high-earning career back in their places of origin. They choose New Zealand for its safety and education for their children, but often find it more feasible to continue earning their living by working back home. As a result, their children tend to live only with their mothers, or sometimes on their own, while the fathers make occasional trips to New Zealand. Regarding (ethnic) Chinese immigrants to New Zealand, Ip concludes that such 'transnationalism tends to be a strategy adopted by default rather than as part of an ambitious global scheme' (2001: 56).

18 His communicative norms (see 'Contextualization cues' in Gumperz 1992) are very much Kiwi-like. Such norms include when to use certain phrases and how to respond to a question verbally and non-verbally. In short, he knows how to communicate appropriately according to mainstream New Zealand English sociolinguistic norms, a sure sign of one's communicative competence (as opposed to simple grammatical competence).

19 Videis CD, which sold in East Asia, but not in Japan. It was less expensive and consumers did not have to have a DVD player, which was expensive then, to watch dramas and movies.

20 It is possible that their liking of basketball is related to *Slam Dunk* (see note 12). Alex also commented, 'A lot of Asians like playing basketball, but now they are getting into soccer as well.'

21 In fact, some participants mention that they don't believe Kiwis would be able to relate to *manga*. Another account given is that 'Asian kids' are used to having fun quietly and privately in an enclosed space, into which *manga* fits well, whereas 'Kiwi kids' would rather drive around, party and go out with girls.

22 *Hana yori dango* (by Kamio Yoko, 36 vols at the time of writing) is a story about the everyday life of a girl from a low socio-economic background in a private high school. Other main characters in this romantic comedy are four wealthy and handsome boys and a high school queen. The title is taken from the Japanese saying *hana yori dango*, meaning that something pragmatic (*dango*='rice cakes') is better than something elegant (*hana*='flower'). However, the author used the *kanji* meaning 'boys' instead of rice cakes for the pronunciation *dango*, creating a humorous effect.

23 In the Korean version names of characters are changed into Korean names. In Chinese versions they often employ the same *kanji* of the characters' names with the Chinese pronunciations. As a result, all versions have different names for the same character.

24 The Asian population is reported to have higher educational qualifications overall than the national average. The 1991 Census shows that 20.4 per cent of the Asian population has a 'university qualification' (as opposed to 8.0 per cent of all New Zealanders) and 22.1 per cent of the Asian population has 'no qualification' (as opposed to 31.8 per cent of all New Zealanders).

25 Participants say 'I love Japanese *manga*' or 'Japanese *manga* is the best', but 'Japanese *manga*' here does not refer to something intrinsically Japanese; rather, the term is largely equated with commodity of good quality and enjoyment in the current market.

26 As Leung (2004) and Ko (2004b) point out, such a shift has already been taking place in TV dramas. The sudden popularity of Korean dramas (and other popular cultural products), termed *hanliu*, seems to have overridden *hari*, 'Japanese fever', in places like Taiwan and Malaysia. At the time of writing, *hanliu* has arrived in Japan and has been vibrant, where Korean dramas in particular have become major hits.

27 Notice also that import of Japanese cultural products was officially banned until 1998, and even after that the issue has always been controversial. Thus, Korean participants' articulation of their preference toward Korean *manga* may be influenced by this national discourse.

28 It is true that there is an increasing number of New Zealanders who are *manga* fans. Still, *manga*-reading is not yet regarded as a significant form of entertainment in New Zealand compared to Japan (cf. Yang *et al.* 1997: 46).

Bibliography

Anderson, B. (1983) *Imagined Communities*, London: Verso.

Appadurai, A. (1996) *Modernity at Large: cultural dimensions of globalization*, Minneapolis, MN: University of Minnesota Press.

Azuma, H. (2001) *Doobutsu-ka suru posutomodan: otaku kara mita nihon shakai* (Animalizing postmodern: Japanese society observed from *otaku*'s perspective), Tokyo: Kôdansha.

Census of Population and Dwellings (2001) by Statistics New Zealand. Online. Available HTTP: http://www.stats.govt.nz/domino/external/web/CommProfiles.nsf/FindInfobyArea/02-rc (accessed 29 June 2005).

Craig, T. J. (ed.) (2000) *Japan Pop!: inside the world of Japanese popular culture*, Armonk, NY: M. E. Sharpe.

Featherstone, M., Lash, S. and Robertson, R. (eds) (1995) *Global Modernities*, London: Sage.

Gumperz, J. (1992) 'Contextualization and understanding', in A. Duranti and C. Goodwin (eds) *Rethinking Context: language as an interactive phenomenon*, Cambridge: Cambridge University Press.

Hudson, A. (1992) 'Diglossia: a bibliographic review', *Language in Society*, 21(4): 611–74.

Ien, A. (1996) *Living Room Wars: rethinking media audiences for a postmodern world*, London: Routledge.

——(2003) '*Terebi dorama ni miru bunka-teki shinmitsu-sei* (Cultural intimacy seen in TV dramas)', in K. Iwabuchi (ed.) *Gurôbaru purizumu: 'ajian dorîmu' toshite no nihon no terebi dorama* (Global prism: Japanese TV dramas as 'Asian dreams'), Tokyo: Heibonsha.

Ip, M. (2001) 'Chinese business immigrants to New Zealand: transnationals or failed investors?', in M. Ip (ed.) *Re-examining Chinese Transnationalism in Australia–New Zealand*, Centre for the Study of the Southern Chinese Diaspora, Canberra: Australian National University.

——(2003) 'Migration city: migration and ethnic diversity in Auckland. Part 2, Chinese in Auckland: historic and diverse', Winter Lecture 3, 3 August, University of Auckland, New Zealand.

Ito, M. (2004) '*Nihon gûzô-geki*' to sakusô suru aidentiî ('Japanese dramas' and complex identities)', in K. Iwabuchi (ed.) *Koeru bunka, kousaku suru kyoukai* (Transcultures, intertwined borders), Tokyo: Yamakawa Shuppansha.

Iwabuchi, K. (2001) *Transnational Japan: ajia o tsunagu popyurâ bunka* (Transnational Japan: popular culture that connects Asia), Tokyo: Iwanami Shoten.

Ko, Y. F. (2003) '*Nihon no aidoru dorama to Taiwan ni okeru yokubô no katachi* (Japanese idol dramas and the desired form in Taiwan)', in K. Iwabuchi (ed.) *Gurôbaru purizumu: 'ajian dorîmu' toshite no nihon no terebi dorama* (Global prism: Japanese TV dramas as 'Asian dreams'), Tokyo: Heibonsha.

——(2004a) 'The desired form: Japanese idol dramas in Taiwan', in K. Iwabuchi (ed.) *Feeling Asian Modernities: transnational consumption of Japanese TV dramas*, Hong Kong: Hong Kong University Press.

——(2004b) '"Hari" kara "hanliu" e (From "*hari*" to "*hanliu*")'. Online. Available HTTP: http://www.jamco.or.jp/2004_symposium/jp/ko/index.html (accessed 29 June 2005).

Kusaka, M. (2000) *Manga-gaku no susume* (Invitation to *manga*-logy), Tokyo: Hakuteisha.

Lee, D.-H. (2003) 'Nihon no terebi-dorama to no bunkateki sesshoku (Cultural contact with Japanese TV dramas)', in K. Iwabuchi (ed.) *Gurôbaru purizumu: 'ajian dorîmu' toshite no nihon no terebi dorama* (Global prism: Japanese TV dramas as 'Asian dreams'), Tokyo: Heibonsha.

——(2004) 'Rimeiku no bunkateki senryaku: "yojo suknyŏ" no jirei (Cultural strategy of remakes: a case study of "yojo suknyŏ")'. Online. Available HTTP: http://www.jamco.or.jp/2004_symposium/jp/lee/index.html (accessed 29 June 2005).

Lee, M.-T. (2003) 'Hong Kong ni okeru "gambaru" onna no toransunathonaru-na shôhi to sôzôryoku (Transnational consumption and imagination by women 'doing their best' in Hong Kong)', in K. Iwabuchi (ed.) *Gurôbaru purizumu: 'ajian dorîmu' toshite no nihon no terebi dorama* (Global prism: Japanese TV dramas as 'Asian dreams'), Tokyo: Heibonsha.

——(2004) 'Travelling with Japanese TV dramas: cross-cultural orientation and flowing identification of contemporary Taiwanese youth', in K. Iwabuchi (ed.) *Feeling Asian Modernities: transnational consumption of Japanese TV dramas*, Hong Kong: Hong Kong University Press.

Leung, L. Y. M. (2004) 'Ajia hôshiki? nihon to kankoku no terebi dorama no hikaku kaishaku (Asian way?: comparative interpretation of Japanese and Korean TV dramas)', the 13th JAMCO website international symposium, February–March. Online. Available HTTP: http://www.jamco.or.jp/2004_symposium/jp/lisa/index.html (accessed 29 June 2005).

McLelland, M. (2001) 'Local meanings in global space: a case study of women's "boy love" web sites in Japanese and English', *Mots Pluriels* 19. Online. Available HTTP: http://www.arts.uwa.edu.au/MotsPluriels/MP1901mcl.html (accessed 29 June 2005).

Nakano, Y. and Wu, Y. (2003) 'Puchi-buru no kurashi kata: chûgoku no daigakusei ga mita nihon no dorama (The petite bourgeoisie's way of living: Chinese university students watch Japanese dramas)', in K. Iwabuchi (ed.) *Gurôbaru purizumu: 'ajian dorîmu' toshite no nihon no terebi dorama* (Global prism: Japanese TV dramas as 'Asian dreams'), Tokyo: Heibonsha.

Ng, W. (2002) 'The impact of Japanese comics and animation in Asia', *Journal of Japanese Trade & Industry*, July/August: 30–3.

Pieterse, J. N. (1995) 'Globalization as hybridization', in M. Featherstone, S. Lash and R. Robertson (eds) *Global Modernities*, London: Sage.

Robertson, R. (1995) 'Glocalization: time–space and homogeneity–heterogeneity', in M. Featherstone, S. Lash and R. Robertson (eds) *Global Modernities*, London, Sage.

Shiraishi, S. S. (2000) 'Doraemon goes abroad', in T. J. Craig (ed.) *Japan Pop!: Inside the world of Japanese popular culture*, Armonk, NY: M. E. Sharpe.

Statistics New Zealand [Te Tari Tatau] (1995) *New Zealand Now: Asian New Zealanders*.

Yamanaka, C. (2004) '"Kankoku *manga*" toiu senryaku: gurôbarizêshon, "han-nichi," jukyô-bunka (Strategy called "Korean *manga*": globalization, "anti-Japan," and Confucianism-oriented culture)', in K. Iwabuchi (ed.) *Koeru bunka, kôsaku suru kyôkai* (Transcultures, intertwined borders), Tokyo: Yamakawa Shuppansha.

Yang, J., Gan, D., Hong, T. and the staff of A. Magazine (1997) *Eastern Standard Time, a Guide to Asian Influence on American Culture: from Astro Boy to Zen Buddhism*, New York: Haughton Mifflin Company.

Yoshihiro, K. (1993) *Manga no gendaishi* (Contemporary history of *manga*), Tokyo: Maruzen.

Part II
Becoming Global

7 'Sportsports'

Cultural exports and imports in Japan's contemporary globalization career

T. J. M. Holden

Introduction

This is a significant moment in Japanese history: a time at which Japan's place in the increasingly interconnected web of nations, products, ideas and practices is mediated in large part by its popular culture; and, in particular, sporting culture. One aim of this chapter is to demonstrate how this came to be and the extent to which it is so. In large part, this process is supported – if not driven – by media which focus on what I call *sportsports*. This moniker is not a simple reference to Japan's athletic imports and exports; rather, it is the array of techniques by which domestic media package and audiences consume information about athletes and athletics. With media as a conscious agent, communications about 'sportsports' have become seminal social texts in everyday Japanese life, with concrete, significant effects.

Sportsports is a twofold phenomenon linked to – if not fuelling – globalization. It involves the flow of sporting 'goods' – in the form of games, players, practices and philosophies – both into and out of nations. Employing select examples, this phenomenon is captured here at the micro, or lived, level. The macro-level analysis has been tendered elsewhere (Holden 2003a). It conceives of globalization as transpiring in stages or 'careers' – distinctly expressed for various theoretically specifiable entities, epochs and activities. In a nutshell, deciphering a nation's career means distinguishing between the 'import' and 'export' of ideas, personnel, diplomacy, trade and military contact, to name but a few, at different historical moments. Japan's past careers have corresponded to the political, economic and social sectors; today, however, it is the cultural sector that drives the country's global career. Specifically, it is the import and (especially) export of sport/stars – most often abetted by indigenous media such as television news, entertainment programming, advertising, the Internet and publishing. Although Japan's popular cultural stage of globalization includes film, music and fashion, the most locally pervasive and influential is *sportsports*.

Japan: the land of the rising sport star

Hideo Nomo was not the first Japanese baseball player to compete in America's professional baseball leagues. That honour went to Mikami Goto, a graduate student who participated in a multiracial team in the now defunct Federal League in 1914–15. Nomo wasn't even the second player, nor even the first pitcher on the US West coast. In 1964–5 Masanori Murakami was loaned by the Yomiuri Giants to its San Francisco namesake 'for seasoning', pitching fifty-four games.

Though not the first, Nomo certainly became the most famous baseball export. His announcement to play in the *dai li-gu* (Big League) met a firestorm of criticism at home – in the popular press and wideshows (Hirai 2001). And then . . . he began winning. 'Nomomania' suddenly captivated a nation. Games he pitched were broadcast live nationwide and shown on the big screen outside Tokyo's Shinjuku station; there, hundreds of Japanese took time out from their workday lives to root for the compatriot who would dare to chuck a comfortable career in Japan for the uncertain – some said foolish – attempt to challenge the big boys across the Pacific. Nomo not only won, he became the National League rookie of the year, returning to Japan in the off-season a hero.

In the decade that followed, the number of Japanese Major Leaguers swelled, reaching fifteen in 2002. Although the number declined to eleven in 2004, there was the largest number of 'position players' ever (four).[1] Following Nomo, Japanese baseball exports won the best newcomer award in 2000 (Kazuhiro Sasaki) and 2001 (Ichiro Suzuki). By 2004 Ichiro had established numerous Major League records: most hits for a rookie (242); first player with over 200 hits in each of his first four seasons; the most hits collected in four seasons (942); and the most hits in a single season (262).

Ichiro's debut year was notable for other reasons. Back in his homeland, Akebono, the first foreign-born *yokozuna* (Grand Champion) in Japan's oldest, most 'traditional' sport, *sumo*, was retiring. He was only the sixty-fourth *yokozuna* since 1757.[2] By the time Ichiro had finishing establishing his four-year records, though, two other foreign *rikishi*, Musashimaru and Asashoryu, were ensconced as the sixty-seventh and sixty-eighth *yokozuna*. Most significantly, in 2003, with the retirement of Takanohana, *sumo* was left with two foreign-born *yokozuna* and no native grapplers to headline the sport.[3] In the conservative world of *sumo*, which views itself as tied to nationhood and Japanese identity, this caused considerable consternation. More, as Asashoryu's domination of the sport became nearly complete – winning thirteen of his first fifteen tournaments as *yokozuna* – *sumo*'s elders became increasingly vocal, carping about the Mongolian's uncouth demeanor, lack of linguistic aplomb and ostensible interest in spurning *sumo* for the less refined sport of K-1 (open weight kick-boxing).

Beyond Mongolian dominance at home and Ichiro's record-setting exploits abroad, 2004 was the year that a diminutive Japanese basketball player, Yuta Tabuse, sought a spot in the National Basketball Association (NBA), the world's foremost professional basketball league. It was Tabuse's second such foray.[4] This time he made the team, becoming the first native Japanese to play pro basketball in America.[5] During the season opener Tabuse scored seven points in ten minutes, thrusting basketball where it had never been before: into the headlines of Japan's national newspapers. Despite the fact that ten other players scored more (six from his own team) and his total was but one-quarter of the game's leader's, Tabuse's effort became the lead story on every sports segment on every evening TV news programme back home.

The following day, in Tokyo, a team of Major League Baseball (MLB) players – most American, along with natives of Canada, the Dominican Republic, Nicaragua and Venezuela – opened a seven game series against a team of Japanese All-Stars. The games were televised nationwide in Japan and news coverage included reports on an MLB visit to a Japanese grade school, participation in calligraphy and tea ceremony lessons, as well as interviews with future Hall-of-Famer Roger Clemens about his technique and training regimen. A major angle was the budding friendship between Clemens and Yomiuri pitching ace Koji Uehara, who videotaped Clemens's workout. Media openly speculated on how these new ideas would bolster the ability of one of Japan's strongest pitchers.

Of the coterminous sporting migrations transpiring today, export is more prominent than import – a reversal of the cultural pattern of past decades. Ultimately, though, these two aspects work in tandem and amount to the same thing. Abetted by news and commercial media, they are fit through and articulate with a univocal filter of national identity. The constant drum-beat of information about Japan's *sportsports* – delivered via TV, newspapers, Internet, advertising, magazines and books – has effectively multiplied discourse about what it means to be Japanese in the contemporary world. Specifically, this has transpired via codification of sports information into conceptions of inside and outside, local (national) and global, Self and Other.

The effects are multiple. First has been the elevation of sports in Japanese society. Second has been the increased notion that Japan is a nation among nations. Unlike years past – physically and then psychologically – Japan is no longer perceived as a country living in isolation. Now, media consumers are daily shown a Japan linked in a chain of interactive partners. Third, the content of messages about *sportsports* has served to magnify the domestic estimate of Japanese performance in this external world. This has led, in turn, to an enhanced perception of the capacity of Japanese people. In a word, media reports of *sportsports* have exerted a profound influence over national psychology and identity.[6]

Demonstrating this falls to exploring the mechanisms by which this occurs. After contextualizing Japan's *sportsports* historically, I identify concrete ways in which *sportsport* mediation transpires today. This includes:

framing, *distortion* (differentiated into *accretion*, *magnification* and *amplification*), *international equivalence*, *global positioning*, *nation centering*, *status shifting* and *foreign gaze*.

Sportsports : a thumbnail history

Japan's globalization was first addressed – if only summarily – by Befu (2000). Highlighting diaspora, he codified three historical eras, beginning in the fifteenth century. My conception, identified above, is broader: articulating distinct moments of militarism, diplomacy, cultural exchange, colonization and economic and cultural distribution. Further, it asserts that, until recently, inflow has been more extensive – and with greater sociological impact, a pattern also true of *sportsports*. A partial litany of economic, cultural and political import includes: Buddhism (in the sixth century); the gun and Christianity (mid-sixteenth century); business from Holland and Russia (the seventeenth century); forced economic and cultural opening by the US (mid-nineteenth century); then US-led military occupation and political reconfiguration (mid-twentieth century). With the economic imports of the late 1950s, however, the globalization patterns seem to have shifted.

Outflow: Japanese sports exports

Until Japan became a global economic power, sports outflow was rather scant. A 1905 Waseda baseball team compiled a seven-win nineteen-loss record against American universities, including Stanford, University of Southern California (USC) and Washington.[7] The country's first official global foray was in the 1912 Olympics in Stockholm. A year later it took part in the First Far Eastern Championship Games,[8] held in Manila.[9] The first government-subsidized international sports event was the Fifth Far Eastern Games, staged in Shanghai, in 1921. That same year there was Davis Cup participation. Otherwise, activity was individual: baseballer Goto, mentioned above, and Miki Tatsuyoshi, a Mixed Doubles entrant at 1934 Wimbledon.[10]

The recent MLB exodus resulted by 2000 in sixteen exports – six of them position players – distributed across the thirty professional rosters.[11] The same trend can be seen in professional soccer, where, after the first export in 2000, the number of Japanese on European rosters increased to four in 2001, then seven in 2002. By 2005 there were nine, dispersed across France, England, Spain, Italy, Holland and Germany.[12]

Although these have been team sports, the media focus has been on individuals. It has emphasized autonomous free agents, heading overseas to perform against the best international competition available. This frame has been bolstered by 'limited export', where individuals leave the country to participate in competitions such as swimming (Kosuke Kitajima and Ai Shibata, above all), marathon racing (Naoko Takahashi and Mizuki

Noguchi), golf (Shigeki Maruyama, Ai Miyazato and Sakura Yokomine), tennis (generally Ai Sugiyama and occasionally Shinobu Asagoe) and table tennis (child sensation, now teen, Ai Fukuhara). It is worth observing essential confluences that have supported such *sportsports*: an increase in the sports that Japanese engage in, heightened public interest in a wider array of sports, more financial backing for 'marginal' sports and, therefore, more opportunities for more athletes from more countries to participate. Add to this equation Japan's economic development, its increasing leisure basis and its increasing geopolitical position in the world, and the *sportsports* phenomenon is better understandable.

Inflow: Japanese sports imports

Contemplating global *sportsport* flow, the door has certainly swung much wider in than out. Baseball's first appearance in Japan was in 1872. By the turn of the century foreign athletic imports began arriving.[13] In 1908, for instance, a team of Major League reserves visited, winning all seventeen of the games against Japanese teams.[14] Since then, baseball squads of all level – MLB, minor league and collegiate – have come to entertain, instruct and compete. One memorable visit included Lou Gehrig, Lefty Grove, Mickey Cochrane and Frankie Frisch in 1931; another brought Babe Ruth. In his seventeen games, 'the Bambino' hit fourteen home runs and drew a crowd of over 75,000 to one game. Negro League teams compiled a record of 46-1 in 1927 and 1932.

Over the years imports have set up shop in Japan. Prior to the Pacific War, three foreigners played for Japanese teams: a Russian pitcher won over 300 games over a nineteen year career; a Hawaiian American won 240 games; and a Taiwanese became the first foreigner to win a batting title. Following the war, a second-generation Japanese-American from Hawaii, Wally Yonamine, was recruited to help pave the way for regular foreign imports in Japanese baseball. Yonamine endured widespread antipathy from Japanese fans,[15] but persevered for ten years.[16] Over the last forty years foreigners have been featured on nearly every Japanese roster.[17]

Following Japan's postwar recovery, the country has served as a site for numerous athletic competitions. This assisted reintegration into the world of nations, and also facilitated the importation of people and practices. Thus, Tokyo hosted the Third Asian Games in 1958 and the Summer Olympics in 1964.[18] As Buruma (2004) has observed, the latter was a watershed: a chance to demonstrate to the global community that Japan was a peaceful, prosperous nation; testament that it belonged among world leaders; validation that it had returned to the world fold. Not only was this the first Olympics held in Asia – rightfully a point of pride for Japanese – it was also the first 'TV Olympics'.[19] For Japanese it was remembered as the games in which their female volleyballers slew the Soviet goliath for gold, an event further stoking national pride.[20]

These early successes were but the beginning of domestically staged global athletics. Subsequent Olympiads were convened in Sapporo (1972) and Nagano (1998). The former was the first Winter Games held outside the European/North American axis. In recent years Japan has been site of many international competitions – most notably, soccer's World Cup in 2002, but also volleyball's World Grand Prix (on numerous occasions since the late 1970s).[21] The First Winter Asian Games were hosted in Sapporo (in 1986), as were the Second (in 1990), and the Fifth were staged in Aomori (in 2003). The Ninth World Swimming Championships were held in Fukuoka in 2001, the World Wheelchair Basketball championships were staged in Kitakyushu in 2002 and since 2000 ten Japanese cities have hosted sixteen international marathons.[22]

Clearly, then, athletic inflow has increased over time. From a nearly closed domestic cultural market in 1960, significant importation of foreign athletes and international competitions has transpired. Moreover, Japan has become a venue for other nations' professional leagues, seeking to transform themselves into world brands. In particular, America's NBA, MLB, National Hockey League, and National Football League have conducted official regular season games on Japanese soil over the past seven years.

Mediation: communicating (and moving) 'sportsports'

It is tempting, in reading the history of *sportsports*, to claim two trends: the centring of globally inflected sports in Japanese society and ever-increasing attention accorded to Japanese *sportsports*. These conclusions, though plausible, cannot be proven here.[23] What can be said is that, today, an inordinate amount of attention is accorded to *sportsports* by Japanese media.

Prior to Nomo's American debut, reports about MLB action were rare on Japanese television. So, too, for soccer; prior to Nakata's Italian transfer, European football was a rarity in Japanese news. Today, the volume as well as positioning of segments dedicated to overseas *sportsports* have noticeably shifted. For instance, on 8 June 2005 *Hodo Station* – a 10 p.m. news programme – not only led its reportage, but devoted nearly its entire hour-long broadcast to Japan's qualification for soccer's 2006 World Cup. The qualifier, against political nemesis North Korea, had been broadcast live from Thailand on TV Asahi, *Hodo Station*'s network. The news hour was filled with live interviews with players, national team executives and coaches, along with in-studio analysis and remote feeds from bars and eating establishments nationwide. Well into the following day, news programmes, morning wake-up and wideshows normally dedicated to celebrity, fashion, gossip and social problems, devoted the bulk of their programming to reports about the soccer team's success.

One week later, *Hodo Station* was back at it, beginning their telecast with side-by-side pictures of Ichiro and Hideki Matsui. Each picture, in turn, dissolved to game footage. First Ichiro was shown blasting a single off the wall, with the excited voiceover of an American television announcer. As he barked that this was Ichiro's one thousandth hit in America, the stadium was shown erupting in a standing ovation. Ichiro was captured acknowledging the ovation by tipping his batting helmet. Cue to the next image: of Matsui connecting with a pitch. Again an American announcer's enthusiastic voiceover could be heard: 'it's out of the infield, it's out of the outfield. Bye-bye baseball. Home run, Hideki Matsui!' Fade to two newscasters seated in the studio, the male announcer gushing, 'Japan's Superstars. We'll show them later in the show. But first . . . ', and then the top (hard) news story of the day began: a story of the wheels that fell off of a Japan Airlines jet upon landing at Haneda.

Aside from the volume of sports-related discourse in contemporary Japan, it is its positioning in the media that is signal; so, too, its tenor and content. Evidence presented elsewhere (Holden 2002, 2003b) suggests that the content heavily emphasizes Japanese over foreign players (though, interestingly, not necessarily domestic over foreign leagues or venues). Part and parcel of this reportage is strong inferences concerning the nature and capacity of the Japanese people and prospects for achievement on a world stage. I aver that this can be explained by Japan's relative historical isolation (or, inversely, its relative lack of past cultural exportation) and the prominent position of information and entertainment media in daily life. In the remainder of this chapter I focus on forces constructing such inferences; the mediation practices that spotlight – if not employ – *sportsports* for particular purposes, producing specific effects.

Framing

For the past decade, every night during baseball season, on every news station on Japanese television a segment has been devoted to the performance of Japanese baseball players in MLB. Each segment is nearly identical: the player is lifted out of the game context and highlighted; either every at-bat is chronicled or, since there are now so many Japanese players playing overseas, their daily 'line' (i.e. number of at-bats, hits and current batting average) is reported – either as script superimposed on the screen or via sportscasters' announcement, or both. The case of Japanese soccer *sportsports* is no different – with every meaningful kick, assist, pass and substitution covered. Invariably, reports on Japan's *sportsports* take precedence over, and receive nearly exclusive attention as compared with the match itself. As I have shown elsewhere (Holden 2003b), such reportage differs in form from that of the domestic game. There, team-centred stories take precedence over the individual-player approach. As such, highlights appear only in the case of extraordinary feats (such as a hitting or pitching milestones) or else as they influence the game narrative. In short, discursive strategies differ between domestic and foreign *sportsports*; foreign coverage exists *only* due to the presence of Japanese players, not because of the games or teams involved.

Media sociologists long ago demonstrated how the form and content of news are both influenced by organizational forces. Implicated were macro forces such as capital investment and corporate or political ideology, as well micro-level activities such as 'newsroom routines' (e.g. Tuchman 1978). One effect is the 'fram(ing)' (Goffman 1974) of news – temporally, spatially and topically. Framing practices often make reference to or reflect the mood of the surrounding world; so, too, the presumed preferences and expectations of the audience (e.g. Gitlin 1983). In this way, certain values are given preference over others and thus legitimated. The notion that 'news frames' embody organizational routines and decisions that help determine the 'what' and 'how' of content reported is discernable in the capsule summaries of Japanese *sportsports*. This predominant formatic frame is not only employed by TV, but also newspapers, which have developed their own strategies for spotlighting Japanese players. Beyond form, the content that fits within such frames tends to be identical, delivering a unity across media genres. The frame is about Japanese performance out in the world. And, to the degree that individual players serve as signifiers for nation, the frame spotlights Japan's performance on the world stage.

Distortion effects

As indicated, the presence of capsules is not limited to any particular day, nor to one specific medium. On the Internet, for instance, *Yahoo!Japan* provides summaries of Japan's MLB *sportsports* that mimics the capsules broadcast on television. So, too, within any one medium *sportsports* capsules are lifted out of and extended beyond a particular genre or time slot. In this way, for instance, player digests that are first aired on traditional late-evening news programmes are rebroadcast in virtually unadulterated fashion the following day – on 'wake-up' and midday 'wideshow' broadcasts. This occurs across the board, on all commercial stations. The effects, I would venture, are multiple, distorting the true picture of Japanese *sportsports*; above all, inflating their presence in and influence over the world outside.

This influence, though, is not of one sort. Indeed, three kinds of distortion can be distinguished: (1) accretion – the process of stockpiling images, lending senses of constancy and ubiquity; (2) magnification – the process by which *sportsports* activities are unduly extolled, the respect due them is over-inflated or their achievements are exaggerated in ways that confer greater significance than perhaps they deserve; and (3) amplification – the process of inflating the size or presence of *sportsports* by according them – individually or aggregately – excessive attention and detail. Briefly, evidence of these effects can be seen in the ways outlined below.

Accretion

To be sure, the fact that reports about and images of *sportsports* have increased is not purely an artefact of Japanese media practices; it reflects actual global movement of athletes. Where once there was only Nomo in baseball and Nakata in soccer, there is now a raft of players to report on. A typical MLB capsule today includes a cross-country 'relay' of reports lasting minutes: in 2005, two Matsuis in New York, Nomo in Florida, Taguchi in St. Louis, Iguchi in Chicago, Ichiro in Seattle, Otsuka in San Diego. A typical European soccer capsule includes multiple border crossings: Inamoto in England, Okubo in Spain, Nakata and Nakamura in Italy, Takahara in Germany and Ono in Holland. While the reportage itself is not 'unreal' (after all, these are actual people in actual places, performing actual tasks) it is contrived. For the continued exhibition of these players – day after day, channel after channel, programme after programme – produces an additive effect. It inflates the presence of *sportsports* in the world beyond Japanese borders. When this over-inflation becomes translated into the perceived *impact* of *sportsports* on their respective sports, this becomes 'amplification'. Accretion differs insofar as it refers to the simple daily appearance of these players on screen – in practice, the interview room, in games (not to mention in advertisements between media reports). The accumulation of such images – not of any one player, but all players together – produces a global awareness, in fact a hyperawareness, of *sportsports* within the consciousness of knowledge consumers.

Taken a step further, it could be said that this incessant appearance of *sportsports* (in TV news capsules, across TV channels, in day-after non-news programming, in advertisements, on magazine covers, in published books and across newspaper pages) functions as a form of operant conditioning. It primes viewers to regard *sportsports* outside Japan; their constant appearance suggests that they are objects worthy of attention, even reverence. Most importantly, such repetition produces a particular mediated effect: aggregated images of exports assists in manufacturing the belief that these Japanese icons possess significance beyond indigenous boundaries.

Magnification

The daily stream of Japanese athletes in the news has the effect of magnifying their centrality in the viewer's visual field – thereby elevating sport, and also the place of these athletes in their respective sporting worlds. How can we gauge such magnification at work? One way is to compare how *sportsports* are reported in media of the host and home countries. As one example, consider reportage about *sportsport* Hideki Matsui on the Internet news service *Yahoo!Sports* in America and Japan. On 21 June 2005, the headline in the US edition was 'Yankees bury Rays with 13 runs in eighth'; the Japanese headline, by contrast, was 'Hideki Matsui praises his [own] effort in a huge comeback victory'. Whereas the former led with a paragraph about 'one stunning inning in which the New York Yankees appeared to exorcize three months of frustration', singling out the contributions of Bernie Williams and Gary Sheffield, the latter news service led with a sentence gushing that 'Hideki Matsui hit his ninth home run (a solo shot) while collecting four hits and two runs batted in'. The thirteen-run inning was the second sentence in the Japanese story, while in the American story Matsui's name appeared in the lead sentence of the ninth paragraph, which read 'Sheffield, Alex Rodriguez and Hideki Matsui hit consecutive homers in the eighth'. A later Japanese version of the story adopted the three consecutive home run angle for its headline, though again leading with Matsui's name, followed by Sheffield and Rodriguez – a shift from the actual scoring chronology.

Such distortion in the framing and reporting process is commonplace. Consider the 18 June 2005 case, where American *Yahoo!* led with Derek Jeter's grand slam while its Japanese counterpart pictured Matsui crossing home plate along with the announcement that he had hit in nine consecutive games. The American report began: 'When Derek Jeter walked to home plate with the bases loaded in the sixth inning Saturday, he had gone 5,770 at-bats over 11 major league seasons without a grand slam . . . ', while the Japanese story simply stated that Matsui batted fifth in the order, collected one hit out of three at bats, and hit in his ninth consecutive game. In contrast to the American report, which was twenty-six paragraphs long, the Japanese article offered four truncated paragraphs. Unlike the American article, which mentioned twenty-five players, the Japanese piece listed only Matsui. While the article did mention the team's five-game winning streak, it contained no mention of Jeter. Unlike the Matsui-centred Japanese article, the American report treated Matsui's contribution in the nineteenth paragraph, the thirteenth player mentioned.

The articles stand as microcosms of differences in perspective: despite mentioning the Yankees' winning streak, the Japanese story was locally-centred, insular, microscopic and individually based; by contrast, the American story was holistic, context-based, macroscopic and historically rooted. Above all, the essential difference lay in the decision to highlight an indigenous player's nine-game hitting streak over an exogenous player's eleven-season history. This was similar to the earlier story, which extracted one home run out of a string of three, elevating its importance and/or increasing its weight above any of the other twelve runs in that one inning or twenty runs for the entire game.

Amplification

Magnification, of course, is not limited to Hideki Matsui. Daily reports of Ichiro in the Japanese press can be found which also depart – often dramatically – from American reports. And, as the next example demonstrates, this can easily lead to over-inflation of achievement. Consider June 2005, with Ichiro advancing toward 1000 hits for his American career. While such a frame might be viewed as contextual – even macro-historical – it was virtually ignored in the American media. After all, there are well over 100 batters in major league history who have garnered 2000 career hits, twenty-five batters with over 3000 hits, and two with over 4000. So, although Ichiro's 1000 constitute the third-fastest tally in MLB history, the number itself has been exceeded by a legion of players too numerous to list (and many long forgotten). Nevertheless, in Japan this was a milestone worthy of assiduous – even fetishistic – attention, a case study of amplification incarnate.

The daily reports counting Ichiro toward his American milestone were not the first instance of amplification involving 'sportsports', or even of amplification in association with Ichiro. There was the most valuable player vote in 2004, when Ichiro was placed fifth by America's sportswriters. These results came as a shock to a large number of fans in Japan. After all, wasn't this the year in which Ichiro set numerous records? The first player to secure 200 hits or more in his first four MLB seasons; the most hits collected in four seasons; and the most hits in a single season. Certainly these records were superior to the exploits of Vladimir Guerrero, with his 206 hits, 39 home runs, 126 runs batted in, and .337 batting average. By comparison, Ichiro collected 262 hits *and* his batting average was 35 points higher than Guerrero's. Such surprise, though, is both a function of and strong evidence for the amplification effect. For, while Ichiro's achievements were reported in the American media, they were not daily fixtures commanding prime daily newscast time. Moreover, even as Ichiro approached his mark, American media didn't accord him the iconic, larger-than-life treatment of the Japanese media, nothing like the Japanese news station that placed a life-size likeness of Ichiro on their set; or the holographic staircase another programme built with Ichiro *daruma*s moving upward with each hit garnered. Even stodgy NHK allowed its announcer to lift his arms triumphantly when Ichiro finally broke George Sisler's eighty-four-year-old record, exclaiming, '*Banzai!*' Thus, given weeks of such concentrated media treatment, is it any wonder that Japanese were surprised with the America's MVP (Most Valuable Player) snub? For Japanese it was hard to fathom American denial of inestimable achievement. Was this a sign of racial bias, many could not help but wonder?

In Japanese media, distortion concerning 'sportsports' is pervasive and continuous. This is not without macro-sociological impact. Daily reproduction of 'sportsports' stems from intentional positioning by institutions of mass communication of particular images in the consciousness of information consumers – what Berger and Luckmann (1967) referred to as the 'symbolic universes' of the media audience. Like the mechanisms of communication themselves, these symbolic worlds are comprised of precious 'information space'. Whatever topic is selected and inserted into that space mitigates the appearance of other topics. In the case of the media themselves, one or more topics must be reduced, cancelled, ignored, silenced, reassigned and/or de-emphasized to accommodate reports on *sportsports*.

It should be observed that it is not only the presence, but also the constant appearance, of *sportsports* that is significant. In the hands of media, *sportsports* become an endemic, if not taken-for-granted, element of everyday life. However, because they appear in an array of communications across a variety of media every day, it is nearly impossible for Japan's information consumers to ignore '*sportsports*' existence. Beyond that, given that the media frame is also one of successful performance (generally overseas) – it is nearly impossible for viewers to elude the 'bigger picture' – to avoid thinking about *sportsports* in macro, essentialized terms; in ways that speak about nation and national success. We will have occasion to view this mediated effect at greater length below.

International equivalence

There is little dispute that the skill level of the average European or South American professional soccer player exceeds that of the average Japanese player. However, when television and newspapers place pictures, highlights or accounts of Japanese *sportsports* alongside their foreign counterparts the effect can be a *de facto* levelling; the engineering of equivalence. Consider the case of weekly soccer digest shows (such as *J Super Soccer Plus*) or sports corners on the evening news. There, extraordinary passes, dribbles, goals and the like by European-based foreigners are followed by clips of Japanese players – often simple touches on the pitch (since there are few goal or assist highlights). While a discerning viewer might appreciate the qualitative difference between a brilliantly struck free kick by Roberto Carlos and a simple midfield run by Nakata, the result for less critical consumers may be a perception of comparability. Shared pitch, in short, may translate into shared ability. Since Japanese players compete in the leagues in which such highlights are produced, Japanese *sportsports* are, logically and via association, capable of such physical feats themselves.

In truth, here stands another distortion process at work: one of exaggeration. This same process of exaggeration can be seen in highlight capsules in other sports, where, for instance, Japanese players are shown striking out (baseball) or finishing well down the list of names on the leaderboard (golf) or losing in two or three sets (tennis). The message communicated goes beyond participation and inclusion, toward effective equivalence; it suggests domestic athletes holding stature and ability on a par with the foreign competitors they challenge.

Global positioning

The year 2005 might have been called 'the year of Ai Miyazato'. In a remarkable fortnight, the diminutive nineteen-year-old paired with Rui Kitada to win the inaugural Women's World Cup of Golf in South Africa, then ventured to Australia for the ANZ Ladies Masters tournament, where she was placed second. The following day, newspapers and television news adopted the identical frame: '*Sekai no Ai-chan*' (The World's Little Ai) and '*Sekai no Miyazato Ai*' (The World's Miyazato Ai). Soon thereafter, the media labelled her 'Japan's Tiger Woods'.

Beyond the amplification and international equivalence at work (after all, Miyazato only managed *second*-place in the Australian tourney), the media frame placed the Okinawan in a world context – an example of what can be called 'global positioning'. The use of *sportsports* for this purpose occurs with great regularity, especially in the case of exports. A strong example of positioning can be found in the nightly sports show *Suporuto* (Sports), which presents European soccer by country (England, Spain, France, Germany, Italy, Holland). After etching geographic boundaries on screen, player portraits – along with name and nationality – are intoned by an announcer (in English and Japanese). Then individual highlights appear. *Hodo Station* has adopted a comparable approach for its baseball reports, placing an over-sized map of the United States behind the newscasters. There, the faces of every Japanese MLB player are posted, located in their city of employment. In this way, Japan is positioned in America via its native sons. Indeed, if the point were lost, one recent night the anchor turned to the sports reporter and asked, 'Well, how did the American-Japanese do today?'

Apart from these obvious attempts at global positioning via *sportsports*, Japan is situated in the world by fairly invisible means: through the nearly endless parade in the media of golfers, baseballers, soccer and tennis players, swimmers, marathoners – playing in foreign venues. The subtext of these daily communiqués is that 'we Japanese play in leagues and competitions around the world. Our sports are global; our nation is not sited in one geographical place; it transpires in many places, at once'. As we will consider below, advertising assists in delivering this message, bridging 'worlds' by placing Japanese *sportsports* in the cities or nations in which they play, though often living and speaking as their Japanese audiences back home.

Nation centering

The chest-thumping involving nation is neither uniform nor totalized. Nor is it entirely jingoistic. Nonetheless, it is pervasive. Consider the 2005 Women's US Open. There, Japanese media – from TV to newspapers to the Internet – devoted full coverage to Miyazato Ai's American debut. For the *Nikkei Shimbun on-line*, Miyazato was among the top six front-page news items for 24 June. No other sports topic was listed on this political-economic journal's start page. Inside, a special golf section was devoted to the tourney, with the headline reading '*Yosen Ochi Shita Nihon Jo-o*' (Japanese Queen Misses Final Cut). The article's lead announced: 'With a two day score of 78,

Miyazato Ai failed to make the cut – the fifth consecutive year that Japan's top money-earner failed to make the final round'.

This example captures how *sportsports* – even in individual sports – are employed as surrogates for nation. One can appreciate, then, that it is nearly unavoidable in the case of nation-based competitions such as volleyball's Grand Prix or soccer's World Cup. Consider TV advertisements for the former, where the entire fifteen-second spot consists of a rippling *hinomaru* superimposed on a grandstand, a voiceover of (presumably) the gathered throng, rhythmically chanting, 'Nippon . . . Nippon . . . Nippon.'[24] As for the World Cup, when Japan's soccer team qualified for Germany 2006 it was not only the top news story; it was the *exclusive* news story on every TV station. Reporters were transmogrified into cheerleaders, gushing, 'Great! Great! We did it!'; news anchors became discussants, exclaiming, 'Congratulations Japan.' Moreover, every morning and wideshow the following day proffered saturation coverage of the nation's qualification – complete with interviews, game strategy and analysis, world reaction and player features. The same game footage played in endless loops behind the discussants in the studio.

A major rhetorical device on Japanese television, Ergül (2003) has argued, is 'infotainment'. Once associated with the tabloidization of 'hard' news and/ or the trivialization of the political, this merging of fun with fact can be seen particularly on wideshows. *Sportsports*, I would argue, reflect another kind of genre spanning: where what were once distinct categories of news – the 'hard' and 'sports' – are now often mixed. This occurs not only in newscasts but in other programming where sports is treated as both information and entertainment. Indeed, *sportsports* may be a proximate cause of genre melding and, thus, boundary blurring.

Examples of this abound. Consider, again, the 2006 World Cup qualification. TV stations devoted nearly the entirety of their news programmes to the story, covering every conceivable angle. Beyond interviews with players and coaches, there was reaction from Japanese fans in bars and on the street, comments from German citizens (whose country would play host to Japan) and reaction from newscasts around the world. It is important to observe that this was something more than a one-off involving a unique event. It reflects the ongoing status shift concerning sports in society. The category 'sports' may once have been a special preserve (within media) – a space, according to Whannel, that is 'separate and apart from the rest of the social world' (1992: 123–4). Once separated from news (in order to defend and communicate conservative ideas and practices – to create the illusion of an apolitical enclave) today we are witnessing a steady march of sports out of that insular space, toward the centre of daily life. Powered in large part by *sportsports*, sports in Japanese media has bled through previously fixed boundaries, taking residence outside defined 'corners' of news programmes or sections of newspapers and magazines.

As demonstrated above, news is a major – if not *the* major – filter of *sportsports*. Less clear, perhaps, is the degree to which subjectivity determines this filtration. In a word, news is produced from an insider's point of view. The reporters are Japanese, who observe and interview Japanese athletes for a Japanese audience. The clips of athletic performances have been selected and spliced together by Japanese information producers for domestic consumption. This should be contrasted with advertising, where subjectivity operates differently. In ads the products are often Japanese, as are the *sportsport* spokespeople. However, the action often transpires *in situ* – in the (overseas) venues where *sportsports* toil – and features commingling between *sportsports* and 'foreigners'. A major theme is how foreigners view *sportsports*. In short, the perspective adopted (by the Japanese ad makers, and communicated to the Japanese audience) is an outsiders' view of Japanese. A few examples will help demonstrate this.

In a series of ads in 2003, Shinji Ono, a soccer *sportsport* in Holland, was presented interacting with Dutch children. The first ad centred on a small girl following Ono in awe through a supermarket. At ad's close she was shown trying to 'lift' a soccer ball in the parking lot, under Ono's watchful encouragement. The next ad employed the same girl, this time joined by a young boy. They lunched and cavorted in a bushy field with Ono, helping him search for a ball he had lost after kicking it in the air. A final ad again featured the two children, aggressively chasing Ono through the streets of Rotterdam. When they reached his practice facility, they held up a hand-painted sign indicating that he is their favourite player. Although the windmills and cobblestone streets lend atmosphere to the ads, the spotlight is on Ono's fluent Dutch, his comfort living in Holland and his adoring fans. The overriding message is the Japanese *sportsport*'s ease in a foreign milieu and, above all, how well accepted and highly regarded he is by people outside Japan.

These themes of acceptance and respect are played out in numerous other ads involving *sportsports*: Hideki Matsui for Kirin beer, Ichiro Suzuki for a health drink, Naohiro Takahara for JCB charge card and Hidetoshi Nakata for Canon cameras and Coca-Cola. In the case of Nakata's camera ads, paired versions posit him in an intricate cat and mouse chase with a lithe Italian model. In the first ad, Nakata seeks to take her picture. In the second, the roles are reversed: she pursues him for a snapshot. The Coke ads similarly depict a desired Nakata, here at a party of attractive, energetic Italians sharing pizza, Coke and laughs. The reaction shots paint a portrait of foreigners enjoying the company of their Japanese friend.

A decade ago such ads were not in advertising's lens. Then, domestic athletes such as the *sumo rikishi* Wakanohana were featured. Any foreign athlete appearing tended to be engaged in locally consumed sports such as K-1. Such was the case of Andy Hug. Today, by contrast, product endorsements most often involve athletes located overseas. Moreover, viewed from a communication point of view it is the perspective that is signal. Whether it is children following Ono, or a woman chasing Nakata, or the slack-jawed café-goers in Seattle gawking in disbelief at Ichiro chasing down a fly ball, the repeated focus of these ads is on foreign gaze: the admiration accorded to Japanese *sportsports*.

Outside over inside

Several questions arise from the previous discussion: what of local Japanese heroes back home? Are the only *sportsports* commanding Japanese media attention sports exports? Is this stage of Japan's globalization career dominated exclusively by external vision? In fact, domestic-based athletes do receive treatment. The most visible exemplar may be Shinjo, a former MLB export who, upon returning to play in Japan, cashed in on numerous product endorsements. It is hard to say whether his widespread appeal is a function of his personality – offbeat by conventional Japanese standards – or his significatory power as a 'foreign import'. Others, such as Bob Sapp, a former US football player (now K-1 fighter), and Akebono, former *yokozuna* and Hawaiian import, have carved out spaces for themselves in the domestic media (mainly advertising and variety show) universe. Other dominant foreign stars – for instance Asashoryu in *sumo* and any number of soccer and baseball imports – are almost entirely ignored.[25] At the same time, it should be noted that few, if any, indigenous athletes – Japanese or foreign – have garnered TV endorsement deals, almost none are featured in daily news recaps; rather, they are highlighted only in the normal course of daily story-based summaries of games.[26]

In this way it must be said that, at present, it is the foreign *sportsport* that is favoured over the domestic. Only on rare occasions are athletes at home spotlighted, with the 2005 case of the Hanada brothers – former *yokozuna* Takanohana and Wakanohana – a solid example. Arguably more proximately 'Japanese' (and, by definition, not *sportsports*) due to their connection to the traditional sport *sumo*, these retired *rikishi* generated a fortnight of non-stop news and wideshow attention over a dispute concerning their father's estate. Aside from valuable stock and stable grounds, it was the stories of sibling hatred, family favouritism and marital discord that stoked media (and public) interest.

Conclusion

In his widely read tract about Japan's modern reinvention(s), Buruma (2004: 7) summarized: 'overconfidence, fanaticism, a shrill sense of inferiority, and a sometimes obsessive preoccupation with national status – all have played their parts in the history of modern Japan'. Certainly these tendencies are all on display in the case of *sportsports*. Through *sportsports* we behold phenomena that both reflect and feed Japan's definitions and perceptions of Self.

As shown, it is the conveyors of information about *sportsports* – the media – that serve as the proximate vehicle for re/producing discourse about national identity. During the postwar era mass communication has served as a 'binding mechanism', linking Japanese citizen to state and also connecting language/cultural communities by re/producing and ultimately inculcating shared beliefs, practices and values. Though Japan is indisputably a poly-mediated nation, no other medium has been more dominant and influential than television.[26] In Yoshimi's words, '[a]mong all forms of media, it is television that has had the most special significance and influence in postwar Japan . . . TV was the central medium in the construction of this postwar nation state' (2003: 460, 484)'.

Today, TV's binding power (or what I call 'bindingness') stems from both form and content: it continuously cycles a nearly uniform set of themes – generally involving shared cultural values, practices and objects; this limited set of objects, in turn, elicits an emotional response from the audience. Among these binding strategies is the phenomenon of *sportsports*. The objects represented in the media form a phenomenological set which under-scores nation and, hence, supports the formulation of national consciousness. This is consistent with Whannel's claim that 'in the world of sport as seen on TV . . . we are united . . . above all, by the constant appeal to our sense of national identity' (1992: 206). As such, this 'popular cultural nationalism' (or, better, 'sports nationalism') would seem another variant of 'nationalism of Japan' to add to the list advanced by McVeigh (2004).

These conclusions underscore how global processes often work to bolster the local. Inside is tied to outside in ways that, though not readily apparent, are surprising in their power. This synergy, certainly, has the capability of blurring or even loosening societal and cultural understand-ings of indigenous and exogenous. Nevertheless, what emerges most clearly from this analysis is how *sportsports* have served to unleash an over-whelming, continuous, unified, macro-oriented discourse. It is an ideational stream centred on Japan's national identity; and, at least in the hands of Japanese media, it is a rather univocal identity, one that centres on Japanese achievement in the world – not simply the sporting world; rather, the sporting world qua social world.

Notes

1 This number was deemed a watermark, of sorts; a validation of Japanese ability in the sport.
2 Accounts of sumo date back to 23 BC but the true origins appear linked to reli-gious rites during the Heian period (794–1185). On the origins of sumo, see Guttman and Thompson (2001: 14–25).
3 With Musashimaru's retirement at the end of 2003, Asashoryu became the sole *yokozuna*.
4 The previous year, Tabuse had been the final player cut from Denver's 2003 pre-season roster.
5 In 1947 Wataru 'Wat' Misaka, a Japanese-American, appeared in three games and scored seven points for the 1947/8 Knicks before being cut.
6 This point has been most clearly made, as this book goes to print, by the satura-tion coverage accorded to team Japan as it competed in, then won the inaugural

World Baseball Classic (WBC). On the field and in the hearts of fans back home, Japan became undisputed world champions of baseball.

7   Robert Whiting (1989: 34).

8   These competitions became known as the 'Asian Games' following the Pacific War.

9   As with this data, much of the information in this paragraph was obtained from 'Sports: promoting health for people and the economy', *Japan Access*, prepared by the Japan Information and Culture Centre, Embassy of Japan in Singapore, http://www.sg.emb-japan.go.jp/JapanAccess/sports.htm (accessed 14 June 2005).

10 This information about Tatsuyoshi can be found in *Japan Now*, a publication of the Japan Information and Culture Center, the Embassy of Japan, vol. 5 (2003): 6. Found online at http://www.us.emb-japan.go.jp/jicc/index.htm (accessed 14 June 2005).

11 2005 data collected from http://www.sanspo.com/mlb/mlb.html (accessed 1 May 2005). For fuller data on these American exports, see 'Japanese major leaguers', at http://aaa43500.at.infoseek.co.jp/m.html (accessed 1 May 2005).

12 2005 data collected from http://www.sanspo.com/soccer/soccer.html (accessed 1 May 2005).

13 Whiting (1977: 141–66; 1989: 27–51).

14 To be fair, Japanese and American teams had been playing sporadically since 1898. The Japanese teams (universities) often beat the American teams (mostly comprised of merchants, missionaries and sailors).

15 As a second-generation Japanese from Hawaii, Yonamine was perceived by Japanese as a traitor who had chosen America over Japan during the war.

16 In 1994 Yonamine was elected into the Japanese Hall of Fame, recompense perhaps for the severe treatment he was subjected to when playing.

17 The rules have traditionally allowed two foreigners on the active roster. This rule has been relaxed somewhat over the last few years. Thus, in 2001 the rule became that there is no organizational limit on foreign players. In addition, four could be on the active roster, divided into two position players and two pitchers. Occasionally, teams field lineups devoid of *gaijin* (aliens) and publicize them-selves as 'pure' Japanese teams.

18 The 1940 Olympics were originally scheduled to be held in Japan, but were scrapped due to the rising hostilities that led to World War II.

19 This is the name accorded it by Nippon Hoso Kyokai (NHK), Japan's public broadcasting company. According to NHK, these were the first games to be broadcast via satellite, the first to be broadcast in colour (albeit only eight events), as well as the first to employ slowmotion VTR. See 'The evolution of TV: a brief history of TV technology in Japan', *NHK home page*: 10, http://www.nhk.or.jp/strl/index-e.html (accessed 8 February 2004).

20 Indeed, this achievement has persisted in national/ist memory.

21 This has been due, in no small part, to the heavy financial backing of Fuji Television. As Ito (2005) has documented, this association has had a great bearing on matters as diverse as gender stereotyping, nationalism and star creation.

22 Data retrievable at *MarathonGuide.com*, http://www.marathonguide.com/index.cfm (accessed 8 February 2004).

23 This chapter does not have the longitudinal data to advance such a claim. Even so, a daily scan of popular media – from newspapers to TV news, advertising to magazine articles – suggests that, with almost full certitude: (1) today it is more commonplace to accord attention to Japanese players located in foreign leagues, or else international sporting events in which Japanese athletes participate; and (2) these events or people are more prominently featured (in terms of time/amount of attention and positioning within the communication) than in the past.

24 Certainly the role and imperatives of the economic institution cannot be ignored here. These ads are promos for the televised coverage of the tournament, which is broadcast by one of the chief sponsors of the Grand Prix, Fuji Television.
25 Although at the time of this writing Asashoryu has just completed his first ad – for Fujitsu laptops, with SMAP star Kimura Takuya.
26 So, too, are individuals featured in extended interviews on all TV stations when they achieve certain milestones, as was the case when Nomura became the third player in Japanese baseball history to gain 2000 hits in June 2005.
27 Consult Holden (2004) for statistics demonstrating this. This includes measures of TV ownership (which exceeds 99 per cent), daily viewership (which tops three hours) and comparison to other daily media consumption: newspapers (at 86 per cent), cell phones (at 73 per cent) and the Internet (at 27 per cent).

Bibliography

Befu, H. (2000) 'Globalization as human dispersal: from the perspective of Japan', in J. Eades, T. Gill and H. Befu (eds) *Globalization and Social Change in Contemporary Japan*, Melbourne: Trans Pacific Press.

Berger, P. L. and Luckmann, T. (1967) *The Social Construction of Reality: a treatise in the sociology of knowledge*, Garden City, NY: Doubleday & Company, Inc.

Buruma, I. (2004) *Inventing Japan: 1853–1964*, New York: The Modern Library.

Ergul, H. (2003) '"Lightening" culture: vanishing borders, hybridized contents, and infotainment in Japanese television broadcasting', paper presented at Anthropology of Japan in Japan (AJJ) Annual Meeting, Ritsumeikan Asia Pacific University, Beppu, Japan, 19 April.

Gitlin, T. (1983) *Inside Prime Time*, New York: Pantheon.

Goffman, E. (1974) *Frame Analysis*, Philadelphia: University of Philadelphia Press.

Guttman, A. and Thompson, L. (2001) *Japanese Sports: a history*, Honolulu: University of Hawaii Press.

Hirai, H. (2001) 'Hideo Nomo: pioneer or defector?', in D. Andrews and S. Jackson (eds) *Sport Stars: the politics of sporting celebrity*, London: Routledge.

Holden, T. J. M. (2002) 'Sports exports/media imports: how Japan engages a globalizing world', paper presented at the 23rd General Assembly and Annual Conference of the International Association for Media and Communication Research (IAMCR), 'Intercultural communication,' Barcelona, Spain, 21–26 July.

——(2003a) 'Japan's mediated "global" identities', in T. J. Scrase, T. J. M. Holden and S. Baum (eds) *Globalization, Culture and Inequality in Asia*, Melbourne: Trans Pacific Press.

——(2003b) 'Nihon-centrism in Japanese international sports reporting', paper presented at the International Communication Association (ICA) Annual Meeting, San Diego, California, USA, 23–27 May.

——(2004) 'Japan', in H. Newcomb (ed.) *Encyclopedia of Television*, vol. 2 (D-L), 2nd edn, New York: Fitzroy Dearborn.

Ito, R. (2005) '"Princess Megu" and "Powerful Kana": Japan's female Olympic stars at the intersection of gender and nationalism', paper presented at the International Association of Media and Communication Research (IAMCR), Taipei, Taiwan, 25–26 July.

McVeigh, B. J. (2004) *Nationalisms of Japan: managing and mystifying identity*, Lanham, MD: Rowman & Littlefield.

Tuchman, G. (1978) *Making News: a study in the social construction of reality*, New York: Free Press.

Whannel, G. (1992) *Fields in Vision: television, sport & cultural transformation*, Routledge: London.

Whiting, R. (1977) *The Chrysanthemum and the Bat*, Tokyo: The Permanent Press.

——(1989) *You Gotta Have Wa*, New York: Macmillan Publishing Company.

Yoshimi, S. (2003) 'Television and nationalism: historical change in the national domestic TV formation of postwar Japan', *European Journal of Cultural Studies*, vol. 6, no. 4, November: 459–87.

8 Writing as out/insiders

Contemporary Japan's *ekkyô* literature in globalization

Rumi Sakamoto

Introduction

During the 1990s, in the context of increasing globalization and growing critique of the dominant myth of Japanese uniqueness and homogeneity, a number of *ekkyô* (border-crossing) writers gained prominence in Japan. In its current usage (and the concept is still in its infancy), the term '*ekkyô* writer' refers to either ethnically non-Japanese authors writing in Japanese in Japan or ethnically Japanese authors writing in Japanese and foreign languages either in Japan or elsewhere. While *ekkyô* encompasses border-crossings both 'into' and 'away from' Japan, more emphasis is placed on inflow than outflow. Writers who emigrated overseas and write exclusively in the language of the host society, such as Kazuo Ishiguro, are not considered *ekkyô* writers even when they write on Japan. In other words, *ekkyô* literature is not just about its producers' physical border-crossings, but is about its place and function in relation to Japan, in particular the function of challenging the 'inside' with some elements of 'outside'. Writing in-between national/ethnic cultures, *ekkyô* writings typically contain a radical challenge to the closed 'inside' of the Japanese nation by employing vivid images of identities that are neither 'here' nor 'there'. Despite their 'outside' elements, they are usually exclusively addressed to 'national' readers and written in Japanese. Although small in number, by the end of the 1990s such writings had become quite visible in the public domain, moving beyond the narrowly defined literary establishment. Their border-crossing lives, as well as their literary exploration of identities negotiated at an intersection of multiple cultural, historical and political forces, seem to have struck a chord with many readers in Japan.

This chapter looks at the autobiographical novels of four *ekkyô* writers who are currently publishing in Japan: Levy Hideo, an American; Mizumura Minae, a returnee from the US; David Zoppetti, a Swiss; and Kaneshiro Kazuki, a second-generation Korean resident in Japan.[1] My purpose is to analyse how these authors and their writings demonstrate the blurring of the boundary between the 'inside' (Japan) and the 'outside' (non-Japan) within the context of globalization. I will first examine the local contexts for the production of meaning around Japanese national identity in the 1990s, locating *ekkyô* writings at the intersection of globalization and the postwar cultural imaginary of homogeneous Japan. I suggest that contemporary Japan's *ekkyô* literature, while sharing elements with 'postcolonial' literature, needs to be understood in relation to the multilateral flows of globalization rather than postcoloniality rooted in the binary power relation between the colonizers and the colonized. I then look at the representation of border-crossing and hybrid identities in the four texts. Particular attention will be paid to their simultaneous insider/outsider positionings and how they challenge the myth of Japanese homogeneity and criticize this exclusivist and discriminatory aspect of Japan without essentializing the position of the outsider.

Challenging the national literature

While non-native writers are nothing new in places such as the US and Australia, and indeed in Japan in the colonial context, today's *ekkyô* writers are understood as a new phenomenon in Japan. This is because, until recently, the notion of Japanese 'national' literature has been self-evident and unchallenged. Postwar Japan, with its myth of homogeneity which centred around the ethnic purity and cultural uniqueness of the nation, has produced a dominant image of the 'national literature' as 'superior linguistic expressions written in "Japanese" by "Japanese" who were born in "Japan"' (Komori 1998: 283).[2] In this framework, literature was considered an embodiment of the supposedly unique Japanese language, sentiment, culture and so forth, accessible only to people who were born and educated as Japanese.

While there were earlier examples of literary transgressions by Korean, Taiwanese and Manchurian writers writing in Japanese, it was only during the 1990s that the practice of writing cross-culturally came to be widely recognized in Japan as a fundamental challenge to the myth of the national literature, confusing ideas of where the borders between national and foreign should be re-established. To understand this, we need to locate *ekkyô* literature in the wider context of Japan within globalization. For what made it possible to see such literature as a new phenomenon (Numano 1996: 386; Iguchi 1996: 84) was not just the simple fact that these 'not purely Japanese' writers are writing in Japanese (which, after all, had considerable precedent), but also reflected 1990s Japanese society's increasing connection with the outside world.

In 1990s Japan the concept of the nation and national identity came under scrutiny from different directions. The death of the Showa Emperor in 1989 and the end of the long-dominant Liberal Democratic Party (LDP) rule in 1993 led to a variety of competing views on Japan's history and its place in today's world. Mounting criticism from newly confident Asian nations over some issues such as the content of Japanese school history textbooks, the so-called 'comfort women' and other war issues led to critical reflections on the nation's collective memory, on the one hand, and a nationalist and revisionist backlash, on the other. Responding to the 1997 United Nations International Decade of the World's Indigenous Peoples initiative (1995–2004), the government passed legislation that acknowledged the Ainu as an indigenous people, departing from its earlier position that no indigenous people existed in Japan. Many publications in the late 1980s and early 1990s challenged the idea of Japanese uniqueness and homogeneity, coinciding with the introduction and popularization of (the largely British version of) Cultural Studies that problematized the essentialist understanding of national and cultural identity. The view that Japan is not really culturally homogeneous came to be widely held within academia.[3]

The emergence of *ekkyô* writers and their challenge to the 'national literature' was understood within this shift from the complacent cultural nationalism of the 1970s and the early 1980s to the increasing awareness of plurality in the 1990s. It was only with the rearrangement of the larger discursive constellation in Japan, as it increasingly became integrated into the global network of knowledge and practice, that *ekkyô* writers' challenge could be recognized as a positive and exciting (and increasingly marketable) phenomenon. The perception of their newness, in short, was partly a function of globalization.

From postcoloniality to globalization

Japan's *ekkyô* writers have been associated with the 'world-wide blossoming of postcolonial and multi-ethnic literatures' (Tachibana 2001: 400), including such postcolonial writers as Salman Rushdie, Ben Okri and Amos Tutola (Numano 1996: 386; Aoyagi 2001: 1; Tachibana 2002: 23). We can certainly consider contemporary Japan's transcultural writings as symptomatic of 'global-scale . . . postcolonial conditions' (Komori 1998: 284). These include the problematization of various forms of social and cultural domination rooted in colonialism; poststructuralist theories of history and deconstruction of the modernist and essentialist notions of the nation; and the liberatory and subversive potential of hybrid or creolized existences and languages. In that their writings contain an element of resistance to the dominant discourse and practice in Japan, articulating mobility and crossovers that challenge the notion of cultural purity, we can also locate them in the context of the worldwide contestation of cultural domination by marginalized minorities, to which postcolonial theory and literature generally attest.

At the same time, however, contemporary Japan's *ekkyô* writers differ from such postcolonial writers as Rushdie, who write within the legacy of nineteenth-century European colonialism. Rushdie and others may rework, negotiate and subvert the narrative of the dominance of the Western colonial discourse to 'take down the master's house using the master's own tools' (Teverson 2003: 332), but they do so within the framework of the dichotomy of the colonizer and the colonized, where one of them can be identified as a 'master'. Postcolonial literature's focus on the relation of domination–subordination between formerly colonized peoples and their former colonizers (Ashcroft 1989) does not apply to Japan's *ekkyō* literature.

Partly because of Japan's historical position as a late-nineteenth-century colonizer which attempted to both resist and to emulate Western imperialism, and partly because of the multi-directional movements that characterize today's globalization, the relations of domination and subordination that inform *ekkyō* writings are multiple and complex. It is not clear who the 'master' is when a white male author writes in Japanese about being 'racially' excluded from mainstream Japanese society while gaining literary prominence by critiquing Japanese homogeneity from the position of the 'authentic in-between'. While such writers as Levy and Zoppetti do write in the language of the Other, their practice of writing in Japanese cannot be equated with the subaltern's 'writing back' (Ashcroft 1989) in the 'language of the oppressor' (Daniels 2001), a typically postcolonial project.

I suggest that the emergence and acceptance of *ekkyō* writers in contemporary Japan need to be seen within the framework of globalization, not that of postcoloniality *per se*. The physical presence of these writers in Japan, as well as their ability to write in a 'non-native' language, reflects the unforeseen level of transnational movement of money, goods, people, images and ideas that characterize today's globalizing world. Without a high level of global cultural flow, Zoppetti would not have picked up his first Teach Yourself Japanese book in Geneva; without a high level of economic globalization, Mizumura's father would not have been sent to the United States, uprooting his daughters from their native land.

Unlike the earlier generation of colonial or *zainichi* (resident Korean) writers, where the choice of language and place of residence resulted from Japan's colonial rule and therefore are inscribed with an element of force, the post-1990s *ekkyō* writers are usually self-chosen immigrants from middle-class backgrounds.[4] Their border-crossings are not limited to movement from the former colony to the metropolitan centre, or from a marginal language to a dominant language. Levy and Mizumura, in particular, moved from the historically powerful America and the English language to Japan and the Japanese language, despite the fact that this restricts them to a relatively small readership. These authors and their works are more the products of multi-directional interconnectivity of globalization than they are of a hugely unequal two-way relationship between the colonizers and the colonized, centre and periphery, or the West and 'the Rest'. They embody the complex movements of the 'ethnoscapes' (Appadurai 1996: 33)[5] and 'global diasporas' (Cohen 1997: 155–76), as well as the uneven cultural productions that do not necessarily correspond to political and economic power.

It seems to me that if we find some 'postcolonial' elements in contemporary *ekkyō* writings this may partly be a product of the 'deterritorialization' and 'interconnectivity' (Thomlinson 1999) of globalization that allows people immediate access to the cultural products of distant places. Postcolonial theory and literature are now part of the globalized knowledge and discourse available to worldwide audiences through the global communication network. It may well be the case that *ekkyô* authors in Japan are making use of globalized ideas and images such as hybridity and in-betweenness that (post)colonial experience has produced elsewhere. If so, their writings are not exclusively products of direct material conditions and local experience within geographical Japan, but have an element of appropriated discourse and 'travelling theory' (Said 1983), inflected and embodied through contemporary and local experiences of globalizing Japan.

The four writers and their autobiographical novels

I have chosen autobiographical writings because their blend of fact and fiction highlights the making/writing of the self in the social context. Autobiographical writings are historical and cultural products rather than purely personal expressions (Folkenfilk 1993: 39–44). For the four texts this chapter considers, globalization and its challenge to cultural nationalism provide the social and historical condition of textual production. The authors collectively offer an insight into the formation of border-crossing identities under globalization and articulate new ways of thinking about national and cultural identities in the globalizing world. Through the autobiographical mode of the works, where each author narrates and constructs the self/character(s), we see beyond the abstract and general principle of hybridity into different hybridity and in-betweenness in lived experience, heavily marked with history, power and specific location(s).

The four autobiographical novels that we now turn to are Levy Hideo's *Seijôki no kikoenai heya* (A room where Stars and Stripes cannot be heard, 1992), Mizumura Minae's *Shishôsetsu from left to right* (I-novel from left to right, 1995), David Zoppetti's *Ichigensan* (First-time customer, 1999) and Kaneshiro Kazuki's *GO* (Go, 2000). Despite their relatively short careers, these authors are quite well known in Japan, having received a number of literary awards, written in national newspapers and appeared in literary and other magazines, as well as on television and other media.[6]

All four authors contain multiple cultures and languages within themselves. Levy, an American of Jewish/Polish decent, spent his childhood in Taiwan and Hong Kong and part of his young adulthood in Japan. He taught Japanese literature at Princeton and Stanford before moving to Japan on his fortieth birthday. He has published a number of novels and collections of essays and interviews, as well as making regular contributions to Japanese literary magazines. *Seijôki* is the story of the teenage son of a US diplomat in Tokyo who escapes from the authority of his father and the Stars and Stripes, finding his new identity in Japan.

Mirroring Levy's trajectory between the States and Japan, Mizumura returned to Japan to become a novelist after twenty years in the States, first as the teenage daughter of a Japanese expatriate and later as a doctoral student of French literature at Yale and a lecturer at Princeton. *Shishôsetsu* is a reflection on her life in New York as a Japanese girl/young woman. It is written in a mixture of Japanese and English, and has been described as Japan's 'first bilingual literature', written horizontally (as opposed to vertically, which is the conventional way of writing books in Japan – hence 'left to right' in the title).

Zoppetti, born in a French-speaking village near Geneva to an Italian-Swiss father and a Jewish-American mother, has been based in Japan since 1988. Following his BA from Doshisha University in Kyoto, he became the first non-Japanese full-time employee of TV Asahi, working as a director and a reporter for a prime-time news programme. Since the success of *Ichigensan*, he has left TV and has so far published two novels and one collection of essays in Japanese, all of which have received literary prizes. *Ichigensan* is a story of a foreign student's experience of Kyoto and his relationship with a blind Japanese girl.

Kaneshiro is a second-generation *zainichi* whose father originally came from Cheju Island, a region that historically suffered from discrimination within Korea. Just like the protagonist in his *GO*, Kaneshiro has changed his nationality from North Korean to South Korean and attended both ethnic (North Korean) and mainstream Japanese schools. *GO* is the story of a *zainichi* boy who falls in love with a Japanese girl who rejects him on finding out that he is Korean.

The four works as popular culture

Before looking at the texts, some explanation of the appropriateness of including these writers in a book on 'popular culture' is in order. Although Levy's and Mizumura's works may not be considered as 'popular' as Kaneshiro's and Zoppetti's in terms of readership, I consider them here in the single category of *ekkyô* writings of contemporary Japan, as a social rather than a strictly literary phenomenon. Partly due to the influence of the global market, the division between the 'pure' and the 'popular' (understood in the Japanese context as 'serious'/'non-serious' or 'critical'/'uncritical') which framed much past discussion on Japanese literature is now breaking down. This means that these days even literature that appeals to educated readers and provides some social evaluation can be seen as one of the many highly differentiated and niche-targeted consumer products (like *otaku* animation or fan-drawn comic books, for example). Japan is a highly developed consumer society where mass literacy is the norm and 'serious' literature can be consumed as an icon or a fashion, as Marilyn Ivy suggested regarding the new 'pop' academic discourse of the 1980s (Ivy 1989). The critique of the myth of homogeneity and the articulation of non-culturally essentialist identities arguably reflect the values and thinking of the cultural/intellectual elite; and yet the same themes clearly exist in Kaneshiro's *GO*, the most 'popular' novel of the four. Conversely, the seemingly more 'serious' literature of Mizumura and Levy appears regularly on blogs and other personal websites.

Their writings are also marketed as part of 'mass' or 'popular' culture, rather than the 'high art'. Marketing has contributed to these authors' visibility and to their becoming a social phenomenon. The knowledge that there are some 'not purely Japanese' authors writing in Japanese, and the perception that this is somehow interesting and exciting, is disseminated through other means than the literary works themselves, including interviews, magazine columns and advertisements. Using catchphrases like *ekkyô-sakka* (border-crossing writer) and *bairingaru-sakka* (bilingual writer), publishers and bookshops often promote their books by emphasizing the authors' ethnic identities and personal histories. For example, in publishers' hyperbole Levy has been dubbed the 'first Western writer of Japanese language' and 'an author who does not have even a drop of Japanese blood'. His past as a Japanologist at elite US universities and as a translator of *Manyoshu* (the oldest extant collection of native Japanese poems) into English is often mentioned. Mizumura's *Shishôsetsu* has also received extravagant publisher's praise, being marketed as the 'first bilingual literature in Japan' and as an 'unheard-of bilingual I-novel'. Details of her life, that she left Japan at the age of twelve, graduated from Yale and taught modern Japanese literature at Princeton and other US universities, repeatedly appear in promotional materials. Selling through additional information (in their cases, through the authors' 'global connectivity') is a common strategy also used in the marketing of other commodities.

From a linguistic perspective, because of its heavy reliance on a language literature can communicate complex and nuanced ideas beyond images and senses, and is therefore a good place to explore cultural or symbolic aspect of globalization. While it is unlikely that consumers of hip-hop music, Hello Kitty or Coca-Cola are receiving complex pictures of globalized consciousness and identities, written texts can communicate such messages and also provide tighter control over meaning at the site of consumption. The rest of this chapter, then, closely examines the four texts to see how cultural globalization worked at the specific time and location: post-1990s Japan. What kind of consciousness and identities are emerging as a result of globalization? How do people make sense of the unevenly interconnected world? In what ways do these authors engage with the myth of homogeneity and with the national and commercial desire to consume *ekkyô* writers as exotic Others and/or fashionable hybrids that confirm Japan's status as a truly 'global' nation with its own versions of Salman Rushdie?

Excluded Others

The four novels all reveal the insular nature of the Japanese community seen from the position of simultaneous insider and outsider. Levy's and

Zoppetti's works clearly take issue with Japanese homogeneity and the complacency that accompanies it. The sense of exclusion their protagonists experience, for example, is expressed in the following scene describing Zoppetti's protagonist's encounter with a group of children on a school trip in Kyoto.

> As soon as I am discovered by one of the children in the group, a voice cries: 'Look, there is a *gaijin*.' Then 'Hey, did you see? There was a *gaijin*.' 'Where? Where? Yes, it's true! It's a *gaijin*!' 'Look, it's a *gaijin*.' '*Gaijin . . . gaijin . . . gaijin . . . gaijin*.' The roar runs through the group from the top to the end as if it is a contagious disease . . . A series of 'hello' 'hello' 'hello' begins . . . After many days like this, I could not but feel a quiet anger and contempt towards those who fire off the cliché of 'It's a *gaijin*, hello, hello!' as if they were pre-programmed robots.
>
> (Zoppetti 1999: 46)

What is described here is the lack of any attempt at real communication from the Japanese children and the stereotyped treatment of a *gaijin* (foreigner) as an object rather than as a person. This lack of communication is not a natural consequence of a language barrier. Ben, Levy's protagonist, states:

> Even if I said something in Japanese, they all look as if looking at a clever doll, and say 'very good' with a Japanese smile, and either answer in English or fall silent. I don't know WHY. I don't understand why this is the way it is.
>
> (Levy 1992: 44)

It is not that communications fail because of an insufficient level of linguistic, cultural or interpersonal skill; rather, the possibility of communication itself is always already closed down because of the pre-assignment of the category of *gaijin*.

The term *gaijin* (literally meaning outsider) is generally used to refer to 'white' foreigners and it involves a particular manner of being excluded from the (imagined) national community of Japan.[7] *Gaijin*, like other minorities in Japan, are certainly a marginalized 'Other' of the cultural construction called Japan, and Levy's and Zoppetti's protagonists suffer from this as they are showered with mindless 'hello, hello(es)' and approached by Japanese only to practice 'English conversation'. But they are not exactly oppressed subalterns. The nature of their exclusion differs from that of other ethnic minorities such as Ainu or Okinawans, because *gaijin*, as 'white' foreigners, have been historically positioned at the higher end of the white–yellow–black racial hierarchy, which the early Meiji Enlightenment uncritically accepted and reproduced.

Much of post-Meiji Japanese history has been dominated by the effort to catch up with, resist, compete with and surpass the West, which was understood as not just a geopolitical but a racialized entity (first Britain and Europe, then America, but always associated with 'whiteness'). While different modes of this West-focused consciousness have existed throughout the history of Japan (from adoration and inferiority complex to competition, jealousy and even outright rejection), the racialized 'West' has remained modern Japan's constant reference point and its dominant Other. Modern Japan has never produced major discourses that discriminate against people with the 'racial' features commonly described as 'white' on the basis of their perceived inherent inferiority to the Japanese. The West was too powerful for Japan to do so in the nineteenth century, and today's construction of *gaijin* as the Other still carries the trace of that history. *Gaijin* exclusion is not a simple, all-out discrimination against the powerless minority by the powerful majority, but is more ambivalent and ambiguous, where desire and attraction are mixed with aversion and indifference.

Levy's and Zoppetti's texts capture the specific form of exclusion that a *gaijin* encounters. Although associated with the historically and discursively powerful West, as individuals their protagonists belong to a 'racial' minority excluded from mainstream Japanese society. Zoppetti's protagonist describes what he experiences as a 'subtle, almost invisible mechanism of differentiation . . . based on appearances', emphasizing that it is not discrimination (*sabetsu*) but *kubetsu*, or 'differentiation' (Zoppetti 1999: 131). Levy writes that Japanese cities 'welcome outsiders with an absolute certainty that they [the outsiders] know nothing, that they cannot know anything' (Levy 1992: 67). In both texts, Japanese characters that do approach them (for example students keen to have an 'English conversation' or a middle-aged salaryman who shows an exaggerated appreciation of the *karaoke* skill of Zoppetti's protagonist) seem to do so simply to reinforce the insider/outsider boundary. Both Levy and Zoppetti are critical of the assumption of the strict and rigid dichotomy between Japanese/foreigner, inside/outside and us/them. Unlike colonized Taiwanese or Koreans, who were encouraged and even forced to 'become Japanese' on one level, for *gaijin* to 'become Japanese' is not an option, for they are considered to be in a clearly separate and incommensurable category. While 'difference not discrimination' may sound like a good multiculturalist celebration of cultural diversity, when the insistence on reifying difference comes from the majority within a community which considers itself homogeneous it clearly has a negative effect on the recipients. All-out discrimination based on the belief of the inferiority of Others and the pressure to assimilate them certainly hurts, but indifference and lack of communication do too.

If the depiction of *gaijin* exclusion in the form of polite but absolute differentiation based on appearances is all there is to Levy's and Zoppetti's texts, we may conclude that they are merely repeating the Orientalist cliché of the inscrutable Japanese, privileging the position of the self. Importantly, however, their critique of the 'inside' of Japan comes from the position not of an absolute outsider, but of a simultaneous outsider/insider. Their protagonists cultivate a sense of belonging and authenticity through acquisition of the language, friendship with Japanese and the concrete daily acts of living in Japan such as slurping up noodles in a favourite little restaurant, riding on overcrowded trains, singing in a *karaoke* bar with a girlfriend or soaking in a public bath. Their life-worlds are undoubtedly very 'Japanese', and they do much more than just encounter the abstract Japanese nation and the ideology of uniqueness. It is from this simultaneous inside/outside position that Zoppetti's protagonist successfully counters the ridicule of a Japanese man by answering him in perfect Kyoto dialect while demonstrating his insider knowledge of Japanese public bath protocol. At this unexpected response, the man quickly disappears, not knowing how to react to such a violation of the Japanese/foreigner boundary (Zoppetti 1999: 167).

Gaijin characters appropriating what is supposedly a part of the unique Japanese culture have the effect of destabilizing Japanese cultural identity and disrupting the national boundary on which national identity depends. This is similar to the critical effect of what Levy calls the 'victory of Japanese' (Levy 1990); that is, the liberation of Japanese language from the assumption of the natural and essential relationship between 'mother-tongue' language and identity by ethnically non-Japanese writers writing in Japanese. Within the boundaries of modern 'national' literature, the images of 'Westerners' were portrayed as an ugly object of hatred on the one hand and as an idealized and beautiful object of worship on the other; both representations were as something fundamentally different from what it was to be Japanese (Tsuruta 1999). In Levy's and Zoppetti's works, however, the *gaijin* protagonists are no longer unrealistic and stereotypical 'Others' of Japan, but instead are subjects whose identities, lives and existence are rooted in the here and now of geographical, cultural and linguistic Japan, and whose critique of the ideology of homogeneity is internal, not external.

For Sugihara, the *zainichi* protagonist of *GO*, exclusion is based on nationality and 'race', not on language or appearance. The text incorporates the discrimination and inconvenience *zainichi* Koreans suffer, including alien registration and fingerprinting, as well as to the colonial history behind the discrimination. Sugihara knows that he 'cannot be a company head because of [his] nationality' (Kaneshiro 2000: 76). A Japanese student provokes him, saying, 'Come on, you Korean; or would you rather run off to your country with your tail between your legs?' (Kaneshiro 2000: 136). An ultimate expression of Japanese discrimination appears in the figure of his Japanese girlfriend's otherwise liberal and understanding father, who had taught her that Korean and Chinese men have 'dirty blood' (Kaneshiro 2000: 178). Sugihara tells his girlfriend that he was born and raised in Japan, 'breathing more or less the same air as you did, eating more or less the same food as you did', rationally and intellectually disputing the myth of Japanese homogeneity and the purity of Japanese blood. This approach, however, proves powerless in the face of his girlfriend's irrational, almost physical, fear. 'I understand the logic of what Sugihara is saying, but I just cannot do it. I am scared ... When I think about Sugihara coming inside my body, I get scared ... ' (Kaneshiro 2000: 181).

Despite the protagonist being clearly an 'outsider', *GO* cannot be reduced to a *zainichi* critique of Japan. It challenges the inside/outside boundary and rejects a simplistic representation of Japanese versus *zainichi* Koreans. For example, Sugihara's best friend in the North Korean school, Shôichi, was brought up by his Japanese mother after his Korean father disappeared when he was three, and is later killed by a Japanese student in a tragic incident. When Sugihara's senior *zainichi* friend visits a council office to have his fingerprints taken, intending to punch the officer in charge to vent his anger over this unreasonable legal requirement, he is met by a disabled officer who repeatedly apologizes for the inconvenience and then by a young woman with a bruise on her cheek, apparently from abuse at an earlier finger-printing session. She makes sure his fingerprinting is not visible to other people at the council office and he ends up muttering, '"thank you" ... at least ten times' (Kaneshiro 2000: 68–9). In yet another episode, a young policeman who stops Sugihara to question him ends up confiding to him that he has been bullied by senior policemen, that his career has stagnated and that he has bad luck with women. Despite its critique of the ideology of Japanese homogeneity and institutional discrimination, the story as a whole tells how Sugihara leaves the 'narrow world' of the *zainichi* community and comes to be accepted by Japanese society as an individual, distinct from the group identity of *zainichi*.

Minae, the protagonist in Mizumura's story, on the other hand, has been living in the United States since she was a teenager, and thus is geographically, culturally and linguistically dislocated from Japan. She is painfully aware that she is a 'Japanese in America', as opposed to a 'Japanese in Japan, who works in Japan, and for whom eating Japanese food and speaking Japanese is normal – a Japanese who is not even aware that s/he is a Japanese' (Mizumura 1995: 59). The experience of living in the United States makes her realize that there is only an 'unreliable and transient link ... between Japanese blood and being a Japanese' (Mizumura 1995: 13). The story reveals how Minae's sense of dislocation from Japan, along with her repeated and fundamental exclusion from mainstream East Coast American society, comes to be compensated for by Minae's nostalgic desire for her (imagined) homeland. At the same time, in a manner similar to that in which Levy's and Zoppetti's protagonists view Japan, America is very much part of Minae's life and identity: 'It was not that there was a human being called me, and then there was America outside me. I realized that I had already been living in America. My everyday life was in America' (Mizumura 1995: 192). The relationship between Japan and America, thus, is not represented as that of two mutually exclusive, essentialized cultures, one of which is naturally and unproblematically closer to her identity; rather, they are both inside her and she is 'suspended in the middle' (Mizumura 1995: 64). The 'gap' she experiences is not that between Japan and America, but that between the 'Japanese-language me' and the 'English-language me', both of which are firmly part of her identity (Mizumura 1995: 192).

Originary homelessness

Thus, although the 'outsider' perspectives in these four texts challenge the myth of Japanese homogeneity and the assumed link between identity, language, blood and geographical location, exposing the narrow-mindedness of the 'insiders', in doing so they do not essentialize the 'outside'. The position of simultaneous insider/outsider in these *ekkyô* writings differs from that of fully and comfortably belonging to the two communities and two identities, moving back and forth between the two. All four texts destabilize a clear-cut distinction between 'here' and 'there', or 'home' and 'elsewhere', and suggest that there is no origin, authenticity or natural belonging in the first place.

In Levy's *Seijôki*, for example, there is no sign that the protagonist, Ben, has a comfortable, unproblematic relationship with America as his 'home' or 'origin'. Ben was 'brought up as a white child in Asia ... as a son of a diplomat' (Levy 1992: 40). Half Jewish and half Polish, Ben cannot readily identify with 'America', the country of the WASP (White Anglo-Saxon Protestant). His 'Jewish' identity is also unstable, as his Jewish relatives cut off Ben's family completely when his father married and had another child with his second wife, who was Chinese. When Ben leaves Asia with his mother after his parents' divorce, this is described as a 'return' to 'unknown [*mishiranu*] America'. He is going 'home', but the home is 'unknown' to him. Back in America, Ben and his mother settle in a 'poor white' area, in a house full of Chinese and Japanese antiques, with his mother slowly going crazy. After graduating from high school, Ben visits his father in Japan, and that is where much of the story takes place. Throughout, there is a strong sense of dislocation and lack of belonging. The sense of dislocation does not simply come from the fact that Ben is in Japan, geographically and temporarily away from his American 'home'. Japan certainly appears as an 'elsewhere', but America, too, is a strange 'elsewhere'. When his father's consulate building is surrounded by Japanese students shouting, 'Yankee Go Home', Ben wonders where they are to go 'home' to. With his Jewish father, his father's Chinese wife and his half-brother with black eyes and black hair, where exactly is he supposed to 'go home' to? 'To Brooklyn, to Shanghai or to the illusion of Jerusalem?' (Levy 1992: 76).

Home, then, is always already dislocated for Ben, and it is from this position of originary homelessness that he begins his search for identity in Japan, escaping from his father's diplomatic residence. At first, Ben cannot decipher the simplest of Japanese letters and characters, and wanders around Tokyo like a 'traveller who can hardly read any signposts'. Japan and the Japanese language seem inscrutable, but he has a strong desire to 'read', to 'enter', to 'blend in and follow'. It is through this desire and through his friend and guide Andô, that Ben eventually learns the language and chooses the city of Shinjuku as his adopted home.[8] Episodes of struggling to eat a raw fish full of bones with chopsticks and swallowing a raw egg in front of his Japanese workmates – and almost vomiting – appear as a self-imposed initiation into the city of Shinjuku. It is his lack of origin (and his rebellion against his father) that allows him to 'enter', appropriate and claim Shinjuku. Despite the strong sense of alienation, Ben, to some extent through his self-imposed acts of initiation, reaches the state where 'I, too, know Shinjuku' and finds his place within Japan. It is this sense of almost instinctive 'knowing' that allows Ben to claim Shinjuku and gain a sense of identity. His adopted 'home' is not a warm place of natural belonging. Far from it, he has to work hard, learning the language and, as in the swallowing a raw egg incident, constantly fighting the message 'You [plural] won't be able to do it'.

The originary homelessness, the lack of nostalgia about 'home' and the partially self-chosen escape from various forms of 'we' seem to distinguish these *ekkyô* writings in contemporary Japan from the large body of diaspora, minority or immigrant literature elsewhere, which is also born out of transnational experiences but for which 'home' or 'community' remains more central. Terms like 'diaspora', 'immigrant' or 'minority' point to the historical experience of dislocation and/or marginalization as a group. In the autobiographical narratives we are looking at, however, the collective aspect of experience is played down. As we have seen, Levy's *Seijôki* is presented as a very individual and personal experience. It is not about the collective experience of Americans in Japan. It is not about immigrant subjectivity, diaspora identity or any such formation of self based on some collectivity, community or orientation towards the 'home'. Similarly, Zoppetti's protagonist describes himself as a 'nomad', for whom 'to keep moving like a Bohemian had become [his] nature and fate' (Zoppetti 1999: 25). Beyond the fact that he came from a 'foreign country', the text mentions very little about his origin.

GO's Sugihara states that nationality is 'like a contract for an apartment – when you've had enough, just leave it', and adopts a Spanish phrase: '*No soy coreano, ni soy japones, yo soy dessarraigado* [I am not Korean, I am not Japanese, I am rootless].' He remains equally distant from Japan, South Korea, North Korea and *zainichi* society. The text is critical of North Korea as a totalitarian and militaristic system solely concerned with 'imposing blind loyalty towards Kim Il-Sung' in order to 'unify the nation into a monolithic solidarity'. Neither is South Korea, 'a Confucian country', depicted in a favourable light; when Sugihara visits South Korea, a taxi driver who finds out that he is a *zainichi* attempts to overcharge him after interrogating him as to whether he can eat *kimchee*. A fight follows, and Sugihara swears, in Japanese, saying that 'the trouble with the Koreans is their short temper', assuming a more or less 'Japanese' position (Kaneshiro 2000: 83–6). He keeps his distance from even the *zainichi* community; when his classmate tries to persuade Sugihara to join a *zainichi* group to advance *zainichi* interests in Japanese society, Sugihara simply tells him that if he does not like discrimination in Japan he can change his nationality to Japanese.

In terms of originary homelessness, *Shishōsetsu* stands out, as Minae's nostalgic love for Japan dominates the text. Despite this fondness for Japan, the novel does problematize the notion of one's origin and 'home' as a comfortable place of natural belonging. For one, Minae's love of Japan and things Japanese is a product of her experience in America. 'Home' is produced 'elsewhere'. Furthermore, Minae's object of nostalgic desire is not the 'real' Japan but the intertextually produced 'Japan' of Meiji literature in which she buries herself in New York. She seeks solace, not in the illusion of Japanese blood or identification with contemporary Japan, but in a literary language of almost 100 years ago which many contemporary Japanese are unable to read with ease. On the one hand, she constantly feels that she is 'in a place where [she] should not be' and misses Japan, which, 'in [her] yearning for home, has swelled up like a monster' (Mizumura 1995: 58). At the same time, she is aware that her Japan is imagined, that it probably 'only exists in a poster advertising national railways' (Mizumura 1995: 9).[9] There is thus a curious balance in the text between the awareness of Japan imagined in New York and the almost irrational but very real desire to go back and finally belong.

These authors' rejection of various 'we's' and their focus on the individually crafted in-betweenness signify a move away from the transnational subjectivity principally determined by the power configuration which originated in nineteenth-century imperialism. Collective identities of the national, ethnic or cultural 'we' are the products of history and power. To identify oneself as *zainichi*, for example, involves accepting the traumatic history and memory of colonization as part of one's identity, and this has been central to much of the past *zainichi* literature. Kaneshiro's protagonist's insistence that 'I absolutely refuse to live while feeling as if I belong to a larger group' (Kaneshiro 2000: 220) may seem naive, or even irresponsible, compared to the earlier-generation *zainichi* literature, which developed around the collective trauma of a colonized nation. At the same time, it also embodies the new consciousness emerging out of the boundary-dissolving and multi-centred globalization rather than out of the all-powerful hierarchical dichotomy of the colonizers versus the colonized, or of centre versus periphery. In the age of globalization, the question of relative centre and periphery in terms of political, economic and cultural power is highly complex. People, money and culture flow disjunctively in different areas (Appadurai 1997), and their movements are neither predetermined nor predictable. In addition, electronic media and transportation technology have created a 'global cultural supermarket' (Mathews 2000), where cultural products from places that are neither 'home' nor a 'host society' are readily and abundantly available. One of the effects of globalization in the cultural arena, then, is the increasing possibility of creating transnational identities

outside the formerly powerful dichotomies 'home' and 'elsewhere' as variations of the centre/periphery. Japan's *ekkyô* writers' works seem to reflect
this global condition.

History, power, collective identities

This does not mean, of course, that the *ekkyô* writers' works suggest that
people are now totally free from history and power, and that identities are
simply a matter of cosmopolitan citizens of the world making individual
choices. Globalization has not created a completely open field of possibility
for individual actors. Rather, it has complicated the context of individual
action and identity formation beyond the formerly dominant centre/
periphery relationship, throwing each individual into multiple and complex
associations and belongings, many of which are symbolic in nature. The
symbolic participation in a cosmopolitan culture multiplies the scope of our
experiences, and this new complexity expands individuals' opportunities to
choose and act (Melucci 1996: 44).

The four texts in question exhibit tension between the desire to escape
from the 'we', and historically and politically assigned collective identities,
and to be nomad or *dessaraigado*. For example, in *GO* Sugihara initially
creates his identity not just out of Japanese and Korean elements but also
from Bruce Springsteen, Nietzsche's philosophy, Billy the Kid, Malcolm X
and a range of other influences, with the only criterion being whether something is 'cool' or not. It is by sharing their 'intuition' into 'cool stuff' (that is,
individual taste and instinct that do not rely on nation or any other forms of
collectivity) that Sugihara and his Japanese girlfriend Sakurai create their
shared experience and identity together (Kaneshiro 2000: 115–17). But they
have a head-on collision with history and collective identity as soon as
Sugihara's ethnic identity is revealed to Sakurai (who signifies Japan, as
'*sakura*' in Japanese means cherry blossom, a symbol of the country).

In *Seijôki*, too, Ben's sense of self is constantly renegotiated in relation to
externally and historically assigned collective categories. Throughout the
story he suffers from the plural 'you', being treated as a representative of
America and Americans, and, on one occasion, even as 'the West itself'
(Levy 1992: 37). He is disowned by the Jewish side of his family, disowned
by the Polish side of his family, brought up in different Asian cities, excluded
in Japan, rejected by his father; and yet he is forever categorized as a
member of a group by others – by those who have a solid 'home' to return
to. Ben is uneasy, sensing a gap between these labels (such as 'American',
'Jewish', 'a white boy with golden hair') and himself. He thinks of himself as
an 'exile' from the 'we' – the 'we' of America, the 'we' of the 'Jewish people'.
But faced with the violence of the assumption of 'home', words fail him.

Ben's claiming of Shinjuku marks the moment when he finally executes
an act of agency by rejecting his earlier state, where he was convinced that
there was nothing but emptiness behind any labels for him. In place of

homelessness and non-identity, he introduces a choice, an action, a subjective intervention that temporarily stops the slippage of his identity and the state of non-belonging. Because of his lack of origin, escaping into 'otherness', for him, constitutes a productive act of creating the self out of not-belonging. And, importantly, this is a self that does not rely on a national or ethnic community or a nostalgic link with his origins. In fact it is rooted in a concrete, local place, Shinjuku. His choice is still overdetermined by the hier-archical relationship between Japan and America that developed over history; but, for him, to move from the relative 'centre' to the relative 'periphery' is a positive act because of his lack of home in the first place.

Escaping into 'Japan' and 'Japanese language' is not an option equally available to Kaneshiro's protagonist, who is a second-generation *zainichi* and a product of Japan's colonial history. The sense of freedom Ben gains by choosing Japan and the Japanese language, rebelling against and escaping from the 'us' of powerful America, is inconceivable to Sugihara. Clearly, for these two 'outsiders' escaping into Japan would mean quite different things. Ben's escape into the language of the (marginal) Other is subversive and empowering because he is leaving, by choice, his father's diplomatic residence and everything that the Stars and Stripes stands for. For *GO*'s Sugihara, neither Japanese (the language of the former colonizer) nor Korean (the language of natural belonging), nor even the use of Spanish ('*No soy coreano . . .*'), can have that subversive quality of voluntarily escaping into the marginal Other, precisely because he is located, by history and power, within the marginalized Other himself.

The presence of history and power is particularly evident in *Shishôsetsu*. Minae and her sister Nanae's formations of self carry (though differently) strong traces of historically specific power relations such as those of gender, race, class and nation. Their identities as Japanese women in America are formulated in the context of a relatively high expectation of assimilation, on the one hand, and the impossibility of 'becoming American' as racially marked 'Orientals', on the other. They do not believe even for a moment that they can be individuals away from their ethnic category of 'Japanese' or 'Asian'. When the sisters agree that 'we cannot become American, anyway. We'll only be Japanese-Americans . . . Or Asian-Americans' (Mizumura 1995: 309), their hyphenated identities are represented as something that is forced on them from outside, not self-chosen. Hybrid identity is often cele-brated as a potential location of resistance and liberation, but Minae's and Nanae's hybridity and in-betweenness are not depicted as a desirable or comfortable (let alone superior) existence. Contrary to the fashionable images of 'bilinguals' or '*kikokushijo*' (returnees) that circulated in Japan during the 1980s as a symbol of Japan's internationalization, *Shishôsetsu* locates the experience of the two sisters within the code of 'coloured' immi-grants and minorities in America as a country of WASPs.

Due to her lack of English-language skill, Minae is put in her school's 'dumb class' along with a student with special educational needs. She compensates for this unfortunate streaming by escaping into the world of Meiji literature and Japanese language at home. Her older sister Nanae, on the other hand, fails both in her attempts at assimilating into American society and at fitting back into Japan through marriage to a Japanese man. She ends up fashioning herself into a mixture of the cliché of Oriental femininity in virtual Western eyes (long black hair that reaches her waist) and overemphasized/misinterpreted American-style sexuality (too much make-up and short dresses – 'boy-crazy' and 'nymphomaniac', as their mother calls her). She also plays out the Japanese cliché of aggressive and flippant American women, using 'vulgar expressions' and 'playing the role of a tough woman' (Mizumura 1995: 26). In Minae's eyes, Nanae has become a 'bizarre being' who could have been 'Hispanic, Filipina, Indian, Chinese, Vietnamese or anything, anything but Japanese' (Mizumura 1995: 127). She means that Nanae has become something that is weird and pathetic and not very 'Japanese' at all. But what Nanae has become is a consequence of her being a Japanese in America. *GO*, similarly, contains a variety of possibilities for being a Korean in Japan: North Korean and South Korean; assimilationist and Korean nationalist; those with Japanese and Korean parents. Just as there is no single and homogeneous 'Japan', there is no single, homogeneous set 'Koreans in Japan' or 'Japanese in America'.

Conclusion

Contemporary Japan's *ekkyô* writers challenge the myth of homogeneity on which postwar Japanese national identity was founded. They denaturalize the link between Japanese appearance, Japanese language use and Japanese culture. In challenging the myth of homogeneity, however, they do not rely on the (imagined) authenticity of 'American', 'Swiss', 'Korean' or other 'non-Japanese' identity. None of the protagonists we have looked at have a comfortable, unproblematic relationship with their 'home' or 'origin'. Rather, it is from the position of homelessness and dislocation and simultaneously being inside and outside that critique of the 'inside' is attempted. These writers' use of Japanese language makes them 'insiders' in relation to Japan, and their autobiographical novels are unmistakably 'Japanese' in terms of their settings and concerns, as well as their characters, whose lifeworlds and sense of dislocation and exclusion are constituted in relation to 'Japan'. The challenge and critique these works issue to the homogeneity myth, then, are internal to Japan.

The four *ekkyô* texts, though in some ways very different from one another, collectively attest to the complexity of transnational and transcultural identity formation in the globalizing world. In each, individuals' relationships to history and power are more complex than the dual axis of subaltern/dominant or colonizer/colonized. The contexts that inform the *ekkyô* writings in contemporary Japan are multiple: the legacy of post-nineteenth-century imperialism and the forceful advent of modernity and

Euro-centrism in the non-Western world; American symbolic domination in post-1945 Japan; the 1970s ideology of Japanese uniqueness and homogeneity; accelerating globalization; the changing Japan–Asia relationship seen in the recent 'Asia boom'; the discourses of multiculturalism and postcolonialism. In the *ekkyô* writers' works, identities are formed where multiple places, memories, histories and power relationships intersect with each other. Many borders are crossed – ethnic, cultural, racial, linguistic and geographical – and they do not always coincide. The characters negotiate their identities with multiple 'here's' and 'there's', carrying within themselves many overlapping and multiple historical and political traces. The categories of 'home' and 'elsewhere' are blurred, but not simply merged into a singular hybridity. Difference, tension and borders are retained inside each identity, each Self.

Despite the possibility of such writings and writers being consumed as a new version of the exotic foreign Other or the authentic in-between that reinforces the 'inside', the potential for a radical critique of the inside/outside boundary certainly exists. For outsiders are already insiders – where it goes from here depends on the readers' engagement.

Notes

1   Another (and perhaps more widely used) term to refer to *ekkyô* literature is *nihongo bungaku* (Japanese-language literature) (Komori 1998; Kôno, 1998). This term, originally proposed by novelist Kim Sok Pom to refer to *zainichi* literature (Takeuchi 2002), has since been used for Japanese-language literature in colonized Taiwan and Korea (Kawamura 1990; Kurokawa 1996) and, to a lesser extent, literature by Japanese immigrant writers overseas; it now also encompasses the type of literature this chapter discusses. I use the term *ekkyô* to emphasize the cross-cultural nature of their writings beyond their use of Japanese language itself, and also to differentiate the post-1990s writings, which I consider products of globalization, from earlier *nihongo bungaku* that appeared in relation to Japan's colonial experience.

2   Up until Japan's defeat in the war in 1945, the Japanese Empire included Korea and Taiwan as its colonies, and, as such, there were a number of literary works written in Japanese by non-ethnic Japanese. However, with the end of the Japanese Empire and its colonies, the myth of homogeneity became dominant. See Oguma's work (1995) for the shift from the 'multicultural' Japanese Empire to the monocultural Japan and the concealment of the multicultural past in postwar Japan.

3   However, the bursting of the bubble economy and the resulting recession in the 1990s, as well as criticism from Asian countries regarding Japan's war responsibility, have led to a sense of an external threat. Globalization (unlike its predecessor 'internationalization', which essentially meant exporting Japanese culture abroad) is often considered to be a threat to the nation-state and therefore has stimulated a call for a stronger nation. Contradictory tendencies towards both globalization and nationalism exist in today's Japan.

4   Kaneshiro, a second-generation Korean resident who has lived in Japan throughout his life and a native speaker of Japanese, does not obviously fit into this category, and is usually discussed along with other *zainichi* writers (Fujita 2000; Takeuchi 2002). This chapter places his novel *GO* in the category of

contemporary *ekkyô* texts in Japan, as it articulates a boundary-crossing experience and identity in globalizing Japan. He consciously and intentionally breaks away from mainstream *zainichi* literature and its victim consciousness (Kaneshiro and Oguma 2001: 265–7), exhibiting more of an individual cosmopolitanism in globalizing Japan, where his Koreanness is just one of the many cultural resources available to him, rather than the defining principle of his identity.

5 On ethnoscapes, Appadurai points out that realities and fantasies about emigration now function on much larger scales, for 'men and women from villages in India think not just of moving to Poona or Madras but of moving to Dubai and Houston, and refugees from Sri Lanka find themselves in South India as well as in Switzerland' (Appadurai 1996: 34).

6 *GO* became a bestseller after winning the Naoki Prize, the most prestigious literary prize awarded annually in the category of entertainment/popular literature. It was also made into an award-winning film and a comic series. *Ichigensan* also became an award-winning film starring the popular actress Suzuki Honami. Mizumura exchanged weekly open letters with a well-established novelist, Tsuji Kunio, in a major national newspaper for over a year (Tsuji and Mizumura 2001). An excerpt from Levy's work even made it to the 'national language' entrance examination of the prestigious Tokyo University in 2001. All four texts are available in cheap *bunko* (pocket-sized paperback edition) versions.

7 Black people are called *kokujin* (black person) and Asians who share similar 'racial' features with the Japanese are in a different category altogether. The term *gaikokujin* is also used for foreign workers from the Middle East, Brazil, etc. (For the concept of *gaijin*, see Christopher 1984: 153–71.)

8 To some extent, this adoption of Shinjuku as his home is about escaping from his father's anger, achieving the self through a difference and separation from the father. Ben's father's opinion that Japanese is not a rational language and therefore not worth learning certainly fuels Ben's determination to learn it.

9 This is a reference to the 'Discover Japan' and 'Exotic Japan' campaigns by Japan national railways. These campaigns represented Japan's remote areas as the object of nostalgic desire and self-exoticising gaze via the West (Ivy 1995).

Bibliography

Aoyagi, E. (2001) *Bungaku-riron no purakutisu* (Practice of literary theory), Tokyo: Shinyôsha.

Appadurai, A. (1996) *Modernity at Large*, Minneapolis, MN, and London: University of Minnesota Press.

——(1997) *Modernity at Large: cultural dimensions of globalization,* Minneapolis, MN: University of Minnesota Press.

Ashcroft, B. (1989) *The Empire Writes Back: theory and practice in postcolonial literature*, New York: Routledge.

Christopher, R. C. (1984) *The Japanese Mind*, London: Pan Books.

Cohen, R. (1997) *Global Diasporas: an introduction*, London: UCL Press.

Daniels, P. (2001) *The Voice of the Oppressed in the Language of the Oppressor*, New York: Routledge.

Folkenfilk, R. (ed.) (1993) *The Culture of Autobiography: constructions of self-representation*, Stanford, CA: Stanford University Press.

Fujita, M. (2000) 'Zainichi bungaku no henyô – kokka kara ko e (Changing *zainichi* literature – from state to individual)', *Shinkan Tenbô*, vol. 44, no. 11: 20–3.

Iguchi, T. (1996) 'Ekkyô – Levy Hideo (Border crossing – Levy Hideo)', *Kokubungaku: kaishaku to kyôzai no kenkyû*, vol. 41, no. 10: 84–5.

Ivy, M. (1989) 'Critical texts, mass artifacts: the consumption of knowledge in modern Japan', in M. Miyoshi and H. Harootunian (eds) *Postmodernity and Japan*, Durham, NC: Duke University Press.

——(1995) *Discourses of Vanishing: modernity, phantasm, Japan*, Chicago: University of Chicago Press.

Kaneshiro, K. (2000) *GO*, Tokyo: Kôdansha.

Kaneshiro, K. and Oguma, E. (2001) 'Sorede boku wa "shiteiseki" o kowasutameno GO o kaita (I wrote *GO* in order to destroy the assigned seat)', *Chuôkôron*, November: 264–336.

Kawamura, M. (1990) *Ikyô no shôwa bungaku: manshû to kindai nihon* (Shôwa literature from a foreign land: Manchuria and modern Japan), Tokyo: Iwanami Shoten.

Komori, Y. (1998) *Yuragi no nihon-bungaku* (Swaying Japanese literature), Tokyo: NHK Books.

Kôno, K. (1998) 'Kokkyô o koeru hyôgen – nihongo bungaku ga hirogatte iku (Border-crossing expressions – expanding Japanese-language literature)', in K. Kanai, K. Kôno, T. Shimamura, A. Kaneko and Y. Komori (eds) *Bungaku ga motto omoshiroku naru* (Literature becomes more interesting), Tokyo: Daiyamondosha.

Kurokawa, S. (1996) *Gaichi no nihongo-bungaku sen* (Selected works of Japanese-language literature from outside), vols 1-3, Tokyo: Shinjuku Shobô.

Levy, H. (1990) 'Nihongo no shôri heisei no toraijin (The victory of Japanese language, a Heisei immigrant)', *Chuôkôron*, January: 314–24.

——(1992) *Seijôki no kikoenai heya* (A room where Stars and Stripes cannot be heard), Tokyo: Kôdansha.

Mathews, G. (2000) *Global Culture/Individual Identity: searching for home in the cultural supermarket*, New York: Routledge.

Melucci, A. (1996) *The Playing Self: person and meaning in the planetary society*, Cambridge: Cambridge University Press.

Mizumura, M. (1995) *Shishôsetsu from left to right*, Tokyo: Shinchô-bunko.

Numano, M. (1996) 'Idô to ekkyô no ekurityûru: Levy Hideo, *Shinjuku no manyôshu* (Writing of migration and border-crossing: Levy Hideo's Manyoshu in Shinjuku)', *Subaru*, November: 386.

Oguma, E. (1995) *Tan'itsuminzoku-shinwa no kigen* (the origin of the myth of homogeneity), Tokyo: Sin'yôsha.

Pieterse, J. N. (1995) 'Globalization as hybridization', in M. Featherstone, S. Lash and R. Roberson (eds) *Global Moderntities*, London: Sage.

Said, E. (1983) *The World, the Text, the Critic*, Cambridge, MA, and London: Harvard University Press.

Tachibana, R. (2001) 'Nomadic writers of Japan: Tawada Yoko and Mizumura Minae', *Proceedings of the Association for Japanese Literary Studies*, vol. 2. 400–19.

——(2002) 'Beyond East and West: Tawada Yoko and Hideo Levy', *Proceedings of the Association for Japanese Literary Studies*, vol. 3. 23–35.

Takeuchi, E. (2002) 'Ekkyô suru nihongo bungaku (Japanese literature crossing borders)', *Sozô to Shikô*, 12 March: 22–8.

Teverson, A. (2003) 'Salman Rushdie's metaphorical other worlds', *MFS Modern Fiction Studies*, vol. 49, no. 2: 332–40.

——(1999) *Globalization and Culture*, Chicago: University of Chicago Press.

Tsuji, K. and Mizumura, M. (2001) *Tegami, shiori o soete* (A letter with a bookmark), Tokyo: Asahi Bunko.

Tsuruta, K. (1999) '*Kindai nihon bungaku no naka no seiyôjin* (Westerners in modern Japanese literature)', in K. Tsuruta *Ekkyô-sha ga yonda kindai nihon bungaku* (Modern Japanese literature read by people who crossed borders), Tokyo: Shin'yôsha.

Zoppetti, D. (1999) *Ichigensan* (First-time customer), Tokyo: Shûeisha Bunko.

9   Japan's original 'gay boom'

Mark McLelland

Introduction

In recent years, the internationalization of gay, lesbian and transgender identities and cultures has been the focus of at times heated debate in both popular and academic contexts.[1] Some have taken the development of lesbian and gay media, particularly literature and film, as well as characteristically Western modes of activism and visibility such as lesbian, gay, bisexual, transgender and queer (LGBTQ) organizations, film festivals and parades in societies as diverse as Taiwan, Hong Kong and Japan, to be evidence of a 'global queering' (Altman 2001: 86-100). As Dennis Altman points out, 'globalization has helped create an international gay/lesbian identity, which is by no means confined to the western world' (2001: 86). This interpretation, drawing on globalization studies paradigms, understands the emergence of ostensibly Western 'lesbian' and 'gay' identities and modes of consumption beyond the boundaries of the Western world as part of a process of 'sexual Westernization'. Assuming the centrality of Western approaches and paradigms, this model posits globalization as a process through which 'the Rest' variously imitates, appropriates and resists 'the West'.

A second view, drawing primarily on ethnographic and historical sources, offers a contrary analysis which tends to reify 'traditional' cultures, positing non-Western societies as repositories of imagined 'authentic', 'local' sexual identities. This binary opposition between what may be termed 'unique local essentialism' and 'global homogenization' analyses of 'global queering' emphasizes the need for more critical theoretical work as well as for more detailed empirical accounts of the development of local Asian LGBTQ cultures and histories.

This chapter argues for a recently ascendant third position which challenges both of the above opposing views. Moving beyond the 'transcultural reductiveness' of approaches which locate the sexual cultures and practices of 'other' societies along a continuum of sameness or difference from those of the West while simultaneously resisting the tendency to see indigenous Japanese categories as somehow more authentic or natural than imported understandings, I argue that *both* Western and non-Western cultures of gender and sexuality have been, and continue to be, mutually transformed through their encounters with transnational forms of sexual knowledge. In seeking to transcend the opposed binaries of unique local essentialist and global homogenization analyses of global queering, the hybridization model offers a more productive framework for understanding transformations of sexual cultures. Through an analysis of the emergence in the postwar period of one Japanese sexual category – that of the *gei bôi* (gay boy) – I argue that this identity is not a simple importation from the West, or the residue of a fixed, unchanging premodern tradition which managed to 'survive' in the face of globalization, but instead is the product of hybridizing global processes.

In an earlier project (McLelland 2000) I traced the spread of the identity category *'gei'* (gay) in Japanese popular culture during the closing decades of the twentieth century. I argued that one of the key events which saw *'gei'* win out over a variety of other competing categories for male homosexuality was the 'gay boom' of the early 1990s, which saw mainstream media (print, television and film) interest themselves in Japan's sexual minorities. The result of the boom was that the terms *'gei'* and *'rezubian'* became widely dispersed throughout the general population and have come to be used in a manner very similar to the identity categories 'gay' and 'lesbian' in English.

However, my subsequent encounter with Japan's postwar 'perverse press' (McLelland 2005; Ishida *et al.* 2005), a large number of monthly magazines published throughout the 1950s with titles such as *Ningen Tankyû, Fûzoku kagaku, Fûzoku zôshi,* and *Fûzoku kitan,* has considerably complicated my understanding of the development of the Japanese category *'gei'.* The perverse press, specializing in stories of 'perverse desire' (*hentai seiyoku*), is a resource barely tapped in either Japanese or English research, and offers a detailed account of postwar sexual categories, identities and cultures, including many accounts written in the first person. Through careful archival work, I was able to trace the development of the Japanese category *'gei'* and uncovered a fact not previously reported, that Japan's original 'gay boom' (*gei bûmu*) occurred in 1958, over a decade prior to the widespread adoption of the term 'gay' in English media.

However, before giving an account of the transmission and subsequent popularization of the term *'gei'* in Japanese, it is first necessary to say something about the complex set of understandings that positioned male homosexuality in the sexual culture of the immediate postwar period.

Japan's postwar homosexual culture

According to reports in the perverse press, the most visible homosexual category to appear immediately after the war was the *danshô*, or cross-dressing male prostitute, who adopted a style similar to the female-role performers of the kabuki, the *onnagata,* who themselves had long been associated with

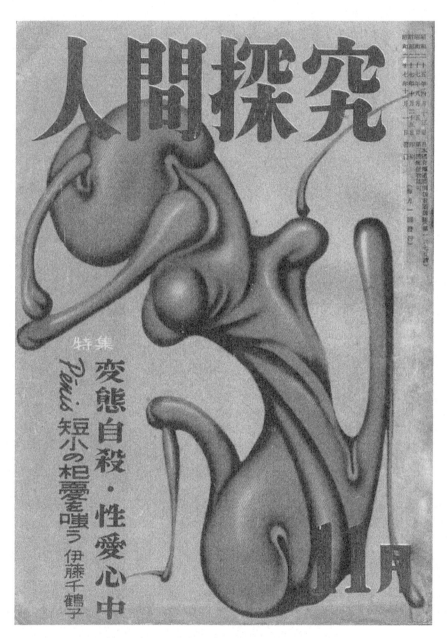

Figure 9.1 The front cover of the 1952 edition of Ningen Tankyû.

male prostitution. However, the most common term for such 'passive' male homosexuals was '*okama*', a slang term for the buttocks (and thereby an allusion to anal sex), which can be traced back to the Tokugawa period (Pflugfelder 1999: 323) and which is still used to refer to homosexuals and other males who behave effeminately today (McLelland 2000: 8). Kabiya, for instance, notes that '[w]hen ordinary people speak about homosexuals in general, they refer to them as *okama*' (discussion cited in Ôta 1957: 421; see also S. Tanaka 1954: 19).

Unlike the premodern paradigm of transvestite prostitution associated with the *onnagata* of the kabuki theatre, contemporary *danshô* were thought to have a predilection for passive anal sex which, although they may have been introduced to it while in the army, was part of their psycho-social make-up. Postwar writers largely followed paradigms established by the sexological writers of the Taisho period (1912–25), who, following the German lead, had attempted to place the sexually perverse into distinct taxonomic categories based upon their supposed psychological or physiological constitutions. The category most commonly used to describe postwar *danshô* was '*urning*' (*ûruningu*), a sexological term that had been devised by German sexologist and homosexual Karl Ulrichs (1825–95) to designate a 'female soul in a male body' and which had achieved widespread currency in prewar sexological writings. *Urning* were considered to have woman-like bodies, small genitalia and an 'innate' (*sententeki*) desire for passive anal sex which led them to turn to prostitution as a way of fulfilling their desires as well as earning a living. They chose to practice as *transgendered* prostitutes because their constitution meant that they were already woman-like and they had a predisposition toward narcissism (*narushishizumu*) and took delight in dressing and making up like a woman.

Both *danshô* and *okama* were transgender categories strongly associated with prostitution. However, a variety of other designations were used by masculine-identified men who wrote in the perverse press about their own same-sex experiences. These include the neologism '*danshokuKA*', which conjoins an alternative reading of the traditional characters '*nanshoku*' (male–male eroticism) and the nominalizing suffix '*-ka*', or '-ist;' hence *danshoku*-ist, or 'practitioner of *danshoku*'. Another term widely used in the immediate postwar years was '*sodomia*', from the English 'sodomite' (or perhaps 'sodomy'), which derived from the Old Testament story of the destruction of the cities of Sodom and Gomorrah, supposedly on account of the poor sexual etiquette of their populations. In the postwar magazines, '*sodomia*' was used not to refer to anal or oral sex (the 'unnatural crime' of sodomy) but to describe male homosexuality in general and could also be used as a designation for individual homosexuals. The term could be used as a noun for individuals identifying themselves as *sodomia* (homosexuals), as an adjective, as in *sodomia* 'interests' (*shumi*) or *sodomii* relations (*kankei*).[2] *Sodomia* could also be used as a group designation or form of address, as in '*sodomia no minna san*', or 'all you homosexuals', and could be conceived of as a state that one could enter into, as in '*sodomia naru*', or 'become sodomitical'.

The English term 'homosexual' was also widely used in transliterated form as *homosekusharu*, often abbreviated to *homo*. The Japanese translation of homosexual into *kanji*, *dôseiai* (literally, same-sex love), which was widely used in the prewar press, also appears in the postwar publications, often conjoined with the suffix '-*sha*', or 'person'. However, *dôseiai* frequently appears with the *rubi* (superscript indicating the pronunciation) '*homo*' written alongside. In fact, *homo*, used as an alternative reading for the characters *dôseiai*, or written separately in the *katakana* script for foreign loanwords, was, by the end of the 1950s, the most common designation describing all men with an interest in same-sex sexual acts.

As the variety of terms – both foreign and indigenous – suggest, in the immediate postwar period it is impossible to discern a pattern in their usage since they are often used interchangeably in the same discussion. For instance, the January 1954 edition of *Fûzoku zôshi* contains an article by Kabiya (1954) entitled '*Danshoku kissaten*', or '*danshoku* coffee shops', which introduces some of the 'brand-new homosexual (*sodomia*) meeting places' where both 'homo' (*homo*) and 'non-homo' (*homo denai*) customers can be found. Kabiya frequently switches between terms, speaking of 'bars for homosexuals', where the designation is *sodomia*; mentioning also *danshokusha*, in which the suffix '-*sha*', or 'person', is conjoined with the traditional term '*danshoku*', hence 'male–male eroticism persons', and elsewhere using '*homo*'.

The ability of the Japanese written language to use characters signifying a certain meaning alongside superscript designating a non-standard pronunciation is a cause of further confusion. While 'traditional' terms such as '*danshoku*' lived on well into the postwar period, the meaning of these terms had obviously shifted. The non-traditional use of nominalizing suffixes such as '-*ka*' (-ist) or '-*sha*' (person), now used to designate specific types of sexual being, occurred alongside the use of *rubi* to suggest new readings of old terms. In the August 1953 edition of *Fûzoku kagaku*, for instance, *danshoku* appears with the reading *sodomia* printed alongside.[3] What nuance this linguistic play added to these terms, or if such nuances were understood in the same way by all readers, is very difficult to discern, but is a clear indication of the hybridity of postwar Japanese sexual categories. Old-fashioned terms such as '*urning*', hangovers from early-twentieth-century German sexology, lived on alongside indigenous terms such as '*okama*' and '*danshô*'. '*Sodomia*', a Latin term which in Europe had strong associations with the Church and was generally used to designate oral or anal acts of 'sodomy', in Japanese became a general rubric for describing all men with same-sex sexual interests. *Sodomia* was frequently used by Japanese men as an identity category and a form of address, and the biblical stigma associated with the term in English seem not to have carried over into Japanese. This very confused situation is evidence of Fran Martin's contention that the circulation of global sexual categories results, not in the displacement of native categories by foreign, but in 'densely overwritten and hyper-dynamic texts caught in a continual process of transformation that occurs with the ongoing accretion of fresh discursive traces' (2003: 251) – a trend illustrated by the popularity of another hybrid term, the '*gei bôi*'.

The rise of the *gei bôi*

The mainly American Allied troops who occupied Japan from 1945 to 1952 and who continued to be based in the country throughout the Korean War included many men with homosexual as well as heterosexual interests. Although the sexual services that were set up during the Occupation to cater for heterosexual men have been well studied (Y. Tanaka 2002; Dower 2000), little attention has been paid to the sexual interactions that took place between members of the Occupation forces and Japanese men. One of the main results of this interaction was the transmission and widespread dissemination in Japanese culture of the English term 'gay' (*gei*) – an interesting example of cultural 'glocalization'.

'Gay', as a signifier for homosexual men, was not widely understood in the US in the 1950s and did not become widespread even in Anglophone societies until the Gay Liberation Movement of the early 1970s. The term had only just established itself as a common referent among homosexual subcultures in the US as a result of the mass mobilization during World War II, which brought a diverse number of homosexual men and women together from all parts of the country and helped to standardize homosexual slang (Faderman 1992: 163; Berube 1990: 117; Cory 1951: 107–8). Yet, as Cory points out, even in the early 1950s the term was 'practically unknown outside of homosexual circles, except for police officers, theatrical groups and a few others' (1951: 108).

Compared with the slow dissemination of the word 'gay' throughout Anglophone societies, where it was to take another twenty-five years to become general currency, the rise of '*gei*' in Japanese was meteoric. 'Gay' (*gei*) entered Japanese immediately after the war via gay men in the Occupation forces who referred to their Japanese partners as '*gei bôi*', or 'gay boys' (Kabiya 1962a: 146), and by the mid-1950s '*gei*', especially as part of the compound '*gei bôi*', was being used in mainstream Japanese media to describe effeminate homosexual men. The sudden popularity of the term was largely due to the fact that '*gei*' (written in the *katakana* syllables used to transcribe foreign loanwords) is a homophone of '*gei*' (written with the character for 'artistic accomplishment' – as in 'geisha'). Gay boys were sometimes spoken of as *gei wo uri* – that is, 'selling *gei*' – and it was easy to make a semantic slip between *geinôjin* (an entertainer, where *gei* is written with the character for artistic accomplishment) and *gei bôi* (where *gei* is a transliteration of gay). *Gei bôi* therefore came to be understood, at least in part, as an occupational category, in a manner similar to *onnagata* or geisha, who were also denizens of Japan's entertainment world.

An illustration of the manner in which *gei bôi* were appreciated for their skills as entertainers can be gleaned from this eye-witness report of a visit to a 'gay bar' in Kanda, Tokyo, named Silver Dragon, published in 1955:

> Once, when cavorting on the second floor of this place, a slim young man who is said to be a master of Japanese dance suddenly stood up, told me to play the record 'The maid of Dôjo temple', and danced a few steps to the rhythm. I recall watching him after everyone there quieted down. Although it was Japanese dance in Western clothes, there was not the slightest oddity about it; it was, on the contrary, a dance full of 'girlish' glamour. However much in demand, this elegance cannot be seen by unrefined company officials at ordinary cabarets in the Ginza area, to which one is taken by the head of a construction company.
>
> (Kabiya 1955)[4]

The superiority of the skills of the *gei bôi* when compared with the abilities of female hostesses was a theme often to be repeated in media discussions of the emerging *gei bôi* culture.

Unlike the *danshô*, who were essentially street prostitutes, the *gei bôi* sought employment in the bar world. In 1957 sexologist Ôta Tenrei published an edited volume entitled *Dai san no sei* (The third sex), based on research he had conducted into the *gei bâ* that had sprung up in Tokyo after the war, pointing out that such bars had not existed before the war. One of the earliest, Yakyoku (Nocturne) in Shinjuku, was reportedly opened as early as 1946 and was much frequented by foreigners (Kabiya 1962b: 102–3; Fujii 1953: 189). In the immediate postwar period, the small bars where young Japanese men went to meet potential partners or clients had been referred to as *danshoku kissaten* (coffee shops) or *sakeba* (drinking spots), but in 1952 a staff member of a Shinjuku *danshoku* bar named Adonis who disliked these old-fashioned designations began to refer to his establishment as a *gei bâ* (gay bar). The term quickly caught on and by the mid-1950s was widely used, even in the mainstream press. While the earliest bars seem to have been more informal, by the early 1950s the bars were staffed by between three and seven professional hosts known as *gei bôi*, who served drinks and provided conversation for customers, often making themselves available for after-hours assignations (Ôta 1957: 306–10).

Ôta discovered nine *gei bâ* in Asakusa, seven in Shinjuku and one each in Ginza, Shimbashi, Ikebukuro, Shibuya and Kanda, a total of twenty-one in all (Ôta 1957: 306). Even compared with a city like New York at this time, this was already a large number. However, according to Ôta's account, most of the bars were modest watering holes with only basic amenities, since earlier attempts to provide more high-class surroundings had failed. This was all to change very suddenly in the next few years, as Japan saw a 'boom' in

お尻のふりかたをご覧ください。「女が女として踊っているよりも、一生懸命女になろうとして踊っているため、色気が出る」と当日出演したある評論家はうなっていました

Figure 9.2 From a 1963 edition of Hyaku man nin no yoru. It describes how gei bôi dance with greater eroticism than biological women. The front cover of the 1952 edition of Ningen Tankyû.

gei life resulting in a proliferation of bars as well as a significant shift in the kind of clientele they attracted.

Japan's original 'gay boom'

In the early 1990s Japanese media were swept up by a 'gay boom' (*gei bûmu*) which saw a rapid escalation in the amount of attention given to minority sexuality issues in the press, on television and in movies. While this develop-ment has been widely discussed in English (see, for example, Hall 2000: 37–43; Lunsing 1997) and Japanese (Yajima 1997; Fushimi 2002), no commentators seem to have noticed that Japan's first gay boom, using precisely this term, had actually taken place thirty-five years previously, in 1958. While in the early 1990s the concept *gei* was beginning to be articu-lated in a more political sense, often in the context of discussion of a *gei* and *rezubian* 'movement' (*undo*), the late 1950s use of this term was quite different and is a clear illustration of how the meanings of terms can shift radically over even short periods of time.

The most significant event that enabled the rapid expansion of the *gei* subculture took place in 1957, when, after years of campaigning, women's groups forced the government to pass an anti-prostitution bill. As many businesses that had relied on heterosexual prostitution closed down or restructured their activities, space was opened up in former red-light areas for new sex-related businesses, including those catering to homosexual men and cross-dressers. Since the law was targeted at the open and conspicuous world of mainstream heterosexual prostitution, its impact upon more covert homosexual practice was less severe and to an extent allowed homosexual operations to move into former heterosexual red-light areas. Since neither homosexuality nor cross-dressing was illegal in Japan and homosexual meeting places were not raided by the police, as was routine in Anglophone societies, Japanese *gei bôi* were able to go about their business without fear of police harassment. The only restriction on *gei bâ* intermittently enforced by the police was the 1948 Entertainment and Amusement Trade Law, which ostensibly forbade trading between midnight and sunrise. Consequently, Shinjuku Ni-Chôme (Shinjuku's second ward), which had been a hetero-sexual red-light district, was gradually taken over by *gei* businesses from this time and now houses the largest collection of bars catering to a homosexual clientele in Japan (Ôtsuka 1995: 14–19; Fushimi 2002: 247–58).

While in 1957 there had only been twenty or so *gei bâ* in Tokyo, catering primarily to a clientele of homosexual men, in 1958 the mainstream press began talking about a 'gay boom' (*gei bûmu*) that had seen the number of *gei bâ* shoot up to nearly sixty, largely due to the crossover appeal of these estab-lishments to a clientele outside the homosexual world (*Shûkan taishû* 1958: 24). *Gei bôi* were no longer catering to an exclusively male (or homosexual) clientele but also provided companionship for women. Ôta points out that, while a large majority of the *gei bôi* working in the bars were by temperament *'urning'*, there were also boys who were not homosexual (*homo de nai*), including students and other 'semi-professionals' who simply worked for a time in the bars in order to earn money (1957: 308–9) and were happy to entertain both male and female clients. Indeed, by the early 1960s evening editions of the tabloid papers regularly featured over twenty advertisements recruiting 'boys' or 'beautiful boys' to work as hosts in private clubs. Known as 'assisted boys' (*enjô sareru shônen*) (Satô 1960), these youths anticipated the 'compensated dating' (*enjo kôsai*) schemes later devised by Japanese high school girls by some quarter of a century.

The growing popularity of the *gei bâ* among a more mainstream clientele makes it difficult to equate these institutions with the developing gay bar subculture in the US and other Western countries. As Nancy Achilles points out, widespread sodomy laws and restrictions on indecent behaviour (such as members of the same sex dancing together) made it difficult for gay bars to advertise their presence in the 1950s and early 1960s in the US, and news of their opening tended to be passed on via word of mouth (1967: 232–3). Esther Newton (1979), in *Mother Camp*, an investigation of 1960s drag shows in the US, does draw a distinction between 'gay bars' where homosexuals met and the more upmarket 'tourist clubs' which put on drag shows for a predominantly heterosexual clientele, but the latter were comparatively few and remained largely subcultural, with little impact on mainstream culture. In Japan, however, the early 1960s witnessed widespread media interest in the *gei bôi* phenomenon.

For instance, an unsigned article in the April 1963 edition of the magazine *Ura mado* refers to the 'touristization' (*kankôka*) that was sweeping through Japan's *gei bâ* scene, wherein 'homosexuals' (*homo*) were being displaced by 'ordinary customers' (*futsû no kyaku*), including many women.[5] An article in *Fûzoku kitan*, also published in April 1963, warns homosexual men who visit 'gay bars' in the expectation of making assignations with the boys working there that some boys also 'service' women.[6] The author suggests that when referring to such boys *'panpan bôi'* (after the *panpan* girls who catered to GIs during the Occupation) would be a better designation; although he does point out that, rather than 'servicing' female clients 'as a man', the boys 'receive caresses like pets'. Transgender performer Miwa Akihiro reported that at the beginning of the 1950s *gei bâ* were rather furtive establishments where customers could be seen passing to and fro waiting for a quiet moment to slip inside (Itô 2001: 2), but by the end of the decade such bars had become avant-garde places of entertainment for a more mainstream clientele.

In 1958 the popular magazine *Shûkan taishû* (Weekly popular culture) wrote about Japan's 'gay boom' (*gei bûmu*), describing it as 'the best in the world' (*sekai ichi*). Unlike the previous category of *danshô*, who were street prostitutes working by night, *gei bôi* were considered to have 'evolved' a new kind of 'gay style' (*gei sutairu*) – one that could 'parade itself in an imposing manner even in daylight'. Communities of *gei bôi* were developing around *gei bâ* all over Japan, estimates running to 2500 in Tokyo, 1000 in Osaka, 500 each in Kyoto and Kobe and another 1000 or so spread throughout the rest of Japan (*Shûkan taishû* 1958: 25). These reports encouraged the conception that *gei* was very much a commercial category, with there being 'in excess of 5000 persons to whom the name gay (*gei*) is applied professionally' (*shoku-gyôteki ni*) (*Shûkan taishû* 1958).

While the 'feminine' style preferred by *danshô* had been a retrospective one, consisting of women's kimono and wigs in which long hair was tied up in a chignon reminiscent of geisha, the *gei bôi* were more contemporary, even pioneering, in their self-presentation. They had little interest in passing as women and did not see themselves as female impersonators, considering their androgynous (*chûsei*), boyish style to be 'a new disposition' (*atarashii keikô*) more in keeping with the modern world (Satô 1960: 60). *Gei bôi* were mostly in their late teens and early twenties, and, although born during the war, would have remembered little from this period. They had no nostalgia for Japan's imperial past but looked abroad instead for inspiration when fashioning their identities. In the late 1950s *gei bôi* were sporting the short-style 'Cecile cut'[7] popularized by actress Jean Seberg, the androgynous star of *Saint Joan* (1957), *Bonjour tristesse* (1958) and *A Bout de souffle* (1959). They wore light make-up and dressed in newly fashionable slacks, under which they wore women's pantyhose. They also had a preference for perfume, especially Chanel no. 5. Jean Seberg represented a new, more androgynous model for women than had previously been popular and the *gei bôi* saw themselves as 'cultural women' (*bunka josei*); that is, they had acquired their femininity by incorporating particular sartorial codes and modes of behaviour associated with cultural constructions of the feminine. *Gei bôi* pointed out that, while the basic categories of 'man' and 'woman' had not changed since the time of Adam and Eve, they represented a new 'sexual idea' (*sei kannen*) – the cultural woman who constituted a third sex (*dai san no sei*).

While the *gei bôi* were clearly keen to differentiate themselves from the *danshô*, both identities illustrate how the feminine was not reducible to the female body, but could be seen as a set of practices able to be expressed by either male- or female-bodied individuals. The femininity of the *gei bôi* was, however, by definition modern and both forward and outward looking. The *danshô*, in continuing to dress and wear their hair like 'traditional' Japanese women, had carried over prewar modes of transgender identity and perfor-mance, but when it came to the performance of femininity *gei bôi* presented themselves as quintessentially modern. Matsumoto Toshio's 1969 movie *Bara no sôretsu* (Funeral parade of roses), the vehicle that launched *gei bôi* 'Peter' on his career, features a fight scene between Peter and his *gei bôi* companions and a gang of real girls, whom they dismiss as *tada no onna* – 'merely women' – in a move recalling earlier paradigms which regarded kabuki *onna-gata* as more accomplished performers of femininity than female actresses.[8] Following Judith Butler, we may ask whether this is 'a colonizing "appropriation" of the feminine' – a question which only has moral force in a belief system which 'assumes that the feminine belongs to women' (1990: 122). Historically, this has not been the case in Japan, where sexual tension had long been generated by the 'dissonant juxtaposition' of feminine gender performance played out with male bodies. *Bara no sôretsu* itself plays with this dissonance in a scene where Peter (or Eddy, as he is named in the movie) and his *gei bôi* companions enter a male toilet and stand together at the urinals – much to the consternation of the other male users. As Newton points out, 'drag questions the "naturalness" of the sex-role system *in toto*; if sex-role behaviour can be achieved by the "wrong" sex, it logically follows that it is in reality also achieved, not inherited by the "right" sex' (1979: 103). What Peter and the 'real' girls are fighting over is not therefore some residual or authentic expression of an inner femininity, but rather the right to enact femininity as a style, or even 'way' of being in the world, a project to which biology has little to contribute.

Although *gei bôi* stressed their modernity, they had much in common with their prewar counterparts and their popularity was enabled by enduring assumptions about gender, particularly as it was played out in the entertainment world, which had survived into the postwar period. Drawing upon previous paradigms of transgender performance developed in the kabuki theatre, there was a tendency to view *gei* not so much as a sexual orientation but more as a kind of artistic skill. The fact that, unlike *danshô*, *gei bôi* were not primarily prostitutes but worked in the bars taking care of and providing entertainment for guests – similar to female hostesses in regular bars – enabled them to develop skills as performers. One aspect of this performance was heightened transgendered behaviour, a trend that accelerated in the next decade. In 1961, for instance, *Fûzoku kitan* (1961: 63) described the 'flourishing' business for 'geisha boys' at high-class restaurants in Tokyo, who, dressing as *onnagata*, performed for an elite clientele. Also in the early 1960s, nightclubs such as Tokyo's Golden Akasaka were frequently staging 'imitation girl contests' which gave contestants drawn from the country's *gei bâ* the opportunity to compete with each others for prizes (*Hyakuman nin no yoru* 1963). In both cases *gei bôi* (homosexual) elides into geisha *bôi* (entertainer) where the stress is not on sexual orientation so much as artistic performance.

Hence, at a time when homophile organizations in the US were keen to stress the 'normality' of the homosexual, developing a quasi-ethnic understanding of 'gay identity' based on citizenship and rights (Epstein 1998; Plummer 1995: 90), Japanese *gei bôi* actually embraced paradigms which emphasized their difference. By the late 1960s emerging US gay activism was characterized by its militancy and chauvinism, rejecting effeminate gender performance and 'discredit[ing] camp and other evasive techniques' (Levine 1998: 26). Transgender paradigms of homosexual identity expression were rejected in favour of a more masculine or at times hypermasculine mode of self-presentation (Levine 1998).

Japan's *gei* culture was, however, going in entirely the opposite direction, capitalizing on the *gei bôi*'s exotic difference. Nineteenth-century German notions positing male homosexuals as a separate 'third sex', contemporary European codes of androgynous beauty and traditional Japanese understandings of transgender performance were fused to create the figure of the *gei bôi*. Japan's *gei bôi* were cultural innovators who, via their role as entertainers, were able to have an impact on society far wider than the confines of the homosexual subculture and whose influence was to remain strong until the early 1980s.

Conclusion

During the late 1950s Japan underwent a 'gay boom' which saw an explosion of homosexual discussion and representation in the popular media unparalleled by developments in any Anglophone society until the early 1970s. '*Gei*' had already been established as a term for effeminate young men who worked in the entertainment industry by the mid-1950s – some twenty years prior to the adoption of the term 'gay' in English-language media. While '*gei*' is certainly related to the use of 'gay' in English – this latter term had *itself* only won out as a preferred term for self-designation within US homosexual communities during the war and was not picked up by mainstream media until the early 1970s. Hence, while it is clear that Japan's encounter with the Allied Forces during the Occupation resulted very quickly in the generation of new types of sexual discourse and the proliferation of new modes of homosexual practice and identity, these Japanese subcultures were very different from the developing 'gay' subcultures in the US at this time, not least in terms of their apparent openness and the freedom with which they were discussed in the press.

While in the postwar period in the US 'gay' was associated with the development of essentialist, masculine male homosexual identities, in Japan the development of '*gei*' as a primarily *transgender* and also a *commercial* category encouraged a movement in the opposite direction. The convenient homophony of *gei* as 'gay' and *gei* as 'artistic accomplishment' only served to reinforce the hybridized manner in which this term came to be used in Japanese to signify a new kind of sexual being: the *gei bôi* who was defined more in terms of his role as entertainer than in terms of his choice of sexual partner. Consequently, the Japanese *gei bôi* was as different from the American gay man as he was different from the *danshô* or male prostitute who had preceded him.

However, in the mid-1980s two simultaneous developments led to a gradual revision in the way *gei* was understood in the Japanese media: the founding in Japan of gay and lesbian rights' organizations which drew upon a now international understanding of 'gay' as a self-referent for largely gender-normative homosexual men; and the emergence of the term 'newhalf',[9] which was to become the new identity category for effeminate homosexual men who lived and worked in Japan's bar and entertainment world. The result was that by the time of Japan's second 'gay boom', which swept the media in the early 1990s, *'gei*, had displaced *'homo'*, emerging as the most common self-referent among homosexual men in Japan. To understand this as a process whereby indigenous Japanese categories of sexual identity were displaced by foreign borrowings, however, would be to efface the complex history of the term *'gei'* in Japanese.

The fact that the *gei bôi* was able to emerge so rapidly as a 'new sexual idea' in the postwar period was in large part due to the fact that prewar nationalist notions of embodiment had collapsed along with the government's rigid regulatory regime at the war's end. The ideology of the prewar regime was so discredited that space was opened up in the ruins of Japan's cities for the celebration of 'the raw, erotic energy of Japanese bodies' (Igarashi 2000: 48), enabling the development of new forms of hetero- and homosexual practice and identity. The *gei bôi* rejected the aggressive masculine gender performance and the procreative imperative of the prewar regime, but, instead of aligning himself with discredited modes of 'traditional' femininity embodied by the *danshô*, he sought to embody the new androgynous ideal of beauty emerging in Europe, which was to dominate the cultural scene of the late 1960s. The hybridized gender performance of Japan's *gei bôi*, then, which drew upon earlier paradigms of the transgender entertainer, coupled with new Western ideals of androgyny, is an instance of what Iwabuchi terms 'transformative local practices' which result in 'the formation of non-Western indigenized modernity' (2002: 40) and is further illustration of Fran Martin's observation that in modern societies sexual discourse is unavoidably 'polyglottic and translational' (2003: 249). The *gei bôi*, like the American gay man, can therefore be seen as a mode of subjectivity enabled by changes taking place in postwar modernity, but *gei bôi* is an indigenous Japanese category which arose in relation to local Japanese conditions, not some copy of a Western original.

Notes

1   See, for instance, the various responses posted to Dennis Altman's (1996) 'On global queering', *Australian Humanities Review*, July. Online. HTTP:http://www. lib.latrobe.edu.au/AHR/archive/Issue-July-1996/altman.html (accessed 4 June 2003).

2   *Sodomiya* occurs in the February 1954 edition of *Fûzoku kagaku* (p. 103), whereas *sodomia shumi* occurs in a letter reproduced in the November 1953 edition *Fûzoku kagaku* (p. 168). The term is also occasionally spelt as *'sodomii'*, as in the October edition of *Fûzoku kagaku* (p. 89), which speaks of *'sodomii kankei'*, and in the September 1954 edition of *Fûzoku zôshi* (p. 102). The rendering *'sodomisuto'* also occurs, although rarely; for example, see the reader's letter in the August 1953 edition of *Fûzoku zôshi* (p. 60).

3   *'Sodomia wa ryûkô suru'* (p. 40).

4   A complete translation of this article by Todd Henry can be found in Mark McLelland, Katsuhiko Suganuma and James Welker (eds) *Queer Voices from Japan*, Lanham: Lexington Press (in press).

5   pp. 138–9.

6   p. 125.

7   Cecile was the name of Seberg's character sporting this hairstyle in *Bonjour tristesse*.
8   Since there was no indigenous tradition of women actors, women's roles in many of Japan's early films, from 1909 to 1919, were played by male actors trained as *onnagata*, which led to lively debates in the media about the relative abilities of male and female actors to perform as 'women'.
9   In 1982 Betty, the *mama-san* of Betty's Mayonnaise, an Osaka *gei bâ*, introduced a new term, '*nyûhâfu*' (new half), as a designation for transgender performers. 'Half', or '*hâfu*' in Japanese, is used to signify individuals of mixed race, usually Japanese and Caucasian, and Betty said of herself that 'I'm half man and half woman, therefore I'm a *new half*'. Like '*gei bôî*', '*nyûhâfu*' was a trendy fusion of two English words, but with a very specific Japanese meaning, and it soon caught on in the press and began to be adopted as a self-designation by many transgender performers (McLelland 2005: 198).

Bibliography

Achilles, N. (1967) 'The development of the homosexual bar as an institution', in J. Gagnon and W. Simon (eds) *Sexual Deviance*, New York: Harper & Row.

Altman, D. (2001) *Global Sex*, Sydney: Allen & Unwin.

Berube, A. (1990) *Coming Out Under Fire: the history of gay men and women in world war two*, New York: The Free Press.

Butler, J. (1990) *Gender Trouble: feminism and the subversion of identity*, New York: Routledge.

Cory, D. W. (1951) *The Homosexual in America: a subjective approach*, New York: Greenberg.

Dower, J. (2000) *Embracing Defeat: Japan in the wake of World War II*, New York: W. W. Norton.

Epstein, S. (1998) 'Gay politics, ethnic identity: the limits of social constructionism', in P. Nardi and B. Schneider (eds) *Social Perspectives in Lesbian and Gay Studies: a reader*, London: Routledge.

Faderman, L. (1992) *Odd Girls and Twilight Lovers: a history of lesbian life in twentieth-century America*, New York: Penguin.

Fujii, A. (1953) 'Kantô, Kansai ni okeru dôseiaisha no shûgôchitai (Homosexual meeting zones in the Tokyo and Osaka areas)', *Fûzoku zôshi*, December: 188–93.

Fushimi N. (2002) '*Gei' to iu keiken* (The experience called being 'gay'), Tokyo: Potto shuppan.

Fûzoku kitan (1961) 'Geisha bôi no ryôtei wa daihanjô (Geisha boy restaurants are flourishing)', February: 63.

Hall, J. (2000) 'Japan's progressive sex: male homosexuality, national competition and the cinema', *Journal of Homosexuality*, vol. 39, nos 3/4: 31–82.

Hyakuman nin no yoru (1963) 'Ware koso wa dansei biinasu no. 1 (We are indeed the no.1 male Venuses)', February, unnumbered photo section.

Igarashi, Y. (2000) *Narratives of War in Postwar Japanese Culture, 1945–1970*, Princeton, NJ: Princeton University Press.

Ishida, H., McLelland M. and Murakami T. (2005) 'The origins of "Queer Studies" in postwar Japan', in M. McLelland and R. Dasgupta (eds) *Genders, Transgenders and Sexualities in Japan*, London: Routledge.

Itô B. (2001) *Bara hiraku hi wo: Barazoku to tomo ni ayunda 30 nen* (Until the rose opens: 30 years walking alongside *Barazoku*), Tokyo: Kawade shobô.

Iwabuchi, K. (2002) *Recentering Globalization: popular culture and Japanese transnationalism*, Durham, NC: Duke University Press.

Kabiya K. (1954) 'Danshoku kissaten (Homosexual coffee shops)', *Fûzoku zôshi*, January: 146–51.

——(1955) 'Gei bâ no seitai sono II (The gay bar mode of life part 2)', *Amatoria*, July: 38–46.

——(1962a) '"Gei bâ" to iu go no meimeisha (The person who christened 'gay bars')', *Fûzoku kitan*, February: 146.

——(1962b) 'Gei masutâ kara kiita koto (Things I heard from a gay bar owner)', *Fûzoku kitan*, December: 102–3.

Levine, M. (1998) *Gay Macho: the life and death of the homosexual clone*, New York: New York University Press.

Lunsing, W. (1997) 'Gay boom in Japan: changing views of homosexuality?', *Thamyris*, vol. 4, no. 2, Autumn: 267–93.

McLelland, M. (2000) *Male Homosexuality in Modern Japan: cultural myths and social realities*, London: RoutledgeCurzon.

——(2005) *Queer Japan from the Pacific War to the Internet Age*, Lanham, MD: Rowman & Littlefield.

Martin, F. (2003) *Situating Sexualities: queer representation in Taiwanese fiction, film and public culture*, Hong Kong: Hong Kong University Press.

Newton, E. (1979) *Mother Camp: female impersonators in America*, Chicago: University of Chicago Press.

Ôta, Tenrei (ed.) (1957) *Dai san no sei: sei no hôkai?* (The third sex: the breakdown of sex?), Tokyo: Myôki shuppan.

Ôtsuka, T. (1995) *Ni-chôme kara uroko: Shinjuku geisutoriito zakkichô* (Ni-chôme rediscovered: notes on Shinjuku's gay street), Tokyo: Shûeisha.

Pflugfelder, G. (1999) *Cartographies of Desire: male–male sexuality in Japanese discourse, 1600–1950*, Berkeley, CA: University of California Press.

Plummer, K. (1995) *Telling Sexual Stories: power, change and social worlds*, London: Routledge.

Satô E. (1960) 'Bishônen no ie: tambôki (Beautiful-boy houses: a report)', *Fûzoku kitan*, August: 58–63.

Shûkan taishû (1958) '5000nin no shitsugyôsha: gendai no kikeiji gei bôi no SOS (5000 unemployed: an SOS from today's freaks of nature – gay boys)', 18 August: 24–7.

Tanaka, S. (chair) (1954) 'Dai ni zadankai: ôsaka – Tôkyô o kataru (Second roundtable: talking about Osaka and Tokyo)', *Adonis*, no. 17; 17–20.

Tanaka Y. (2002) *Japan's Comfort Women: sexual slavery and prostitution during World War II and the US occupation*, London: Routledge.

Yajima, M. (1997) *Dansei dôseiaisha no raifuhisutorii* (Male homosexuals' life histories), Tokyo: Gakubunsha.

10 Subcultural unconsciousness in Japan

The war and Japanese contemporary artists

Yoshitaka Môri

Introduction

> How are we to arrive at a knowledge of the unconscious? It is of course only as something conscious that we know it, after it has undergone transformation or translation into something conscious. Psychoanalytic work shows us every day that translation of this kind is possible. In order that this should come about, the person under analysis must overcome certain resistances . . . the same resistances as those which, earlier, made material concerned into something repressed by rejecting it from the conscious.
>
> (Freud 1995/1915: 572–3)

The twenty-first century has seen the birth of a new fine arts movement in Japan which the art critic Sawaragi Noi coined Japanese Neo Pop (JNP) (Sawaragi 1998, 2002).[1] JNP is an artists movement, which was initiated in the 1990s by artists born in the 1960s. It owes its creative force to pop subculture, in particular animation films (*anime*), comics (*manga*) and special effects films. Some of the artists, such as Murakami Takashi, Aida Makoto and Yonobe Kenji, have been well accepted not only in Japan but also in the Western art market, which enthusiastically looks for new talent.[2]

JNP is intriguing to me, first of all, because it raises a question concerning the distinction between high art and popular culture. It suggests that the distinction between the two in Japan is always blurred and has not been strictly established in the same way as in Western art. JNP artists are trying to revise Japanese art history, which has generally marginalized and excluded pop culture.

I would like to examine JNP, second, because it proposes a new relationship between culture and the national. Thanks to the current prevalence of Japanese popular culture in the world, the stereotypical images of Japaneseness, represented by Mt Fuji, geisha, Noh, kabuki and *ukiyoe*, have been dramatically replaced by new icons of popular culture, such as comics, animation, video games and so on. JNP can be situated within this context of the changing nature of the definition of Japanese culture.

Third, I am interested in the way in which ideological formations lie behind the success of JNP both in Japan and in the West. Two issues in particular will be addressed. My first concern is how the use of war images relates to the establishment of a national identity through understanding World War II. As we will see, JNP artists often use images of war, the immediate postwar period, atomic bombs and air raids. Next I will examine a concept named 'super-Flat' or 'superflat', which a leading figure, Murakami Takashi, proposed alongside the Derridian critic Azuma Hiroki, as a theory that analyses JNP and other contemporary *otaku*-related culture (Murakami 2000; Azuma 2001).[3] It seems to me that the concept of 'superflat' is not merely a theoretical framework explaining contemporary Japanese culture, but rather one of the ideological formations which have appeared under postmodern conditions since the 1980s.

Through the analysis above, I would like to consider the current relationship between the globalization of artistic culture and the emergence of new and 'authentic' Japanese national culture. It can be stated that globalization produces new transnational hybrid cultures which are created not only by the 'culture industry' but also through voluntary and often international cultural exchange among artists, musicians and audiences. At the same time, and paradoxically, through the globalizing process authentic and often stereotyped 'national' culture is reinvented as a new cultural commodity. This is a product of the discourse of multiculturalism which essentializes a cultural identity within national boundaries and distributes it in the international market. Examining the 'authentic' and the 'national', I illustrate this new culture's nationalist limitations and demonstrate the possibility of an alternative transnational culture.

JNP and Murakami Takashi

Let me start my argument by looking at art works by JNP artists and their backgrounds. I would like to focus on Murakami Takashi as a central figure, because he has provocatively offered some theoretical frameworks for JNP and he is the most commercially successful artist.[4]

Today, Murakami is known as an artist influenced by Japanese subculture such as comics, animation and special effects films. His paintings are full of Japanese cartoon-like characters. For instance, one of the pop icons which he created, DOB, is a character designed like Disney's Mickey Mouse or Sega's Sonic. He has also produced three-dimensional figure 'sculptures' of cute hypersexual girls by transforming animation mania's male heterosexual fantasies into art works. In short, the characteristic feature of his recent works is basically to transform an expressional form of Japanese popular culture into fine art works.

Murakami also presents himself as a kind of pop icon and is extremely adept at manipulating the media. The news that his work was priced at $624,000 at a Sotheby auction was reported as illustrative of the fact that

Japanese popular culture is now recognized as fashionable. He also worked with Louis Vuitton, designing his own version of their merchandise, and often appears on TV chat shows as a celebrity on the New York art scene. His performative activities, along with his art, have made him a provocative figure who claims that the distinction between high art and low culture can be radically resolved.

It would be helpful to look at Murakami's career to understand his theoretical background. Born in 1962, he grew up in a period of high economic growth in Japan. This was a time when Japanese visual culture was being increasingly homogenized, thanks to the medium of television in particular. Murakami was not exceptional, in that he spent his time with TV *anime*, *manga*, special effects films and other visual pop culture media.[5]

Murakami was educated as a traditional Japanese art (*nihonga*) painter and was granted a PhD from Tokyo National University of Fine Arts and Music, the most established national university in Japan. At college he tried to pursue a contemporary avant-garde style of Japanese painting, while learning traditional methodology. He eventually discovered a continuity between traditional Japanese paintings and *anime* and *manga*, in that they share the specific aesthetics of two-dimensional expression, which he would call later 'superflat'.

Murakami's cultural experience is more or less shared among the JNP artists of his generation. They love both contemporary fine art and popular culture. In most cases, however, while they were art students the preference for popular culture was repressed in the educational institutions of art in which they studied. JNP is unique because it is the first Japanese art movement which openly expresses influences emanating from subculture and popular culture in its artistic practices.

Revising Japanese art history: the war paintings, visual pop culture and JNP

Sawaragi Noi, working with Murakami as an advisory critic, is a key theorist of JNP. According to Sawaragi, the impossibility of making the distinction between high art and low culture in Japan is not a new phenomenon, and indeed forms the very nature of Japanese art, since World War II in particular (Sawaragi 1998). He suggested that this inability is caused by the fact that Japan has not experienced a proper process of Western modernization, and he called Japan 'a bad place (*warui basho*)' where all modern categories are easily resolved (Sawaragi 1998: 8–26).

He began his argument in his seminal book, *Nihon/Gendai/Bijutsu* (Japan/Modern/Art), by discussing the difficulty of writing a chronological history of Japanese modern art. The slash marks between 'Japan', 'Modern' and 'Art' represent, he says, this problem (Sawaragi 1998: 8–9). Even if superficially a lineage of Japanese contemporary art seems to follow Western art history, it is more like a series of simulations or kitsch of Western art and therefore only repeats itself cyclically within a closed circle; hence it cannot progress. In his argument, the history of Japanese art is a series of *ahistorical* events in a 'bad place'. He did not, however, only criticize Japanese art, but instead, tried to re-establish the possibility of Japanese art under these particular conditions, by de/re-categorizing all cultural elements of fine art and popular culture.

Interestingly, Sawaragi attributed the *ahistorical* condition of Japanese art to the activities of artists who either voluntarily or reluctantly drew *Senso-ga* (war paintings) or *Senso-kiroku-ga* (war report paintings) during World War II (Sawaragi 1998: 322–49). Japanese military authorities mobilized most of the contemporary established artists to draw propaganda paintings which would report and celebrate the war, sometimes by sending the artists as war correspondents with troops. Hundreds of paintings were produced by most of the established artists at the time.

After the war, most war painters faced severe criticism, often even accusing each other of having supported the military authorities. The war painter purge forced some to stop being artists and others to keep silent on their paintings. The memory of the war paintings was totally repressed among contemporary artists. Although a large collection of the war paintings gathered by General Headquarters (GHQ) was returned to the Japanese government in the mid-1970s and has been kept at the National Museum of Modern Art, Tokyo, they have not been open to the public, partly because the museum did not want to be involved in political debates and partly because the artists' families feared the renewal of accusations against the artists. The issue of war paintings has been the biggest taboo in postwar Japanese art history. Sawaragi suggested that the war paintings have to be accurately situated at the very beginning of postwar Japanese art history, because collective amnesia over war painting is the very cause of the *ahistorical* condition of Japanese modern art.

The re-evaluation of the war paintings is not, however, Sawaragi's original idea. In 1977 an artist, Kikuhata Mokuma, who had initiated the neo-dada-styled Japanese avant-garde art movement known as *kyushu-ha* in the 1960s, published a provocative book entitled *Fujita yo nemure* (Rest in peace, Fujita). Focusing on the most established artist, Fujita Tsuguharu, in the book, Kikuhata (1977) tried to re-evaluate the war paintings from an artist's perspective.

Fujita Tsuguharu (known as Tsuguji, or later Leonard in Europe and the US) is one of the best examples of the war painters in the sense that he was the most established artist, domestically and internationally, and his deep commitment to the war paintings has confused Japanese art history. Fujita was born in 1886, moved to Paris in 1913 and became successful as one of the central figures of the Ecole de Paris in the 1920s. After coming back to Japan with international fame in 1929, during World War II he was sent to battlefields in China and South Asia with troops and drew several battle scenes. He was severely criticized for this by other artists after the war, moved back to Paris in 1949, acquired French nationality in 1955 and died in Switzerland in 1968.[6]

By and large, there were two different political positions concerning Fujita's war paintings before Kikuhata's publication. Some accused Fujita of commitment to the war. It is said that he left Japan mainly because *Nihon bijutsu kai* (the Japanese Artists' Organization) asked him to take responsibility for war crimes (because he painted pictures that supported the war effort) and not to work in the Japanese art world. This position was, if often reluctantly, largely shared in the art world because Fujita did not publicly apologize for his political commitment. A minority of close friends and family, on the other hand, argued that Fujita was forced to draw the war paintings against his will and that it was impossible to refuse to support the war at the time.

In any case, his perceived commitment to former Japanese imperialism raised an intense debate concerning art, politics, the war, peace, artists' political responsibility and their morals. Even though these two positions were too politically polarized to generate any productive debate, they shared a certain aesthetic understanding of Fujita's (and others') war paintings: neither took the war paintings seriously as Japanese fine art in an aesthetic sense.

Kikuhata proposed a third way to understand Fujita's paintings. He saw potential in Fujita's war paintings, in particular those which were drawn during the late war period when Japan was almost defeated. Kikuhata suggested that Fujita drew the war paintings in the beginning because the military authorities asked him to do so, but eventually he did so only for the sake of his creative aesthetics. This does not mean that he simply celebrated the war as the other war artists did, but that he went beyond the original purpose of the war paintings.

In fact, his late war paintings depicted all the bloody cruelty, carnage and death of devastated battlefields in Southeast Asia. They were painted with dark brown colours in such a documentary-like, realistic manner that they created in viewers deep repugnance. Unlike other war paintings at the time, it is hard to see Fujita's works as a celebration of the war because they were so offensive. In fact, some military authorities criticized Fujita's works because the paintings might have discouraged people as they were too real and brutal (Kikuhata 1977: 37).

Kikuhata suggested that Fujita drew his war paintings in a way that was beyond moral judgment of whether he was either pro-war or anti-war. That is, he could not overlook the theatre of war as the best motif for his expression of what the war meant to him. From today's perspective, Fujita's paintings of, for instance, Japanese soldiers killing US soldiers in chaotic battlefields are so real that they can be understood as a kind of anti-war painting.

Kikuhata's argument is fascinating to me, not because he insisted on the autonomy of art, but because he discovered the condition of autonomy only through the process of negating moral judgment. To Kikuhata, Fujita's work has to be positioned at the very centre of high modernity in Japanese art history. There is no priority for art or politics, the beautiful or the good. They are tangled in a complicated, conspiratorial but sometimes contradictory way.

About thirty years after Kikuhata's argument, Sawaragi found continuity between the war paintings and JNP's works. Certainly some of the war paintings, and Fujita's works in particular, show significant similarity of expression to that found in today's animation films and comics. Realistic or even hyper-real two-dimensional drawings of war scenes, which are often dramatically aestheticized, seem to share a common artistic consciousness with contemporary Japanese subcultural visual expressions, which are full of images of violence and cruelty.

The JNP artists take war images as their creative motifs. For instance, Murakami made three-dimensional objects in his early work by using tiny plastic models of soldiers, which Japanese children often played with in the 1960s and 1970s. Later, he sometimes appropriated images of atomic bombs into his cheerful cartoon-like drawings. *Time-bokan Sexual Violet* is the best example. It is a painting which depicts a human skull as if it were the mushroom cloud of an atomic bomb. Although the work looks comical and even funny at first glance, it nevertheless reminds the viewer of the cruelty of war. A mushroom, a motif which is repeatedly found in his works, obviously connotes sexual desire, representative of the phallus as well as the memory of atomic bombs in Hiroshima and Nagasaki.

Murakami is not the exception. As Sawaragi suggested, the JNP artists are overshadowed by their imaginary experiences of the war. Yanobe Kenji's project *Atom Suites*, in which he wanders about while wearing a bright yellow anti-radiation suit, is filmed in ruined Chernobyl. It is easy to see the association with Japanese experience of the atomic bombs. Aida is more clearly conscious of the history of the war paintings. In a series of his works entitled *Sensoga Returns*, he parodied the style of the war paintings and drew a fictional Japanese air raid on New York City and a war between Japan and Korea acted out by cute girls in high school uniforms.

The JNP artists are unique not only because they are openly influenced by contemporary popular subculture, but also because they are the first group that, within the context of Japanese art history, has publicly referred to their own relationships with the memory of war. One question still remains. How can we fill in the gap between the war paintings in World War II and JNP's works? Since the provocative work of Kikuhata in the 1970s, artists, art critics and art historians collectively have remained silent on the war paintings, although there have been numerous peace or anti-war art works.

Sawaragi argued that the missing link can be found in the field of pop subculture: while the memory of war painting has been repressed in the mainstream of fine art, it has survived in the form of subcultural imagination. He suggested:

Why do we remember 'the world's end' and 'the ruins/the ruins of fire (*haikyo/yakeato*)' subconsciously, although we have not seen or experienced them? I have no clear answer. But the one thing I can say is that post-war Japanese repeatedly experienced, more or less, 'the world's end' and 'the ruins/the ruins of fire' through pop culture such as TV programs, films, comics and animations; *Godzilla*, being wakened by radioactivity after a long sleep, destroys Tokyo; *Spaceship Yamato* tries to save the earth which is dying from radiation; The Metropolis is devastated in 'Psychic Wars' in *AKIRA*; Children are forced to join commandoes as a 'student mobilization' in the war against unidentified 'apostles' in *Neon Genesis Evangelion*. We have seen that Tokyo and Japan have been destroyed many times and experienced cruel wars with heroes who try to survive in the 'subcultural imagination'.

(Sawaragi 2002: 388)

It is not accidental that comic and film artists repeatedly applied images of the war in their works. Most of the artists in the early postwar period admittedly tried to incorporate their wartime experiences into their works. *Godzilla*, released in 1954, is the best example in the sense that the ruined image of Tokyo directly came from the image of Tokyo after the air raids during the war. The film's anti-war and anti-nuclear weapons political message is very clear when we see *Godzilla* awaken after a nuclear test.[7] It is not difficult to find more cases. In the book *Bakushinchi no geijutsu 1999–2001* (The art at Ground Zero 1999–2001), Sawaragi pointed out the fact that a special effects film artist, Narita Toru, who became famous for the success of the series *Ultraman,* made by Tsuburaya Production, was impressed and influenced by Fujita's war paintings (Sawaragi 2002: 400). To sum up, Sawaragi's project on JNP was to reconstruct a new linear history of Japanese art by starting with the war painting, incorporating subcultural works into it and then ending at JNP. His perspective offers a new idea of art history which is different from the existing Japanese postwar art history that we know.

Subculture, JNP and unconscious nationalism in pop culture

I appreciate Sawaragi's detailed examination of the relation between popular culture and JNP, and his rediscovery of the war paintings, which have remained untouched since Kikuhata's argument. He clearly brought the unconscious of Japanese contemporary art to light. The term 'the unconscious' denotes a place where something which is forcibly forgotten is stored, in a Freudian sense. I also agree with him that no clear distinction between high art and low culture can be found in Japan. His project to remake history by incorporating different categories of culture is provocative and also persuasive to a certain extent in explaining the condition of postwar culture in Japan.

However, I am frustrated with his tendency to privilege the condition of Japanese culture as something unique. Even if it is a fictional and constructionist one, as he admits, his project of re-establishing a Japanese (art) history is essentially nationalist, in the sense that he imagines Japan as a homogeneous entity, and it appears that he is trying to establish a new authentic national culture himself. His argument that Japan is 'a bad place' ironically reproduces another 'bad place' where all critical arguments are cyclically repeated only within a Japanese context and without any outside reference or reflexivity.

The problem is more serious when he discusses Japan's cultural situation in contrast with the West's. If we look at art history in non-Western countries in Asia or Africa, for example, we find that almost none of them have either a fixed category of 'high art' as such or even the idea of 'modernity' and 'modernization' in a Western sense. I would argue that his dichotomy between Japan and the West has to be replaced by a more general couplet linking the West and the non-West.

I would like to point out some problems in Sawaragi's historicization of Japanese art/culture from a more transnational perspective. On one hand, I agree with him that the war paintings, and Fujita's works in particular, should be situated at the starting point of Japanese postwar art history. On the other, I would argue that Fujita's works should not be exclusively monopolized as an originary artefact by Japanese postwar art history discourse. As we have seen with Fujita's career, he spent almost half of his life in France and acquired French nationality. He won his international fame first in Europe as one of the contemporary 'European' artists, not as a 'Japanese' artist, who brilliantly drew portraits of European women, animals and landscapes, while maintaining a good friendship with Picasso and Modigliani. Even though he was born in Japan, fluently spoke Japanese and may be considered 'racially Japanese' – which is a very dubious category in contemporary arguments both in social and medical science – how could we so easily and reductively categorize him as a 'Japanese' artist?

Fujita has to be seen as an international artist as well as a 'Japanese' artist, in the same way as Picasso is seen as 'Spanish'. The privileging of the artist's cosmopolitan positioning beyond national boundaries should not be underestimated. In this context, then, his problematic and complex relationship with the war paintings has to be understood from both a national and a transnational point of view, even if this may raise contradictions.

As Roland Barthes and other postmodern literary critics have already suggested, meanings of all texts do not exclusively belong to authorship (Barthes 1980). All textual meanings are always produced in inter-textual, interactive relationships between authors, readers and other cultural, social and political (con)texts in different places and in different times. Furthermore, as the postcolonial critic Homi Bhabha suggested, any dominant discourse is produced only through hegemonic negotiations between the dominating and the dominated. Thus the meanings cannot be homogeneous, but are always and already hybridized because they are inevitably involved with other, subordinated meanings, even if they may be interwoven in-between texts under unequal power relationships (Bhabha 1993).

Fujita's war paintings and his political ambiguity have to be understood within these contexts. The meanings of paintings are diversified so that they often go beyond the artist's intention, which is already pluralized in itself, with resulting contradictions. Fujita's works can be easily read both as war paintings and as anti-war paintings to the extent that they confused and annoyed Japanese military authorities. In fact, if we do not know in advance who the artists are we cannot distinguish, in terms of morality, Fujita's cruel, detailed and descriptive paintings from other famous anti-war paintings such as Picasso's *Guernica* or Iri and Toshi Maruki's collaborative works entitled *Hiroshima Panels*, anti-war paintings in which they depicted their night-marish experiences just after the atomic bomb in Hiroshima.

Neither is it my aim to judge Fujita's ambiguous works simply as guilty or innocent from a moralist perspective, nor to argue, sticking to the idea of the autonomy of art, that modernist categories such as 'the true', 'the good' and 'the beautiful' should be kept separate, as Jürgen Habermas suggested. Rather, I would argue that art and politics, aesthetic judgment and moral judgment co-exist in contradiction at the very centre of modernity. As Paul Gilroy found by examining J. M. W. Turner's controversial painting entitled *The Slave Ship*, in which Turner depicted dying slaves thrown into the sea in the storm (Gilroy 1993), a problem of racism lay at the heart of the aesthetics of British modern art. Similarly, I argue that Fujita's war paintings should be located at the centre of questions of modernity, not only in Japan but also in a broader, transnational context. The specificity of Fujita's war paintings should not be monopolized by Japanese art history, but instead should be open to other countries in Asia and in Europe, and to the US, and should be critically re-examined in both aesthetic and political terms, as we saw with Gilroy's examination of Turner.

Sawaragi's project of positioning war paintings as a repressed origin of Japanese postwar art raises the second, more serious, problem. He is right to suggest that negation of the war paintings' significance as an origin of postwar Japanese art has concealed two different types of violence during the war: Japan's violence towards Asian and other countries' peoples; and the violence which the Japanese themselves suffered. However, against Sawaragi's ambitious project, the difference between the war paintings and subcultural expression is clear. If we look at the Japanese pop culture which Sawaragi identified with the followers of the war painters, we find them heavily obsessed only with the violence of the latter part of the war, in particular the atomic bombs in Hiroshima and Nagasaki and the air raids on Tokyo. The examples to which Sawaragi refers – *Godzilla*, *Spaceship Yamato*, *AKIRA*, and *Neon Genesis Evangelion* – certainly all depicted images of a postwar city, air raids and radioactive contamination, but they hardly touched upon the violence which Japan perpetrated abroad. What is missing in the postwar subcultural imagination is the memory of the war in Japanese colonies and outside Japan. Yet most of the war paintings are full of images of battles abroad.

It seems that Japan lost its colonial memory together with its colonial territory after the war. This nationalist sentiment can be clearly seen in most pop cultural works. For instance, *Godzilla* was released in 1954 when the worldwide anti-nuclear movement emerged following the US nuclear test at Bikini Atoll and the subsequent accident in which a Japanese fisherman's ship, *Daigo Fukuryumaru*, was exposed to radiation. In the film a monstrous figure which subsequently destroyed Tokyo was born as a result of the nuclear test. This megahit special effects film reminded Japanese consciously or unconsciously of the cruel experience of the Tokyo air raid and the atomic bombs in Hiroshima and Nagasaki ten years earlier. In this context, Godzilla was seen metaphorically to represent the US (Sato 1992).

The nationalist sentiment was further intensified in the development of visual pop culture in the 1970s. *Spaceship Yamato*, originally broadcast as a TV series in 1974 and screened in cinemas in 1977, was an explicitly nationalist work of critical importance, in the sense that it had an enormous impact on the first generation of *otaku*-related culture that followed it. In the story, the earth is devastated with radioactivity after a debilitating attack by aliens. The Earth Defence Force finds a legendary Japanese World War II battleship, *Yamato*, which sank during World War II, and converts it into a spaceship. They travel to a far planet, Iskandal, where *Cosmo Cleaner* is waiting to clear radioactivity and save the earth, while they fight a war with aliens from Gamiras Empire.

It has to be noted that all crews on Yamato have only Japanese names, while Gamiras's soldiers, having German-like names, behave like Nazis. We can easily find a twisted desire in which the author wanted to overcome nightmarish memories of World War II by transforming Japanese military forces into saviours. It is also intriguing to see that the 'Evil Empire' that devastated the earth is described as if it were German. This particular political displacement of the subcultural imagination is an example of how Japanese remembered the war and situated themselves in international relations. Azuma Hiroki called this particular tendency in Japanese pop subculture '*Otaku* Nationalism', but until recently this was not recognized by many Japanese, as people were reluctant to question the assumptions that formed the basis of everyday Japanese life.[8]

This amnesia has been shared not only by subcultural practitioners but also, to a certain extent, by liberalists and even leftists. For example, anti-war peace movements, and in particular the anti-nuclear movements in the 1960s, which were the most successful social movements in postwar Japan, were supported by a national consensus of anti-war sentiment. As Fujiwara Ki'ichi suggested (Fujiwara 2001), the peace movements in Japan have had a nationalist tendency, in the sense that they have exclusively emphasized and privileged the experiences in Tokyo, Hiroshima and Nagasaki within Japanese national territory. In doing so they have marginalized and even repressed the memory of cruel battles in Asia and other areas abroad. It was only through the period of rapid economic growth in the 1970s that Japanese started to discuss their own responsibility as a war aggressor.[9] In short, the peace movement as a national movement was possible only through the process of portraying the Japanese people as 'victims of war'. It was also a time for people to re-evaluate the anti-nuclear movement in Japan and critically assess why the successful domestic Japanese anti-nuclear movement could neither expand to become a global movement nor find any support abroad.

The nationalist sentiment can be more clearly seen in JNP, and in particular in Murakami's work. He said in the interview with Kelmachter:

> We retain a powerful sense [*sic*] of trauma in the depth of our culture as an after effect of defeat in World War II. The fact that we faced the end of the war by the dropping of atomic bombs is very symbolic and influential, not only for people who experienced the war but also for my generation who didn't. In a sense, the Japanese have the principle of living for the moment.
>
> (Kelmachter 2002: 101)

Murakami suggested that this principle did not appear only after the war but rather has been a long-held element of Japanese mentality, and continued:

> Already in the Edo period, there was a proverb that said 'the fame of the city of Edo ("Today's Tokyo") is founded on its ashes', which means that the Japanese have long been able to react positively to catastrophes such as fire. People often contrast Europe, with its stone architecture, and Japan, where the buildings are wooden. And it's certainly true that the Japanese have a powerful sense of living in a provisional state. That's also because of earthquakes.
>
> (Murakami 2000: 101)

Murakami owes his international success not only to his artistic qualities but also to his ability to theorize. He discovered early elements of current Japanese aesthetics in the Edo period in contemporary artworks such as *ukiyoe*, and demonstrated continuity between the premodern and the postmodern. By doing so, he is trying to establish a linear, if fictional, Japanese art history by gathering historical elements at random in a postmodernist way and then presenting himself as a representative 'Japanese' artist who can be situated at the end of a line of authentic Japanese art history. In Murakami's explanation, however, the ambiguity which we find in Fujita's war paintings and the critical viewpoint on nuclear issues in early pop culture such as *Godzilla* have disappeared altogether, while he appreciates the war experience simply as something that guarantees contemporary Japanese uniqueness.

It is rather disappointing to see the depoliticization of Murakami's works, as his works in the early 1990s shared a much more politically critical connotation before he adopted subcultural practices as a methodological reference. For instance, he was more critical of Japanese history in his early work *Randosel Project*, in which he exhibited several colourful small backpacks. *Randosel* are commonly used for primary school students.[10] It was interesting to me because, while normally *randosel* are made of black or red leather, his works were produced in colourful leather from animals which were proscribed under the Washington Convention on International Trade in Endangered Species of Wild Fauna and Flora (CITES).[11] It also should be noted that the first *randosel* was originally made for a Japanese emperor, and that the leather industry has been historically managed by an outcast group known as *burakumin*.[12] The project can be understood as a critical evaluation of Japanese modern history and education as well as beautiful art. Sadly, his political acumen has declined as his success in the international art world has grown.

Superflat and the new ideology of cool Japan

The concept of 'superflat' or 'superflatness', which Murakami recently proposed, is more problematic to me, as it completely lacks critical reflexivity to Japaneseness and national history. It was originally manifested in an exhibition which he organized at Parco Gallery, Tokyo, in 2000 and then continued at the MoCA gallery, in Los Angeles and other museums abroad, in the following year. Murakami asked thirteen artists, including fine artists, a photographer, a comic artist and animation artists, to participate in the exhibition under the theme of the 'superflat'.

Murakami's idea is that, following the history of Japanese traditional paintings, from *ukiyoe* to contemporary comics and animation films, one can establish a linear linkage of expressions of 'flatness', a concept that is two dimensional and lacks any depth within it. In emphasizing this linkage, he tries to create a genealogical history of 'superflatness'. The idea of 'superflat' represents not only being extremely flat but also the 'flatness of flatness'; that is, something which goes beyond its physical flatness to challenge the whole idea of 'history'. He characterized the Japanese condition of postmodern culture as superflat and suggested that 'the world of the future might be like Japan is today – superflat' (Murakami 2000:5).

The show was successful although it was relatively small, but the concept of 'superflat' was more successful, in the sense that it has been used to represent a characteristic feature of Japanese contemporary culture. The term 'superflat' is prevalent in contemporary Japanese discourse, producing different connotations in different fields.

For instance, Azuma Hiroki, working with Murakami on the exhibition 'superflat', elaborated the concept of 'superflat' to explain an epistemological transition from the modern to the postmodern in Japan. According to Azuma, the postmodern society in which we live today can be characterized by the term 'database'. In 'database' society, we do not experience the depth which we had before in the modern age, such as possessing hidden ideologies, grand narratives of history or even modern values: the good, the beautiful and the true. Everything is on the surface, where we can access anything from anywhere. There is no hierarchical fixed value system, but instead everything is fragmented as an element and located on the 'superflat' surface without any value judgment (Azuma 2001).

According to Azuma, what postmodern artists should and can do is not to create art works inspired by their own ideas, authorship or even ideology but to appropriate and reappropriate existing works in the 'database' and to construct and re/deconstruct the 'database'. In this argument, he is thinking of a tradition of *otaku*-related culture: *niji-sosaku* (Secondary Creation). *Niji-sosaku* is an important practice of *otaku*-related culture, in particular of comics and animation films, in which people (re)produce works by appropriating images, characters and stories from past works.

I prefer Azuma's argument to Murakami's because Azuma at least tried to theorize Japanese postmodern conditions within a broader international context, and in doing so acknowledged hybrid elements in Japanese contemporary culture, mainly through American influence. I do not deny that there are certainly people whose subjectivity is constructed under the 'superflat' postmodern condition which he analyses. This is the very reason why his argument has been widely accepted in the last couple of years. It explains convincingly the location and identity of middle-class, privileged, urban-dwelling males in an advanced society like Japan. However, I would argue that the concept of 'superflat' or 'superflatness' is not a theoretical framework by means of which a contemporary cultural condition can be analysed, but rather an ideological formation which is articulated within specific historical conditions in Japan.

First, I am sceptical of his argument, in which he over-generalizes. I am thinking of the other side of postmodern conditions since the 1970s. If we look at the process of postmodernization, not only in the field of visual culture but also in politics and in the economy, the last two decades were not a time when everything was equalized, homogenized and even 'flattened' in society as it is in the 'database'. Thanks to the success of neo-liberalist and neo-conservative ideology under post-Fordist economic conditions, the gap between the rich and the poor has significantly widened in Japan, as it has in other parts of the world. The terms *'kachigumi'* (winner) and *'makegumi'* (loser) have become fad words. The unemployment rate, which has been rising, and the number of *freeters* (young part-time workers), which also has increased, have accompanied the ruination of cities and towns in rural areas due to the lasting economic recession. It was a period when society was radically divided into two contrasting poles. Azuma uncritically appreciates the postmodern condition but completely misses the other side of postmodernity. Worse, the euphoric idea of 'superflat' functions as an ideology which conceals social, economic and political crisis in Japan.

Second, it is an ideology of fundamentalist multiculturalism on a global scale. Within the concept of 'superflat', 'Japan', 'Japanese', 'Japanese culture' and 'Japaneseness' are all absolutely essentialized as a homogeneous set of values and are simultaneously set up as an international commodity to be consumed by overseas consumers. This is one reason Murakami and the idea of 'superflat' have been successful not only in Japan but also abroad.

It should be pointed out that the 1990s were a time when the art world experienced a surge of interest in globalization and multiculturalism.[13] While in this context globalization started with criticism of the Eurocentric, white, male-dominated art world, it was accelerated by the lack of superstars in Europe and in the US at the time. Multiculturalism in art also is a relatively new phenomenon. Until the 1970s, by and large, an artist's nationality was not seen to be relevant to Japanese observers. Japanese artists were not concerned about their own nationality as identity, particularly when they worked abroad. Kawara On, Arakawa Shusaku and Yoko Ono are examples of artists who believed that art can be more or less a universal language which transcends our spoken language. Today, artists' cultural backgrounds and nationalities are increasingly seen as important in international exhibitions and art fairs in the age of globalization. Murakami and other JNP artists are strategically introduced as 'Japanese' artists. I find it problematic that artists are divided by national boundaries in an essentialist way, because there remains a particular kind of power relationship between the West and the non-West, which Edward Said called Orientalism (Said 1979).

The problem of Orientalism is that it reproduces an uneven power relationship between the West and the non-West through the process of knowledge production and categorization. The idea 'superflat' satisfies an orientalist perspective by (re)producing a stereotypical, exotic and mysterious image of Japan and Japaneseness, which David Morley and Kevin Robins named 'techno-orientalism' when they analysed postmodern images of Japanese people, associating them with stereotypes of Japan as a high-technology, economically successful culture populated with business-oriented, faceless and 'inhuman' characters (Morley and Robins 1995).

Murakami deliberately and strategically appropriated the orientalist perspective to subvert the Western art system at the beginning of his career, but I am suspicious as to whether he has succeeded, because it seems to me that eventually he has been domesticated within an existing system which is still Western oriented, by having his art located safely as a new exotic object. His complex relationship with Western fine art from Francis Bacon to Andy Warhol is often marginalized by him being confined only within a Japanese cultural context.

I believe that all artists should pursue the production of both cosmopolitan and local languages in order to de/reconstruct art history. Otherwise, the modern dichotomy between the West and the non-West, universalism and particularism, and the dominant and the dominated remain the same and cannot be overcome. The idea of 'superflat' has to go beyond national boundaries by eliminating its essence of Japaneseness.

Third, and finally, the concept of 'superflat' is now an ideology which underlies Japanese government policy for the culture industry. In 2003 the government established the Intellectual Property Strategy Programme in order to develop new industries in education, information technology, media and entertainment.[14] Until then, Japanese pop culture as a business had not been taken seriously because its market was thought not to be large enough, but now it is seen as one of the most important exports in terms of culture as well as financial returns. In 2002, just before the Intellectual Property Strategic Programme, Douglas McGray suggested in an essay entitled 'Japan's gross national cool' in *Foreign Policy*:

> Japan is reinventing superpower – again. Instead of collapsing beneath its widely reported political and economic misfortunes, Japan's global cultural influence has quietly grown. From pop music to consumer electronics, architecture to fashion, and animation to cuisine, Japan looks more like a cultural superpower today than it did in the 1980s, when it was an economic one.
>
> (McGray 2002: 44)

McGray was not the only person to point out the importance of popular culture. This sentiment was shared by those who had been less confident of Japan's future due to the long-lasting economic recession since the end of the so-called bubble economy. Popular culture was suddenly 'discovered' as a hope for Japan's economy.

Murakami is seen as one of the best examples of new Japanese exports; he symbolizes the 'authenticity' of Japanese pop culture, in that *manga* and *anime* are now regarded as 'authentic' Japanese culture exhibited in museums around the world. Governmental and capitalist languages now reappropriate Murakami and JNP's strategic manifest without any reflexivity. There is none of the ironic gesture which Murakami's statement originally contained in a governmental policy which celebrates Japanese popular culture as a new industry. All we can see is an imperialist desire to organize the world by putting Japan at the centre.[15]

Towards transnational cultural histories

In this essay, I have tried to examine JNP and its relation to Japanese postwar history and contemporary postmodern conditions. It is interesting to see how memories of the war have been repressed, kept in the storage of the unconscious in a Freudian sense and displaced within visual cultures from fine art to pop culture in Japan. It is also intriguing that postmodern conditions enable us to re-evaluate the hidden history of war paintings as part of the creative imagination for pop culture and JNP. However, it has to be pointed out too that, despite interesting political and cultural possibilities in the re-examination of the Japanese war paintings and other history, most of the arguments over 'superflat' have been disappointingly nationalist in terms of assuming Japanese culture as a homogenous and pure entity. While memories of the war may have remained in pop culture, the domination of the experience as victims within Japanese territory has produced a new nationalist sentiment. Unfortunately, such cases are increasing, in particular over the past couple of years, backed by the government policy outlined above.

However, when we look at the contemporary economic, cultural and social conditions in which we live, we can see that Japanese popular culture is not purely 'Japanese' but is indeed more hybridized than Azuma argued. For instance, the Japanese animation film industry relies heavily on production networks in Korea and China, due to the global restructuring of production. Korean dramas are now overtaking Japanese trendy dramas, which were once dominant in East Asia in the early 1990s. The production, distribution and consumption of popular culture are not restricted within national boundaries, but are instead more fluid and hybridized than ever.

I would argue that it is more exciting to extend the argument that over the last decade Japanese have become more entrenched in a transnational context. For instance, if we discuss the issue of Fujita's war painting not only within a small Japanese circle but also with Asian artists or art historians, or even with Western historians, we will find much more fruitful, if not critical, arguments on how we should understand modernity and its relationship to aesthetics and politics.

Notes

1   The term 'Japanese Neo Pop' originally appeared in a Japanese art journal, *Bijutus Techô* ('Pop/Neo Pop' issue), in March 1992, in which Nakahara Kodai, Murakami Takashi, Nara Yoshitomo, Taro Chiezo and others were featured.
2   There are not many academic essays on JNP written in English. Murakami's own manifest 'A theory of superflat Japanese art' in *Super Flat* (Murakami 2000), Midori Matsui's essay in Murakami's exhibition (Matusi 1999) and an anthology on Japanese contemporary culture in relation to art, *Consuming Bodies: sex and contemporary Japanese art* (Lloyd 2002) will give a good introduction to the JNP movement.
3   Azuma's argument entitled 'Superflat Japanese postmodernity' can be also seen on his Internet home page: http://www.hirokiazuma.com/en/texts/superflat_en1.html.
4   The following argument is based on his interview in the *Kaikai Kiki* Exhibition Catalogue at the Serpentine Gallery in London (Kelmachter 2002).
5   Otuska Eiji's analyses of the *otaku* generation are helpful to an understanding the common media experience in the 1970s (see Otsuka 2001, 2004).
6   There is considerable research, both academic and journalistic, on Fujita's life story, although most have not touched on his commitment to war paintings (see Kondo 2002).
7   An anti-nuclear political message was already clear from the beginning in the advertisement for *Godzilla*.
8   See Sato (1992) and Azuma's home page (cited in note 3).

9 There had been, of course, huge arguments on Japanese responsibility for the war, in particular the question of *tenkô* (conversion), among intellectuals since the end of the war. But, at a mass level, why the Japanese came to (mis)identify themselves as 'peaceful' people after World War II has yet to be discussed.

10 *Randosel* (*randoseru*) is a box-shaped bag which almost all Japanese primary school students use in school. It is called *randosel* as its style is similar to a Dutch military bag, '*ransel*'.

11 Murakami did not make clear whether it was real or fake, but it seems to me that it is fake, judging by its appearance.

12 *Buraku* is a Japanese word which originally referred to a village or hamlet, but in the Meiji period it acquired a particular connotation in relation to former outcast communities in the Edo period. Although they were officially emancipated in the early Meiji period, the discrimination against them has continued in society, in particular in inequality of job opportunities and marriage.

13 A typical example of multiculturalism in art can be seen in the exhibition 'Magiciens de la terre' held at the Pompidou Centre, Paris, in 1989.

14 It is known as the *Chizai* project, an abbreviation of *Chiteki Zaisan Senryaku*, which is located at the cabinet office.

15 It would be unfair to overgeneralize about the JNP artists. For instance, Aida's more controversial appropriation of the war paintings seemingly still contains a critical edge of Japanese authentic culture and history.

Bibliography

Azuma, H. (2001) *Dôbutsuka suru posutomodan* (Animalizing postmodernity), Tokyo: Kôdansha Gendai Shinsho.

Barthes, R. (1980) *The Pleasure of the Text*, trans. R. Miller, London: Hill and Wang.

Bhabha, H. (1993) *The Location of Culture*, London: Routledge.

Freud, S. [1995] (1915) 'The Unconscious', reprinted in P. Gay (ed.) *The Freud Reader*, London: Vintage.

Fujiwara, K. (2001) *Senso o kioku suru: Hiroshima, horokôsuto to genzai* (Remembering wars: Hiroshima, Holocaust and the present), Tokyo: Kôdansha.

Gilroy, P. (1993) 'Art of darkness: black art and the problem of belonging to England', in P. Gilroy *Small Acts*, London: Serpent's Tail.

Kelmachter, H. (2002) 'Interview with Murakami Takashi', in *Murakami Takashi, Kaikai Kiki Exhibition Catalogue*, London.

Kikuhata, M. (1977) *Fujita yo nemure* (Rest in peace, Fujita), Fukuoka: Ashi Shobô.

Kondo F. (2002) *Fujita Tsuguharu: ihôjin no shôgai* (Fujita Tsuguharu: a life of an alien), Tokyo: Kôdansha.

Lloyd, F. (ed.) (2002) *Consuming Bodies: sex and contemporary Japanese art*, London: Reatkin Books.

McGray, D. (2002) 'Japan's gross national cool', *Foreign Policy*, 130: 44–54.

Matsui, M. (1999) 'Towards a definition of Tokyo pop: the classic transgression of Takashi Murakami', in T. Murakami *The Meaning of Nonsense of the Meaning, Exhibition Catologue*, New York: Bart College.

Morley, D. and Robins, K. (1995) *Spaces of Identity: global media, electronic landscapes and cultural boundaries*, London: Routledge.

Murakami, T. (2000) 'A theory of super flat Japanese art', in T. Murakami (ed.) *Super Flat*, Tokyo: Madora Shuppan.

Otsuka, E. (2001) *'Kanojo tachi' no rengô-sekigun* ("Girls'" Japan Red Army), Tokyo: Kadokawa Shoten.

——(2004) *Otaku no seishinshi: 1980 nendai ron* (Intellectual history of *otaku*: on the 1980s), Tokyo: Kôdansha.

Said, E. (1979) *Orientalism*, London: Penguin.

Sato, K. (1992) *Gojira to yamato to bokura no minshushugi* (Godzilla, Spaceship Yamato and our democracy), Tokyo: Bungeishunjûsha.

Sawaragi, N. (1998) *Nihon/Gendai/Bijutsu* (Japan/Modern/Art), Tokyo: Shinchôsha.

——(2002) *Bakushinchi no geijutsu 1999–2001* (The art at Ground Zero 1999–2001), Tokyo: Shôbunsha.

11 The 'most crucial education'

Saotome Katsumoto, globalization and Japanese anti-war thought

Matthew Penney

Introduction

Tahara Sôichirô's *Nihon no sengo* (Japan's postwar), a recent work of Japanese popular history from one of the country's bestselling and most widely read journalists, bears the provocative subtitle 'Were we mistaken?' (Tahara 2005). This question, asked of the entire postwar period, is representative of a significant current in contemporary Japanese thought – the idea that Japan has strayed from the 'correct' path and failed to live up to international 'norms'. In recent years, Japanese debates about war and peace, on both sides of the ideological divide, have been influenced by this view. Conservatives play up the idea that the Japanese constitution, which explicitly forbids participation in armed conflict and the maintenance of military forces, means that the nation has not been able to play a role in world affairs appropriate to its economic might. Progressives criticize the Japanese government's failure to adequately apologize and compensate the victims of colonialism and war for aggression and atrocities. In both views, Japan is abnormal and incapable of living up to 'universals' – either the 'universal' right to self-defence and duty to participate in international conflicts like the 'war on terror', or the necessity to inculcate the view that 'war is wrong' and the idea that past crimes must be dealt with honestly in the public sphere.

In the 11 September 2005 election the Liberal Democrats won a landslide victory, capturing 295 seats in the Diet. Progressive parties like the Japanese Communist Party and Social Democratic Party, whose representation plummeted in the 1990s, were held to a mere nine and seven seats, respectively. Nevertheless, when polled about the Liberal Democratic Party's goal of constitutional revision 62 per cent of Japanese questioned responded that they would not approve of the elimination of the 'peace-clause' (Tabuchi 2005). This suggests that, while progressives have failed to secure seats in the Diet, their fundamental position on war and peace has considerable currency. A significant reason behind this is the prevalence of anti-war images in Japanese popular culture.

Author Saotome Katsumoto wrote in 2002 of the 'war on terror': 'Terrorism is, of course, a form of violence difficult to forgive, but the war being waged in retaliation is also violence . . . where and in what way can we put on the brakes?' (Saotome 2002a: 3–4). For Saotome, war is wrong, and the 'war on terror' an unjustifiable threat to world peace. Saotome, a survivor of the 10 March 1945 American air raid on Tokyo that killed over 100,000 civilians and left as many as 5 million homeless, became a popular anti-war author. He is also a veteran grass-roots socialist activist and a life-long supporter of progressive politics. After writing for *Akahata* (Red Flag), the Japan Communist Party paper in the 1960s and the 1970s, Saotome moved into a career as a writer of non-fiction (Saotome 2004: 252–3). He is one of Japan's most prolific authors on subjects of war and peace, having written volumes for some of the most significant non-fiction series in the Japanese language – the Shinsho series from Iwanami Shoten, aimed at adults, and the Iwanami Junior Shinsho and *Kusa no ne haha to ko de miru* (Grassroots mother and child see) series for children. These works are a staple at public and school libraries across Japan and at major booksellers.

Saotome's work highlights peace as a 'universal' value. For example, he wrote:

> The twentieth century is often said to be the century of war. Of course, in the first half there were two world wars and in the second there were various civil wars and conflicts which did not go away, but we must also turn our eyes to a movement in human history to outlaw war.
>
> (Saotome 2002a: 3)

He points to the failed League of Nations and to the United Nations (UN) as significant steps in the direction of this 'universal' anti-war ideal (Saotome 2002a: 3). He also emphasizes the UN charter and the promise '[t]o save succeeding generations from the scourge of war, which twice in our lifetime has brought untold sorrow to mankind' as embodying a 'universal' goal (Saotome 2002a: 3). Saotome quotes Oscar Arias Sanchez, the former president of Costa Rica, a country that he admires for disbanding its military, who says, 'You cannot protect us by digging trenches or putting up high defensive walls. Instead, we need to educate human hearts to believe in goodwill, harmony, human tolerance, generosity, and sympathy' (Saotome 2002a: 4).

Saotome has long emphasized the importance of anti-war education: '"Those who cannot learn from history are doomed to repeat it" is the warning of philosopher George Santayana and at present, I think that the first thing that we can do for the sake of peace is to know and to learn' (Saotome 2002b: 67). Through education, 'universal' values and the 'universal' goal 'to save succeeding generations from the scourge of war' can be achieved. Saotome's perspective is not only rooted in local narratives and the image of the Japanese people as victims of war. It draws upon a wide variety of anti-war images. His books include *Haha to ko de miru: nankin kara no tegami* (Mother and child see: a letter from Nanking) and *Betonamu*

200 man nin gashi no kiroku: 1945 nen nihon senryô no moto de (A record of the starvation of 2 million in Vietnam: 1945 under Japanese occupation).

Writing on the atomic bombs and the firebombing of Japanese cities, Saotome sympathetically portrays the plight of Japanese victims. This 'victim's narrative' exists, however, side by side with powerful statements of Japanese as assailants in war. In the hands of writers like Saotome, perspectives like victim and assailant, inside and outside are not dichotomous but can constitute a comprehensive critique of war. The suffering brought about through the use of organized violence, be it the suffering of the Japanese people in war, the suffering of others at Japanese hands or suffering as manifested in international anti-war symbols like Auschwitz and Vietnam, are all conveyed to readers.

I will examine three of Saotome's major works to highlight the central themes of his perspective on war. The 1979 children's title *Tokyo ga moeta hi* (The day Tokyo burned), while primarily concerned with the suffering of Japanese civilians in wartime, also shows the Japanese as assailants in war, thereby providing a critique of Japan-centric narratives. In a similar vein, *Betonamu 200 man nin gashi no kiroku: 1945 nen nihon senryô no moto de* offers a critique not only of past actions by the US and Japan, but also of contemporary Japan. Finally, *Ikiru koto to manabu koto* (Living and learning), published in 1997, uses war to illustrate Saotome's philosophy of education and his understanding of war and peace. In sum, Saotome deploys both global and local themes to zero in on both international wars and Japan's war experiences.

The day Tokyo burned

In 1979 Iwanami Shoten, Japan's leading progressive publisher, inaugurated a non-fiction series for children patterned after its most popular line, the Shinsho series. The series introduces historical and cultural themes. The editors wrote:

> You, the young generation, are standing at the starting line of your lives ... modern society is burdened with many contradictions ... the threat of the annihilation of humanity through nuclear war, human inequality beginning with the gap between rich and poor ... for the peace and development of mankind, you urgently need to apply yourselves and gain new wisdom.
>
> (Iwanami Shoten Henshûbu 2002).

Saotome Katsumoto's *Tokyo ga moeta hi*, the fifth volume in the Junior Shinsho series, which has since swelled to nearly 500 titles, remains in print today. Saotome explained: 'I wrote this book with a desire to tell of my experiences at 12 years old, on that day, 10 March, to my own child who has suddenly become a middle school student of that same age, and to other members of that generation' (Saotome 1979: 212).

These comments fit into a larger trend in Japanese popular thought – resistance to what has been described as the *fûka* (weathering) of war experience and the importance of teaching the lessons of the Pacific War to 'children who do not know war'. The latter phrase is the title of a hit 1968 folk tune which struck a popular chord in its description of a Japan in which over half of the population were born after the end of the war (Kitayama 1998: 4). The necessity to teach about the 'tragedy of war' to this group became an important factor in discourses about education and in historical writing for children (Yoshida 1995: 106–8). This was a major concern of Saotome's, expressed most clearly when he wrote:

> If you ask 'what day is 10 March?' I wonder how many people can quickly recall the Tokyo air raid? Just recently, while working for a certain broadcaster, I put the microphone in front of Tokyo primary school students and when I asked that question, the children just turned their heads and looked blank. I thought that there would at least be one child who knows about the Tokyo air raid but the result was zero. Although it was something I had envisioned, I was still surprised and depressed.
>
> (Saotome 1979: 209)

Saotome begins his anti-war appeal and argument for the importance of remembrance and education with the idea of the Japanese people as victims of war:

> Like the sorrowful tragedy of the atomic bombings of Hiroshima and Nagasaki, I had wanted to think that children would be encouraged to keep in their hearts, in some form, the memory of 10 March Tokyo air raid in which 100,000 lives were lost in a single night, as an example of the importance and dignity of human lives. However, I wonder if this was only my hope?
>
> (Saotome 1979: 210)

This attempt to bring about the 'peace and development of mankind' begins by recalling the firebombing of Tokyo alongside the experience of Hiroshima and Nagasaki. *Tokyo ga moeta hi* vividly describes the mindset behind the indiscriminate bombing of civilians. Of General LeMay, who orchestrated the American bombing campaign, Saotome writes:

> We can well understand how much General LeMay valued the lives of his subordinates [and such an attitude] was not just limited to General LeMay . . . If the life of one person was treasured so greatly, what can be made of the 100,000 lives lost in a single night by indiscriminate bombing? Was it the same as wiping out small bugs?
>
> (Saotome 1979: 204–5)

He continues:

> However, if we are going to condemn the indiscriminate bombing of ordinary civilians, it is not only LeMay and America. We also cannot lose sight of the fact that in 1937, the year of the outbreak of the war between Japan and China, the Japanese army, after occupying the Chinese capital of Nanking and massacring civilians there, chased Chiang Kai-shek's government to ... the city of Chongqing and from February of the following year carried out indiscriminate bombing raids that included non-combatants as targets some 46 times.
>
> (Saotome 1979: 206)

With the Chinese example, Saotome transcends the 'Japanese as victim' conceptualization to universalize the plight of civilians in wartime bombing. The suggestion, common in the English-language press and in monographs like Erna Paris's *Long Shadows: truth, lies, and history* (2001), that Japanese authors exclusively project the image of Japanese as victims in war is overly simplistic. Saotome looks at the problem of indiscriminate bombing of civilian populations from a variety of angles, showing Japanese people both as victims and assailants.

Saotome extends the discussion of LeMay and civilian bombing to the Vietnam War: 'LeMay, using the B52 strategic bomber . . . in place of the B29, rained North Vietnam with fire – genocidal indiscriminate bombing – all the while saying "I'll bomb them back into the stone age"' (Saotome 1979: 206).

The bombing of North Vietnam provided a rallying point for anti-war thinkers, including Saotome. Saotome emphasizes not only American aggression in Vietnam but Japan's supporting role. From the firebombing of Tokyo and the nuclear bombing of Hiroshima and Nagasaki to Japanese atrocities in China and provision of support for US bombing of Vietnam, Saotome presents a compelling palette of US war crimes, complementing his critique of Japanese crimes in the Pacific War. In the 1980s Saotome condemned Japanese war atrocities in the same terms he used to promote awareness among young readers of the bombing of Tokyo.

Starvation under occupation

In 1993 Saotome published a book aimed at adults entitled *Betonamu 200 man nin gashi no kiroku: 1945 nen nihon senryô no moto de* (Saotome 1993). As is usual in Saotome's non-fiction, he begins by relating his own experiences. He writes about wartime rationing, about how school supplies for children were far from a priority during the war years and about feelings of dejection (Saotome 1993: 7–9). The first part of the work, which describes Japanese mothers crying because they did not know where they would get the rice to feed their children, sets the stage for the discussion of Vietnamese hardships (Saotome 1993: 8). The image of Japanese suffering is an effective jumping-off point for Saotome's subsequent commentary. This is an important element of the work's structure and a technique that Saotome has exploited frequently. After outlining rice shortages in wartime Japan, he tells how rice taken from Vietnam (then under Japanese rule) precipitated famine there that some believe may have claimed over 2 million lives. This figure has been challenged in a number of contexts. Two million dead was the figure accepted by the Vietminh, but in 1945 Vietnamese government officials estimated the total at around 400,000 (Ogura 1997: 345). The statistical debate, however, takes nothing away from the power of Saotome's account.

Saotome states that his research helped him 'to understand the true form of the "Greater East Asia Co-Prosperity Sphere" that Japanese militarism had built up in Indochina' (Saotome 1993: 177). He paints a startling picture of starvation in words and photographs to bring out the full force of the tragedy.

However, Saotome is interested in doing more than showing the Japanese army as assailants of the Vietnamese population. Most of the rice taken from the Vietnamese, the cause of mass starvation, was consumed by Japanese civilians (Saotome 1993: 129–44). Saotome makes this point in part to force his audience to think about the issues of agency in war, about victims and assailants, and in part to inspire reflection on Japan's prosperity and place in the world in 1993. He writes:

> Starvation, refugees, and the poverty problem are not just things of the distant past. According to a UNICEF report from late last year, 35,000 children die of malnutrition and disease every day . . . I hope that this book will help us consider the human condition from the past to the present and into the future.
>
> (Saotome 1993: 180)

Saotome deploys historical examples as the basis for a contemporary critique designed to inspire reflection on global poverty and to emphasize Japan's responsibility to provide aid for the less fortunate.

'The elite' – Auschwitz and Unit 731

In 1997 Saotome published *Ikiru koto to manabu koto* (Living and learning) in the Iwanami Junior Shinsho series (Saotome 1997). The work deals with war but focuses on the critique of elitism – elite students or elite bureaucrats. 'Elite' status and the assumption that justice and rationality go along with it, he argues, are behind the scientific and organized killing that took place at Auschwitz (Saotome 1997: 8–10).

Saotome describes his first visit to Auschwitz in powerful terms: 'I still can't forget the violent shock that I received when I first visited here' (Saotome 1997: 9–10). It was the mountains of eyeglasses and children's toys that made the biggest impression on the author.

Saotome links the crimes of Auschwitz to elements of the Nazi organization and the 'elite' status of its leaders. Saotome does not blame what happened on the 'German character' but, rather, on flawed values that are not limited to Nazi Germany. 'I am just another human being; if I was placed in the same position, I wonder if I would have done the same thing' (Saotome 1997: 12).

Saotome's comments about Auschwitz and universal responsibility serve as a jumping-off point for a discussion of Japanese war crimes: 'If we move our eyes from Europe to the nations of Asia, Japanese militarism's fangs of aggression were being bared with rage' (Saotome 1997: 13).

He discusses Unit 731, a branch of the Japanese army charged with developing biological and chemical weapons in Manchuria and North China, which carried out human experimentation, ending in the murder of more than 3000 Chinese and other victims. The elite status of the doctors and the 'scientific progress' represented by their experiments legitimated the atrocities, which Saotome describes in horrific detail. He also introduces an analogy that strikes close to home for Americans, writing that the scientists 'assumed that they had made a contribution to Japanese medicine. This is just like the researchers devoted to the development of weapons of mass destruction like the atomic bomb' (Saotome 1997: 14).

In his discussion of 'the elite', Saotome not only presents the Chinese as victims, but suggests an association between Nazi terror in Europe, Japanese aggression in Asia and US firebombing and atomic bombing of Japanese civilians.

Conclusion

Saotome Katsumoto's anti-war commentary reflects a deep personal conflict. He writes of his own war experience: 'I can't say "I was just a kid so I was a victim of war" and leave it at that. Even if just for a short time, I worked in a weapons factory – I have an assailant's side as well. How should I think about this?' (Saotome 2003: 2). He has attempted to answer this question in a lifetime of anti-war education – appealing to Japan's direct responsibility even while exploring global anti-war symbols such as Auschwitz, Hiroshima and Vietnam.

Saotome examines the interplay between the Japanese people as victims of war, as in the Tokyo and Hiroshima bombings, and as assailants, as in the China war and signature atrocities such as the 'comfort women' and Unit 731, and ranging over past and present both to appeal to a common humanity and to highlight Japan's responsibility.

Others have deployed 'universal' symbols of war and atrocity for precisely opposite ends. Since 1996, members of the *Atarashii rekishi kyôkasho wo tsukurukai* (Society for the Creation of a New History Textbook) and like-minded writers have also employed globalized images in their writing. Their aim, far from documenting Japanese responsibility for war crimes, however, has been to downplay Japanese imperialism and aggression as no more than trivial examples among far greater atrocities. Nishio Kanji, in his influential *Kokumin no rekishi* (History of the people of the nation), for example, plays up examples from other countries, noting that '[t]his book is overflowing with interest in foreign countries as there are even more references to China, Europe and America than to Japan' (Nishio 1999: 768). Nishio's examples, particularly those of European and American imperialism, are designed precisely to excuse Japan's brutal colonial domination throughout Asia as a reaction to the 'Western' threat in a period when imperialism was considered a given and thus entirely justifiable (Kibata 2000: 245–7). The universal example in Nishio's hands provides a rationale for all Japanese wartime behaviour. Similarly, in the popular *Sensôron* (On war), *manga* artist Kobayashi Yoshinori uses the abuses of Western imperialists in Asia to justify Japanese actions (Kobayashi 1998: 27–34). These arguments stress that Japan is not unique and that what critics present as its flaws are instead 'universal values'. Ironically, such views emphasizing the universality of colonialism, war and atrocity are frequently coupled in the work of writers like Kobayashi and Nishio with insistence on Japanese uniqueness, usually in the form of glorification of the wartime rhetoric of freedom and cooperation in 'Greater East Asia'.

In the end, however, revisionist viewpoints have, in the works of Saotome Katsumoto and other likeminded authors, a powerful popular counterpoint. The awareness that Japanese have been both victims and victimizers in war is not limited to Saotome. It can be found in the works of noted Japanese scholar-activists such as Oda Makoto, Ienaga Saburo, and Fujiwara Akira. It is also an important dimension of many works published outside Japan, such as John Dower's *War without Mercy*, which discusses cruelties on all sides of the Pacific conflict (Dower 1986). Other works, such as the collection *Censoring History*, edited by Laura Hein and Mark Selden, also bring this problem into focus (Hein and Selden 2000). The view of the Japanese as both victim and aggressor has also surfaced in works such as Gomikawa Junpei's bestselling novel *Ningen no jôken* (The Human Condition). Saotome's importance lies not in the uniqueness of his ideas but in the breadth and depth of his approach. Drawing on images of the Japanese as both victims and assailants in war, as well as myriad international anti-war symbols, Saotome has written popular works for adults and children for over three decades. In this time, he has challenged revisionists, pushed for the preservation of the 'peace clause' of the Japanese constitution and taken steps to ensure that Chinese and other Asian voices are heard in the chorus of Japanese war remembrance.

Japanese academic writing has offered a prolific and nuanced critique of wartime atrocities. Academic works, however, are rarely accessible to popular audiences, particularly to children. Reaching these readers demands a very different tone and means of articulating ideas about history. It is here that Saotome Katsumoto's genius for communicating difficult themes to all levels of Japan's reading public becomes evident. Saotome has successfully drawn upon the image of the Japanese side as both victim and assailant in war in support of a comprehensive anti-war critique. He has also demonstrated a gift for bringing historical themes into contemporary focus. His use of the Nazi and Unit 731 examples to question the nature of Japanese education is a powerful case in point. In this way, his anti-war themes transcend a purely historical discussion and become part of a far-reaching social critique. Saotome's basic message that 'war is wrong' and that education must guard against it may be a simple one, but in a time when rightwing sound bites have become increasingly strong, and in the context of the Japanese government's continued ambiguity and silence on issues of aggression and atrocity, it is significant. Theodore Adorno, in a 1966 radio broadcast entitled 'Education After Auschwitz', commented that '[t]he demand that Auschwitz must never happen again is the most crucial education. It is so much more important than anything else that I don't feel I have to or should justify it' (Rathenow 2000: 73). This is a vision of education, of anti-war thought and of reflection on past atrocities to inform the present. It is also striking in its simplicity. Saotome Katsumoto's writings promote a similar simple message. This, however, is his strength, his talent for bringing to mass audiences the idea that 'war is wrong', a point that, supported by a variety of anti-war images from within Japan and without, he considers the 'most crucial education'.

Bibliography

Dower, J. (1986) *War without Mercy: race and power in the Pacific War*, New York: Pantheon Books.

Hein, L. and Selden, M. (eds) (2000) *Censoring History: citizenship and memory in Japan, Germany, and the United States*, New York: M. E. Sharpe.

Iwanami Shoten Henshûbu (2002) 'Inawami jyunia shinsho no hossoku ni sai shite (On the occasion of the start of Iwanami Junior Shinsho)', in Iwanami Shoten Henshûbu (ed.) *Bokutachi no ima* (Our now), Tokyo: Iwanami Shoten.

Kibata, Y. (2000) 'Kokumin no rekishi no seiôzô to nihon teikoku shugi (The view of the West of *History of the People of the Nation* and Japanese imperialism)', in Kyôkasho ni Shinjitsu to Jiyû o' Renraku-kai (ed.) *Tettei hihan: kokumin no rekishi* (A complete criticism of *History of the People of the Nation*), Tokyo: Ôtsuki Shoten.

Kitayama, O. (1998) 'Sensô o shiranai kodomotachi (Children who do not know war)', in *Nihon no uta* (The songs of Japan), vol. 4, Tokyo: Nobarasha.

Kobayashi, Y. (1998) *Sensôron* (On war), Tokyo: Gentôsha.

Nishio, K. (1999) *Kokumin no rekishi* (History of the people of the nation), Tokyo: Sankei Shinbunsha.

Ogura, S. (1997) 'Monogatari Betonamu no rekishi (The Story of Vietnamese History)', Tokyo: Chuokoronsha.

Paris, E. (2001) *Long Shadows: truth, lies, and history*, London: Bloomsbury.

Rathenow, H. (2000) 'Teaching the Holocaust in Germany', in I. Davies (ed.) *Teaching the Holocaust: educational dimensions, principles and practices*, London: Cassell.

Saotome, K. (1979) *Tokyo ga moeta hi* (The day Tokyo burned), Tokyo: Iwanami Shoten.

——(1989) *Haha to ko de miru: nankin kara no tegami* (Mother and child see: a letter from Nanking), Tokyo: Kusanone Shuppankai.

——(1993) *Betonamu 200 man nin gashi no kiroku: 1945 nen nihon senryô no moto de* (A record of the starvation of 2 million in Vietnam: 1945 under Japanese occupation), Tokyo: Ôtsuki Shoten.

——(1997) *Ikiru koto to manabu koto* (Living and studying), Tokyo: Iwanami Shoten.

——(2002a) *Kataritsugu sensô: 15 nin no dengon* (Passing on the war: the testimony of 15 people), Tokyo: Kawade Shobô.

——(2002b) 'Ima sensô o kangaeru (Considering war now)', in Iwanami Shoten Henshûbu (ed.) *Boku-tachi no ima* (Our now), Tokyo: Iwanami Shoten.

——(2003) *Sensô to kodomo-tachi* (War and children), Tokyo: Ôtsuki Shoten.

——(2004) *Saotome Katsumoto*, Tokyo: Nihon Tosho Sentâ.

Tabuchi, H. (2005) 'Japan seeks to amend pacifist constitution'. Available HTTP: http://news.yahoo.com/s/ap/20051006/ap_on_re_as/japan_constitutional_revision;_ylt=AoAs2vcSzBgiMfK77XdPw0sBxg8F;_ylu=X3oDMTBiM W04NW9mBHNlYwMlJVRPUCUl (accessed 6 October 2005).

Tahara, S. (2005) *Nihon no sengo* (Japan's postwar), vol. 1, Tokyo: Kôdansha.

Yoshida, Y. (1995) *Nihonjin no sensôkan* (Japanese views of war), Tokyo: Iwanami Shoten.

12 Loochoo Beat(s)

Music in and out of 'Okinawa'

James E. Roberson

Introduction

Over the past decade, Okinawa has rightly, if belatedly, received renewed Western scholarly interest as 'islands of discontent' dissatisfied with their continuing postwar position as 'Cold War islands' caught between and subordinated to Japanese and American geopolitical influences and interests (see Hein and Selden 2003; C. Johnson 1999; Hook and Siddle 2003). At the same time, especially within Japan but to some extent outside as well (see Roberson 2003; H. Johnson 2001), Okinawa has become the focus of interest as 'islands of song' (*uta no shima*; for recent discussions in Japanese, see Aoki 2000; *Eureka* 2002; Matsumura 2002). Okinawan music has tended until very recently to enter mainland Japanese and global imaginaries as Japan's contribution to 'world music', 'ethnic' or 'roots' music from the Ryûkûs (Potter 2001), composed either of still vital Okinawan musical traditions or of an authentic new local hybrid combining these with modern Western influences. This kind of listening all too frequently imposes an exoticizing, externally composed aural hegemony on 'Okinawan music' that is both homogenizing and ahistorical, suggesting that authentic 'Okinawan' music either is that which is traditional and relatively unchanging or is 'modern' only in its ethnically marked hybridity. I have elsewhere (Roberson 2003) offered a critique of the apolitical deafness of such assumptions as regards the genre of 'Uchinâ Pop'.

In this chapter I consider certain of the implications of the complex interrelationships among globalization, locality, music and identity in (or with) contemporary Okinawa. In doing so, I hope to dislocate Okinawan musics, bringing into question just what is 'Okinawan music' by restoring history and further inserting other genres into the mix of musics in and out of Okinawa. I focus on the emergence, especially since the late 1960s, of a series of performers in and (from) outside of Okinawa whose music requires more complex understandings of 'Okinawan music' and of 'Okinawa(n identity)'.

Music, identity and globalization

Music is one set of personalized cultural practices through which self-identities are constructed and through which the identities of others are assumed or assigned. DeNora thus notes that a person's self-identity 'is locatable in music' (2000: 68) and that 'music provides a material rendering of self-identity; a material in and with which to identify identity' (2000: 69). Focusing on the issue of ethnicity, Stokes argues, as do others, that musical practices 'provide the means by which ethnicities and identities are constructed and mobilized' and through which boundaries of identity and difference are recreated and recognized (1994: 5; see also Mitchell 1996: 89). At the same time, it is also necessary to be wary of the dangers of what Middleton (1990: 146–7) calls 'ethnomusicological exoticism', and to move away from essentialist assumptions of the relations between cultural practices and identities toward understandings that recognize more complexly situated 'articulations' of cultural identities and practices (Negus 1996: 100). Such locally situated articulations of identity are increasingly constructed through musical practices 'by means of a hybridization of local and global musical idioms' (Mitchell 1996: 2).

Music thus provides one of the media (or mediascapes; Appadurai 1996) through which local identities, individual and cultural, are composed within conditions of globalization. However, contemporary local–global dynamics are not singularly or simply those of, to borrow terms from Geertz (1983), the 'experience-near' localization of influences, forces and flows that originate (that are original) in 'experience-far' global centres. Instead, as Tomlinson emphasizes, '[t]he paradigmatic experience of global modernity for most people . . . is that of staying in one place but experiencing the "dis-placement" that global modernity brings to them' (1999: 9). In this 'mundane experience of deterritorialization' (Tomlinson 1999: 113), local everyday experience and identity become intimately interconnected with the quotidian penetration, taken-for-granted presence and hybridizing reterritorialization (Tomlinson 1999: 141ff) of global cultural processes.

Thus, Mathews suggests, on the one hand, that in contemporary Japan 'the taken-for-granted realm has increasingly become that of the global cultural supermarket – albeit a supermarket many of whose forms continue to be seen as foreign' (2000: 67) and, on the other hand, making specific reference to music, that 'there is a sense in which forms such as rock and jazz music . . . are at present not foreign but part of the taken-for-granted fabric of contemporary Japanese life' (Mathews 2000: 60). In Japan, as indeed in many other places, understanding musical practice as articulating localized/ing global identities and identifications requires also an awareness of taken-for-granted, everyday 'soundscapes' (Feld 1996) that resound with ongoing 'glocalized' cultural (re)production as people ongoingly attempt to 're-establish a cultural "home"' (Tomlinson 1999: 148).

The question that I want to address in this chapter, then, becomes that of how to understand the interrelations of music and identity in Okinawa within ongoing globalizing processes of localized cultural identity construction, where globalization implies also the 'mundane deterritorialization' of musical forms and practices. What *is* 'Okinawan' music within such conditions of everyday globalization? I approach this question through the delineation of the deconstructive complexity of musical forms and practices in/out of Okinawa.

Loochoo Beats: Okinawan musical mixed-plate

One of the complicating issues implied by and imbricated within the notion of hybridity is that of authenticity. Hybridity itself is, of course, not just a matter of playful and creative cultural creolization; it has often been the product of (sometimes very violent) political economic histories of racism, colonialism and imperialism – that is, of particular localized and embodied experiences and practices of globalization, a point to which I return throughout the chapter. Conversely, as Negus notes, 'many so-called indigenous or traditional musical cultures, which are often revered for their purity or authenticity, are actually "hybrid" forms' (1996: 175). If even supposedly 'pure' or 'authentic' cultures and cultural practices are really 'hybridity all the way down' (Rosaldo 1995; Tomlinson 1999), then it becomes important to recognize that 'authenticity' 'is a discursive trope of great persuasive [and therefore political] power' (Stokes 1994: 6–7) invoked to make claims about (Self) identity as distinct and different (from Other). What is considered 'authentic' thus participates in ongoing internal cultural debates regarding 'identity' and such claims and counterclaims have great representational, economic and political significance (see also Gilroy 1993).

In the case of contemporary Okinawan musics, such considerations of hybridity and authenticity, as experienced and expressed, are important markers of the nature of music in the always already globalized local cultural space of Okinawa. Claims of authenticity thus mark a distinctive 'Okinawanness' but also often belie more complex global cultural contexts and complications. As with other peoples, Okinawans 'participate in so many communities and cultures all the time that expressing their "essence" means exposing the plurality of their cultural and personal identity' (Lipsitz 1994: 64). If so, what, again, *is* 'Okinawan' music?

Music from the global village: Shima-uta and Uchinâ Pop

Although there are historically older schools and repertoires of music in Okinawa, including regional folk (*min'yô*) and classical court (*koten*) musics, that are also used as markers of Okinawan musical authenticity and that index earlier processes of hybridizing globalization (see Kaneshiro 1997 for an overview), Okinawan music has over the postwar period more popularly become associated with what I will refer to as 'Shima-uta' (literally, village/island songs) folk music and 'Uchinâ Pop'.

Also referred to as 'Okinawa(n) Pop' (see Kumada 1998), I use the latter term to refer to hybrid musical forms which became especially popular in the 1990s and which combined older Okinawan musical influences with those of Western pop, rock and reggae (see Roberson 2003 for a discussion). The key musicians creating 'Uchinâ Pop' have included China Sadao (especially as producer of the vocal group the Nenes), Kina Shoukichi (with his band Champloose) and Teruya Rinken (leader of the Rinken Band), but also notably Daiku Tetsuhiro and Ara Yukito (with his band Parsha Club). Although Kumada and Shinjô (2003) suggest that the Uchinâ Pop boom has ended, others have noted that Uchinâ Pop remains an important stream (*nagare*) in Okinawan music (see Kojima 2003) or have noted the emergence of newer bands and performers, such as Begin, Shakari, Tingara, Yonaha Tôru, Kamiya Chihiro, Natsukawa Rimi and others, who while using traditional Okinawan influences are working even more fully from rock/pop bases (see *Street Sounz* 2003; M. Tanaka 2003).

Regardless, Uchinâ Pop music has gained no small part of its popularity because of its hybrid musical creativity and association with so-called world music (see Roberson 2003 for a critique). In addition to the more common use of rock/pop influences – beginning with China Sadao's early cynical reggae-based look at the post-reversion exodus from Okinawa in 'Bye-Bye Okinawa' and Kina Shoukichi's garage-rock-like 'Haisai Ojisan' – Uchinâ Pop musicians have been experimenting with a variety of hybrid sound combinations, drawing on global musical resources and influences. For example, the Nenes' 1995 CD *Nârabi* contains a song called 'Saisai Bushi' which employs an Indonesian *gamelan* accompaniment, as do several songs on the Rinken Band's 1992 CD *Ajimâ*. Hidekatsu's music, meanwhile, is an arabesque of broadly Asian musical influences and indexes.[1]

In addition, a number of Okinawan musicians have incorporated contemporary Hawaiian musical influences in producing a hybrid trans-Pacific island music – which, following Japanese musician Kubota Makoto, might be called a 'Hawaiian Champuru'. Most prominently, Hirayasu Takashi has combined with guitarists Bob Brozman and Yoshikawa Chûei on three CDs to produce Hawaiian-textured 'Okinawan' music. Yoshikawa has also produced CDs with/for female singers Ganeko Yoriko and Natsukawa Rimi that include his Hawaiian slack-key guitar-influenced accompaniment. The instrumental virtuoso Yano Kenji (an original member of the near legendary Rokuningumi) has together with vocalist Shima Sachiko produced a number of CDs which draw instrumental inspiration from Hawaiian music (slack-key and, really West Coast USA, 'surf' music). And Amami Oshima born (Nakano) Rikki's 1998 CD *Miss You Amami* features some wonderful work by slack-key master Yamauchi 'Alani' Yuki.[2]

These musical mixings, Okinawan Plate Lunch or Hawaiian Champuru (remembering also that the word '*champuru*' is of Indonesian origin), reveal two important aspects of the global dimensions of Uchinâ Pop music. The first of these is that of an ethnicized self-awareness that, while risking self-exoticization (see Kumada 1998, 2000), is also very knowledgeably drawing on global musical resources in composing new creole creations. The local musical scene in Okinawa is simultaneously the location of global/world music influence and knowledge. Second, within this, various of these hybridizing contemporary musical experiments index and recreate Ryûkûyan historical experience and memory. The use of Indonesian *gamelan*, for example, recalls and musically revives cultural connections of some historical depth, Ryûkyûan traders having travelled throughout Southeast Asia, especially in the fourteenth to sixteenth centuries (see Kerr 1958). The use of Hawaiian slack-key guitar and other elements, while exploiting the popularity of Hawaiian music in general in Japan and while perhaps more playfully or naively employed, must also be seen within the historical context of Okinawan migration to and continuing diasporic connections with Hawaii (see Roberson n.d. for a discussion of the musical narration of the Okinawan diasporic experience).

Such contemporary 'world music' creolizations, moreover, are not the first (or only) cases of the incorporation of global musical influences in Okinawan music during the modern era. Shima-uta folk-song writer and producer Fukuhara Chôki was already during the prewar period recording (in Osaka) what has since become known as Okinawan 'new folk' (*shin-min'yô*) music, which included the use of Western musical instruments, particularly violin and mandolin. The violin continues to be featured on Okinawan Shima-uta CDs such as those by Kadekaru Rinji and Tamaki Kazumi, while Kameya Chôjin has been well known for use of the mandolin throughout his career.[3] In addition, localized global influences may also be seen in Noborikawa Seijin's postwar invention, based on the twelve-string guitar, of the '*rokushin*', a six-stringed version of the traditional three-stringed sanshin (see Kohama 1991: 94).

In both Shima-uta folk songs and Uchinâ Pop, two overlapping genres, the quotidian experiences of and experiments with globalization are reflected in musical practices and products that in their hybrid, *champuru*, mixing reflect processes of globalization's (mundane) deterritorialization and reterritorialization. The overall 'LooChoo gumbo' (to use the title of a song by Japanese musician Hosono Harûmi)[4] of Okinawa, however, is more complex, including also genres based not on Okinawan scales, instrumentation, or lyrics, but on more recently located global musical forms.

Music from the keystone: Okinawan Jazz and Rock

Giddens (1990) suggests that military power constitutes (together with capitalism, industrialism and surveillance) one of four central institutional dimensions of contemporary global modernity. Especially in Okinawa, it is important to recognize both the extraordinary violence of militarized globalization and other (potentially) less brutal consequences of the quotidian militarization of local social-cultural spaces by global military interests and forces.[5] The historical and ongoing experience of these overlapping, contradictory consequences of the world military order are embedded/embodied in Okinawa as site of the horrific loss of life during the 1945 Battle of Okinawa, as 'Keystone of the Pacific' during the American Occupation lasting until 1972 and as continuing 'host' to massive American military bases (see Angst 2001; Keyso 2000; M. Ota 2000).

Without denying the exploitation, oppression, discrimination and (sexual) violence that have accompanied the continuing American military presence in Okinawa, in the everyday localized confluence of American, Japanese and Okinawan cultural influences Okinawa has emerged, as Ota contends, as a 'highly creolized culture of contact zone' (Y. Ota 1997: 152). Music has been a central cultural practice and product of this, though such music itself need not be characterized by a localizing creolization as is more prominently the case with Uchinâ Pop. Instead, there is an aspect of the musical hybridity of Okinawa that has been constructed by the simultaneously conjunctive and disjunctive presence of a variety of distinctive musical genres associated with American roots; in particular, Okinawan jazz, (acoustic guitar-based) folk and rock musics. Here I look only at Okinawan jazz and Okinawan rock.[6]

In his book *Blue Nippon*, Atkins notes that. 'the production and consumption of jazz . . . were decisively shaped in the first two postwar decades by institutional, psychological and sociocultural impulses set in motion by the Occupation' (2001: 167). In Okinawa as in mainland Japan, it was the personally, institutionally and technologically embodied cultural presence of American Occupation forces that was especially important in the emergence of local jazz scenes (see Bise 1998). In addition to 'members only' clubs such as the Harbor View and VFW and Legionnaire clubs, the major American bases on Okinawa had three types of camp clubs – for enlisted men, for non-commissioned officers and for officers. Most of the early Okinawan jazz bands, starting in 1950 with the Duke Dorsey Orchestra, played in American military camp clubs (Bise 1998: 186–8). Noted pianist Yara Fumio and female vocalist Yoseyama Sumiko both got their starts in clubs on American bases (Nishi 1998; Okinawa Prefecture 1995). Into the early 1960s, musicians from mainland Japan and the Philippines (with its American connections) were brought into Okinawa under contracts intended also to support the introduction of skills (*gijutsu dônyû*). Influential as well in the golden era of Okinawan Jazz during the 1950s and early 1960s were contacts with visiting American musicians, playing primarily for military audiences, and the direct importation of American records, which entered Okinawa months ahead of mainland Japan (Shigeta 2003).

From the early 1960s the American popular music scene, including that in and around American military bases in Okinawa, shifted as rock 'n' roll music became increasingly influential. There was a multiplicity of conjunctures at work in the rise of Okinawan Rock that, as with Okinawan Jazz, reveal the quotidian operations of globalization, mediated and embodied by the presence in Okinawa of the American military. On the one hand, by the mid-1960s there were some 80,000 American military personnel and dependants in Okinawa (Rabson 1989: 9). Especially with the escalation of fighting in Vietnam from the mid-1960s, Okinawa became a staging and rest-and-relaxation base for American soldiers, creating a demand for the entertainment provided by bars and clubs on and off base that employed Okinawan rock musicians.[7]

On the other hand, the already long-established everyday presence of the American military occupation of Okinawa created quotidian conditions of cultural contact that drew a number of key Okinawan musicians to perform rock music. This is especially the case for musicians who grew up in Koza (now Okinawa City), which is located adjacent to Kadena Air Base. Kyan Yukio, for example, recalls being a child in the early 1950s, when 'the first music I listened to was American music. I listened to it every day. Because, Americans brought chewing gum, chocolate and at the same time jukeboxes. Straight American culture' (Okinawa City 1998: 137). Hirayasu Takashi also describes musical memories from Koza in a recent song called 'Tojo Nite' ('On the Road'):

> From Radio KSBK, I listened to Caravan
> From the jukebox, 'Knock on Wood,'
> James Brown, Aretha Franklin, The Temptations
> Ben E. King, Wilson Pickett, Otis Redding
> In those days I was still 20.[8]

While Hirayasu here interestingly primarily recalls rhythm and blues performers, he sings of everyday contact with American musical culture technologically mediated by radios and jukeboxes. A similar trope of the direct, primary, leading familiarity of Okinawa(ns) with American music is reflected in comments by musicians like Miyanaga Eiichi (nicknamed 'Chibi', he played drums and sang in Condition Green and Murasaki), who describes being lent records by Americans to learn songs from, which records were thus available to him and other Okinawan musicians well before they entered mainland Japan (my fieldnotes, 2003; Okinawa City 1998: 44).

In addition to such jukebox, radio and record mediated everyday contact with American music, there are other embodied dimensions of the Americanness of Okinawan Rock that bear comment. First, for many of these musicians, their close and constant contact with America(ns) facilitated their English-language abilities. George Murasaki (leader of the band Murasaki) is bilingual, the son of a second-generation Okinawan-American father from Hawaii. George went to American schools on the US military bases and spent two years at UCLA in the late 1960s (my fieldnotes, 2003; Okinawa City 1998). Such language ability was immediately important as the Okinawan bands were performing cover tunes in bars and clubs for Americans, and it also has provided a linguistic authenticity (relatively, and claimed to be) different from mainland Japanese bands.

The connectedness of these early Okinawan rock bands with America is literally embodied in other key Okinawan musicians as well. Both Miyanaga Eiichi and singer Kyan Marie are the children of Okinawan mothers and American GI fathers. Embodying a somewhat differently conceived intimate globalization of Okinawan personal and cultural space, the Shiroma brothers (Toshio and Masao), founding members of Murasaki and later of their own band, Island, are the sons of an Okinawan mother and Filipino father, who before returning to the Philippines worked as a cook for the US military (Sunamori 2000: 19).

Returning to music as such, the first true rock 'n' roll band in Okinawa is generally said to have been the Whispers, formed in 1964 by Kyan Yukio and Katchan (Kawamitsu Katsuhiro). Like others of the time, this band was influenced by the 'electric sound' of American and British groups. The 1965 visit of the American band the Ventures was an especially important event in early Okinawan rock history (Tonegawa 1988; Okinawa City 1998). Miyanaga describes being 'hit in the head by the Ventures' (Ogura 1998: 178). Keyboard player George Murasaki, meanwhile, describes his later interest in the British band Deep Purple as the result of feeling that they were doing the kind of music he had been wanting to do himself, incorporating Western classical and rock music influences (Okinawa City 1998: 24).

In addition, the audiences for performance by these Okinawa rock bands of the 1960s and 1970s were, as noted above, dominated by American servicemen. Most early Okinawan rock bands performed both in clubs in the base towns of Koza and Kin and on the military bases themselves. Bands perfected their skills by performing four to six sets per night in front of young American soldiers who, the musicians claim (my fieldnotes, 2003; Okinawa City 1998), were direct and at times violent in their criticism of poor performances. Like Okinawan jazz musicians, these local Okinawan rock musicians claim to have gained a distinctive Americanized/Westernized musical authenticity through their everyday local Okinawan experience of and relationships with the American presence – personal, cultural and military – in Okinawa.

Yamatu-yu? Okinawa Indies and Yamatunchu Shima-uta

On 15 May 1972 control over Okinawa 'reverted' from the United States to Japan. In 1975, the Vietnam War finally ended. With reversion, as George Murasaki notes (Okinawa City 1998), mainland musicians, music media representatives and scouts began coming to Okinawa. As a result, there were post-reversion booms in Okinawan folk music (*min'yô* or Shima-uta) and, from 1975, in Okinawan Rock. Both mainland promoters and audiences tended to treat Okinawan bands almost as though they were foreign bands, describing their arrival on the mainland as a 'landing' (*jôriku*; my fieldnotes, 2003). Ogura suggests that '[t]he culture industry commercialized Okinawan rock as "real hard rock"', but that such mainland commercialization 'deprived Okinawan rock of its social context', dominated by the US military bases (2003: 268).

The band Murasaki debuted spectacularly, releasing two albums in 1976, after the first of which Murasaki was number one in the rock music chart of Music Life (Ogura 2003: 466). In an era in which mainland Japanese rock bands might sell but 10,000 LPs, Murasaki had sales of 40,000 plus (Okinawa City 1998: 28). Condition Green made their mainland debut in 1977 (they also played a few dates and recorded an album in California), Marie with Medusa following in 1981 (Okinawa City 1998). By the mid-1980s, though, the first Okinawan rock invasion had ended.

The 1990s and the early 2000s have seen a number of other 'tales of ascent'[9] that differently implicate the relationships of Okinawa to Japan and to (within) the changing and diversifying global musical scene. On the one hand, from the mid-1990s the Okinawa Actors' School, under the direction of Makino Masayuki (see Oyadomari 1997), produced a series of singers and acts, including Amuro Namie, Chinen Rina, SPEED, MAX and DA PUMP, who have all had success as essentially mainstream Japanese pop music, dance-beat and hip-hop performers (though DA PUMP have recently added some 'Okinawan' flavor into their hip-hop; see Fujita 2004).

On the other hand, from the late 1990s and into the early 2000s there has been a band boom in Okinawa, which has resulted in an Okinawan Indies scene that has also gained nationwide notice (see Kenko 2003; Kumada and Shinjô 2003). These bands are playing a range of styles, from 'Okinawa Core' punk to hip-hop, and include (among many others; see *Street Sounz* 2003) groups such as Mongol 800 (whose second independent release *Message* reached number one on the national Oricon chart and sold some 2 million copies! K. Takahashi 2003: 31), IN-HI (formerly Indian-Hi), Orange Range (now arguably the most popular band in Japan) and HY (whose *Street Story* was the first Indies first-release CD to reach number one in the Oricon album chart; Miyajima 2004: 27).[10] In part, the popularity and success of such Indies bands is, as Aoki (2000: 174) points out, related to advanced CD and Internet technologies that allow artists to record and market their music themselves and that, together with the taken-for-granted-ness of changes in the global music scene, indicate the 'mundane deterritorialization' of popular music in Okinawa.

Between these two groups of Okinawan musicians and performers are (among others) Kiroro, a female duo performing piano-based ballads, and Cocco, a unique female singer-songwriter whose music has a hard, if not punk, edge (on the former, see Fujita 1998; E. Takahashi 2003; on the latter, see Okudaira 1998).[11] All of these younger acts, in one fashion or another, reveal overlapping processes of globalization, since all are working within musical genres of Euro-American origin and world scope, and since a number have recorded songs with English lyrics. Simultaneously, processes of nationalization may also be heard at work here, as all these Okinawan performers are singing primarily in Japanese if not performing primarily in mainland Japan or for mainland audiences. At the same time, especially for the latter group of Indies bands, but also for others such as Kiroro and Cocco, while these performers are 'not stuck on Okinawa' (Kumada and Shinjô 2003: 32) and while some in the first instance mobilize 'Okinawan' musical or visual markers to market themselves as distinct from other (mainland) bands (Kumada and Shinjô 2003; Wakanosuke 2003: 87), they variously also maintain some sense of and pride in their being from Okinawa or, as Tamaki Chiharu of Kiroro put it, in being '*Ryûkyûjin*' (a Ryûkyûan; Fujita 1998: 19).

Other musical border crossings between Yamato (mainland Japan) and Okinawa involve differently positioned and composed processes of cultural appropriation and assimilation.[12] There have been, for example, a number of mainland Japanese musicians who have experimented with, incorporated, or appropriated 'Okinawan' musical influences, usually drawing on the traditional Shima-uta folk and Uchinâ Pop genres discussed earlier. There are three aspects to this mainland musical borrowing and appropriation that I would like to point to here. First, there have been a number of Japanese musicians, including singers Katô Noriko and Otaka Shiszuru, who have recorded arrangements of originally Okinawan songs. The first contemporary mainland musician credited with covering a contemporary Okinawan composition was Kubota Makoto, whose band Kubota Makoto & Yûyake Gakudan recorded a reggae- and Hawaiian-influenced version of Kina Shoukichi's hit song 'Haisai Ojisan' on their 1975 LP, *Hawaii Champroo* (Kitanaka 1998a: 104). Also notable are recordings of Okinawan (-based/ inspired) songs by keyboardist Sakamoto Ryûichi on his 1987 *Neo Geo* and 1989 *Beauty* CDs that, together with other songs on each CD, featured vocals by Okinawan female singers Koja Misako, Ganeko Yoriko and Tamaki Kazumi.

Although himself erasing the identities of these three important singers and incorrectly suggesting that their 'Okinawan voices stand in here unproblematically for "Japanese"', Currid's remark that the coherence he hears between Sakamoto and the 'Okinawan Chans' (as they were called) on 'Asadoya Yunta' 'depends on the erasure of present and historical difference' (1996: 94) is more insightful, pointing to the need to critically consider the politics of incorporation and dominance potentially, at least, reflected in mainland Japanese musicians' appropriations of Okinawan music. At the same time, however, Okinawans themselves may hear things differently. Thus, Kumada and Shinjô (2003: 10–11) suggest that in putting together the Nenes (featuring a four-woman chorus, including Koja) China

Sadao was influenced by Sakamoto. Koja has said of her experience recording and touring (through Japan, America and Europe) with Sakamoto that:

> Before working with Sakamoto-san, I was just singing because I like to. I didn't know whether the songs [Shima-uta] I was performing were good or not, but when I went out into the world [*sekai ni deta*] I for the first time looked anew at my songs/singing and was able to view Okinawan music from a different angle.
>
> (Aoki 2004: 16; see also Aoki 2003a: 50–1)

In addition to covers and adaptations of Okinawan songs by mainland Japanese musicians, there are, second, a number of mainland artists, including Shang Shang Typhoon, the Shishars and Ang-Chang Project, who have composed original songs using Okinawan musical influences and inspirations (see Potter 2001; Kitanaka 1998b; H. Tanaka 2003). Sakamoto's former partner in the techno-pop band YMO (Yellow Magic Orchestra), Hosono Harûmi, has maintained a long-term musical engagement with Okinawa, starting with his early *Tai-an Yôkô* (1977) and *Paraiso* (1978), continuing with his 1985 soundtrack for the Takamine Gô movie *Paradise View* and with his more recent (1993) *Medicine Compilation* CD, which features Teruya Rinken and Uehara Tomoko on the song 'Mabui Dance #2'. Kuwata Keisuke, leader the Southern All Stars, has written a number of Okinawan-inspired/influenced songs, including two that invoke or (in the latter case) critique Okinawa's (post)war experience – 'Machikasanu Renka' (on the 1990 CD entitled *Southern All Stars*) and 'Heiwa no Ryûka' (a single released in 1997).[13]

The third, overlapping, dimension of mainland Japanese engagements with Okinawan music that I want to mention points to a reflexivity of sorts, as among the Okinawan-influenced songs originally composed by Japanese musicians there have been a number that have in turn been reincorporated back into the 'Okinawan' repertoire. For example, the song 'Satokibibatake' – which describes a child's remembrance of her father, killed in the 1945 Battle of Okinawa – composed by Terashima Naohiko and originally recorded by Moriyama Ryôko, has (among other things) recently been re-recorded by Okinawan singer Natsukawa Rimi. The Nenes, under the direction of China Sadao, included the Southern All Stars' song 'Heiwa no Ryûka' on their 1997 CD *Akemodoro*.[14]

Most significant, however, have been the work of Nakagawa Takashi and his band Soul Flower Union (or Soul Flower Mononoke Summit) and of Miyazawa Kazufumi and his band the Boom (see also Potter 2001). Both of these mainland musicians have recorded with Okinawan musicians and have written songs that are now 'Okinawan'. Nakagawa and Soul Flower Union have recorded with (and produced CDs for) Noborikawa Seijin and Hirayasu Takashi. The latter translated Soul Flower Union's song 'Mangetsu no

Yûbe' into Okinawan and in doing so 'made it into an Okinawan folk song [*min'yô*]', according to Kitanaka (1998b: 47).

The Boom have been even more influential. Miyazawa has worked with Kina Shoukichi and with singer Ganeko Yoriko, whose CD *Kui nu Hana* includes an Okinawan-language version of the Boom's song 'Shima-uta', with original Okinawan lyrics by Yoriko's father, Seiei. The Boom's 'Shima-uta' (recorded in both Japanese and Okinawan versions) has since its release in 1992 sold over 1 million copies (Kitanaka 1998b), been used in a commercial by an Okinawan awamori liquor maker, and included in a compilation of the top 100 selected Okinawan songs (Radio Okinawa 1994). It is often used in Okinawa as an Eisâ drum-dance number and a karaoke favourite (Radio Okinawa 1994: 115; see also Aoki 2003b). The continuing relation of this mainland band with Okinawa is further reflected in their 2002 CD *Okinawa: Watashi no Shima.*[15]

The articulations of Okinawa and Japan imbricated within and indexed by these mainland musical appropriations and appreciations of Okinawan music are complexly composed. Feld thus writes of the 'double voice' of musical appropriation, one being that of 'admiration, even homage and respect, a fundamental source of connectedness, creativity, and innovation', and the other being that 'of power, even control and domination, a fundamental source of asymmetry in ownership and commodification' (Keil and Feld 1994: 238).

Thus, while recognizing genuine Japanese appreciation of Okinawa(n music/culture), Japanese recordings of 'Okinawan' music may also be seen as problematic practices in which economically and culturally empowered mainland musicians appropriate the musical products and heritage of peripheralized and internally colonized Okinawa(ns). This imbalance of power (influence, profit) is typical of relations of musicians differentially positioned in global fields of socio-cultural and political-economic power. As Taylor notes:

> When western musicians appropriate music from somewhere else and use it in their music, or even work with nonwestern musicians, the old subordinating structures of colonialism are often reproduced in the new music, though in complex ways that need to be analyzed carefully.
>
> (Taylor 1997: 40)

These questions and issues remain relevant in relations between Japanese and Okinawan musicians, regardless of the intentions of the former in working with Okinawan musicians and in drawing on or appropriating Okinawan influences. At the same time, that those intentions and interests may be informed by criticisms of war and Japanese domination (as is the case with Soul Flower Union, the Boom and the Southern All Stars) must also be recognized, as must the reflexive value and relative empowerment provided Okinawan performers (and others) through such exchanges (as, in part, is also the case with Sakamoto and Hosono, Kubota and others).

Okinawa Latina: Okinawa as diaspora space

The final complexity of globalization manifest in Okinawan music that I want to very briefly touch on is that of the presence in Okinawa of a number of Latin music bands and performers. This location of Latin music within the Okinawan landscapes of music and identity was symbolized at the third Worldwide Uchinanchu Festival in 2001, at which a 'Music Fest' focused on Latin music and featured four bands, three from Okinawa: Kachimba 1551, Tamgolomango and the Diamantes.[16] As in 1995, the theme song for the festival was 'Katate ni sanshin wo' (originally 'Con el sanshin in la Mano') by the Diamantes, a song of Okinawan (return) migration (see Roberson n.d.).

Tamgolomango combines Okinawan and Brazilian influences in creating a 'global' jazz sound (Third Worldwide Uchinanchu Festival Executive Committee 2001: 48). Kachimba 1551 is a salsa band comprised of eight Okinawans and one (*nisei*) Latin-American Okinawan, who play both original (mostly Spanish lyric) tunes and salsa remixes of Okinawan songs. The oldest and most important of these Okinawa Latin bands is the Diamantes, whose leader is Alberto Shiroma, a third-generation Okinawan Peruvian who moved to Japan in 1986 and from there to his grandparents' homeland, Okinawa (Hosokawa 2003; Matsumura 1999: 267ff.). At the time of their major debut the Diamantes included eight members, three Okinawan Peruvians and five Okinawans (Isoda 1995). The Diamantes' home base remains their club in Koza, Pati, where, initially at least, many of their fans and customers were (American) Latino soldiers from the nearby US military bases (Higashi 1998: 112–13).

Though occasionally including some Okinawan elements, Shiroma sings primarily in Spanish and Japanese. The band's music is an energetic mixture of what Shiroma has called 'tropical-style' Latin American and Caribbean sounds (see Higashi 1998; Hosokawa 2003: 326–8), though Shiroma also describes growing up in Lima listening to the Beatles, American pop music (including Gloria Estefan) and Japanese music (Higashi 1998; Matsumura 1999). Reflected also in 'Katate ni Sanshin wo', Shiroma's Latin American return migrant experience is perhaps most clearly articulated in the Diamantes' first real hit, 'Gambateando'. This much-discussed song (see Hosokawa 2003; Roberson n.d.) describes the experiences of hard work, discrimination and hope among '*dekasegi*' Latin American Nikkeijin return migrant workers in Japan, of whom there are now some 250,000 (see, for example, Roth 2002; Tsuda 2003).

As Hosokawa Shuhei notes, such Okinawa Latin bands raise 'questions about the inter-relationships among cultural identity, musical express, and migratory experience' (2003: 322). Both personally and musically, Shiroma, the Diamantes, Kachimba 1551 and Tamgolomango embody and reflect their

'Okinawa Latina' nature. In (being seen as) not just constructing but also personally embodying a colorful, energetic 'shared "southern-ness"' (Hosokawa 2003: 329) between Okinawa and Latin American, these musicians and bands are (together with the examples of Hawaii discussed above) part of the composition of Okinawa as a hybrid (*champuru*) 'diaspora space' (Brah 1996). Here, embodied diasporic experience and the reflexive internalization of a 'diaspora consciousness' (Clifford 1997: 255ff.) that musically incorporates and indexes that experience together constitute further elements of the mundane deterritorialization of contemporary Okinawan globalization.

Conclusion: global *gajumaru*

Hosokawa suggests that what is intriguing about the fusion of influences among 'Okinawa Latina' bands such as the Diamantes is its and their 'slippery relationship to Okinawa' (2003: 326), reflecting leader Alberto Shiroma's (and the other musicians') 'multiple identities' (Hosokawa 2003: 327). With 'Okinawa' further bracketed, indexing the constructedness of 'Okinawa' and 'Okinawan(s/ness)', the same may be seen in much of the music and many of the musicians discussed throughout this paper. While all variously maintain, refuse to be bound by, or rediscover connections with 'Okinawa', their experiences and musical expressions of their multiple identities as 'Okinawan but of a different kind' (see Inoue 2004) complicate any singular or unilinear tracing of 'roots (music)'. Instead, like actor/comedian Tamaki Mitsuru's mobilization of the image of the *gajumaru* (banyan tree) in posters for his twenty-fifth anniversary 'Wan Live' performance in 2003, Okinawan roots are multiple and multiplex.

These complexities and multiplicities of Okinawan identities, here discussed in reference to circulations of sound involving Okinawan, American and Japanese music(ian)s, are the ongoing consequences of Okinawan modernity as constituted within and through the 'mundane deterritorialization' of global cultural processes. This everyday globalization or globalization of the everyday is an inherent element and dimension of contemporary Okinawan experience and identities, including those of and in musical practices, and indexes the reflexive globalized/ing imbrication of Okinawa, Japanese and American (and other) influences, forces and flows in the continuing composition of Loochoo Beats in/out of Okinawa and Japan.

Notes

1   See China Sadao (1994/1978) *Akabana*, Pony Canyon, PCCA-00581; *Kina Shoukichi and Champloose* (1989/1977) Japan Record, 25JC-357; Nenes (1995) *Nârabi*, Ki/oon Sony Records, KSC2 112; Rinken Band (1992) *Ajimâ*, Wave, SRCL 4272; Hidekatsu (1996) *Shinmitsu naru Yoake*, BMG Victor, BVCR-679.
2   See Kubota Makoto and Yûyake Gakudan (1998/1975) *Hawaiian Champuru*, Show Boat, SWAX-18; Hirayasu Takashi and Bob Brozman (2000) *Jin Jin/Firefly*, Riverboat, TUGCD 1020; Hirayasu Takashi and Yoshikawa Chûei

(2001) *Uto Ashibi*, Respect Record, RES-54; Ganeko Yoriko and Yoshikawa Chûei (2002) *Uta Ashibi*, Respect Record, RES-67; Natsukawa Rimi (2002) *Hae*, Victor, VICL-60856; (Nakano) RIKKI (1998) *Miss You Amami*, Sambinha RICE ORR-701; Yano Kenji and Shima Sachiko (1994) *Sons of Ailana, Vol. 1*, Qwotchee Records, QRCD-001.

3 See Kadekaru Rinji (1998) *My Sweet Home Koza*, B/C Records, BCD-1; Tamaki Kazumi (1997) *Tinin*, Disk Akabana, APCD-1003; Kameya Chôjin (1993) *Kameya Chôjin*, Marufuku Record ACD-41.

4 Hosono Harûmi (1995/1977) *Tai-An Yôkô*, Nippon Crown, CRCP-137.

5 The current (2004) situation in Iraq is testament to the potential for brutality and violence to become ongoing local consequences of the presence of global militarized power. I have no intention, even in the Okinawan case, of suggesting a uniformly benign local occupation by or presence of American military forces and personnel; though I conversely, in the Okinawan case, do not want to suggest a unilaterally negative evaluation of the personal, social, and cultural consequences of American occupation and presence there.

6 Okinawan folk music using Western acoustic guitar-based music has its origins in the early to mid-1970s. In 1972 the seminal album *Okinawa Folk Mura* was released, while in 1975 another omnibus album, *Koza '75*, was produced by another set of musicians including Chinen Ryôkichi and Kurokawa Shûji. Although Chinen has also subsequently released a CD of folk-blues, singer-songwriter Sadoyama Yutaka remains the most important Okinawan folk musician (see Bise 1998).

7 The four major Okinawa rock bands are Murasaki, Condition Green, Marie with Medusa, and Kotobuki. Recordings (CDs and LPs) include: Murasaki (1976) *Murasaki*, Tokuma Japan Communications TKCA-70485; Condition Green (1978) *Life of Change*, Pony Canyon, PCCA-00681; Marie with Medusa (1989) *I was Born in Okinawa*, Tokuma Japan Communications TKCA-70488; see also the compilation double CD *Okinawa Hard Rock Legendary* (2003) Imperial Records, TECN-35904–35905.

8 Lyrics from Hirayasu Takashi and Bob Brozman (2001) *Nankuru Naisa*, Riverboat Records, TUGCD1023.

9 To borrow from the title of the Okinawan folk song 'Nubui-kuduchi', meaning ascending (nubui=nobori) to the capital, a song that narrates a journey to Japan from Okinawa during the days of the Ryûkyûan Kingdom.

10 See Mongol 800 (2002) *Message*, High Wave/Tissue Freak Records, HICC-1201; IN-HI (2003) *We are the Champloo*, Universal UPCH-1224; Orange Range (2002) *Orange Ball*, Spice Records, DMS-001; HY (2003) *Street Story*, Climax, CLCD 20002.

11 For compilation CDs, see Kiroro (2002) *Kiroro no Uta 1*, Victor, VICL-60835; Cocco (2001) *Best + Ura-Best + Mihappyôkyoku-shû*, Victor VICL-60770–1.

12 Representative CDs for the artists referred to in the following include Katô Noriko (2003) *Okinawa Jôka*, Universal, UICZ-4065; Sakamoto Ryûichi (1987) *Neo Geo*, CBS/Sony, CSCL 1279; Sakamoto Ryûichi (1989) *Beauty*, Toshiba EMI, TOCP-53050.

13 See Hosono Harûmi (1978) *Paraiso*, Alpha ALCA-9068; Hosono Harûmi (1985) *Paradise View*, Teichiku Records, TECN-15339; Hosono Harûmi (1993) *Medicine Compilation*, Epic/Sony Records, ESCB 1302; Southern All Stars (1990) Southern All Stars, Victor, VICL-1; Southern All Stars (1997) *Heiwa no Ryûka*, Victor, VIBL-5.

14 See the following CDs: Natsukawa Rimi (2003) *Sora no Fûkei*, Victor VICL-61094; Nenes (1997) *Akemodoro*, Antinos Records, CDORBD 096.

15 Music discussed in this paragraph may be found on the following: Soul Flower Union (1996) *Electro Agile Bop*, Ki/oon KSC2–164; Noborikawa Seijin (2001)

Spiritual Unity, Respect Record RES-45; Hirayasu Takashi (1998) *Kariyushi no Tsuki*, Respect Record, RES-25; Ganeko Yoriko (1995) *Kui nu Hana*, VAP, VPCC-81075; The Boom (2002) *Okinawa: Watashi no Shima*, Toshiba EMI, TOCT-24823.

16 For Kachimba 1551 and the Diamantes, see, for example, Kachimba 1551 (2001) Va a Pasar, 3rd Wave, NMCL-1-12; Diamantes (1997) *Lo Mejor de Diamantes*, Mercury, PHCL-5083.

Bibliography

Angst, L. (2001) 'In a dark time', unpublished PhD thesis, Yale University.

Aoki, M. (2000) *Okinawa uta no tabi* (Okinawan song Journey), Naha: Bôdâinku.

——(2003a) 'Koja Misako' [interview], in M. Tanaka (ed.) *Shimanchu damashî* (Island spirit), Tokyo: Shufu to Seikatsusha.

——(2003b) 'The Boom', in M. Tanaka (ed.) *Shimanchu damashî* (Island spirit), Tokyo: Shufu to Seikatsusha.

——(2004) 'Koja Misako' [interview], *Coralway* 92: 6–7. Naha: Japan Transocean Air Co., Ltd.

Appadurai, A. (1996) *Modernity at Large*, Minneapolis, MN: University of Minnesota Press.

Atkins, E. T. (2001) *Blue nippon*, Durham, NC, and London: Duke University Press.

Bise, K. (1998) 'Sengo Okinawa ongakushi 1945–1998 (Postwar history of Okinawan music 1945–1998)', in F. Tadashi (ed.) *Uchinâ no uta*, Tokyo: Ongakunotomosha.

Brah, A. (1996) *Cartographies of Diaspora*, London and New York: Routledge.

Clifford, J. (1997) *Routes*, Cambridge, MA, and London: Harvard University Press.

Currid, B. (1996) '"Finally, I reach to Africa": Ryuichi Sakamoto and sounding Japan(ese)', in J. W. Treat (ed.) *Contemporary Japan and Popular Culture*, Honolulu: University of Hawaii Press.

DeNora, T. (2000) *Music in Everyday Life*, Cambridge: Cambridge University Press.

Eureka (2002) 'Tokushû: Shima-uta (Special issue: Shima-uta)', vol. 34, no.10: 53–175.

Feld, S. (1996) 'Waterfalls of song: an acoustemology of place resounding in Bosavi, Papua New Guinea', in S. Feld and K. H. Basso (eds) *Senses of Place*, Santa Fe, NM: School of American Research Press.

Fujita, T. (1998) '(Interview Kikaku) Uchinâ no uta: mirai to nekko (Special interview on Uchinâ song: its future and roots)', in F. Tadashi (ed.) *Uchinâ no uta* (Uchinâ song), Tokyo: Ongakunotomosha.

——(2004) 'Okinawa ongaku no ima: Da Pump (Contemporary Okinawan music: Da Pump)', *Coralway* 92: 6–7. Naha: Japan Transocean Air Co., Ltd.

Geertz, C. (1983) *Local Knowledge*, New York: Basic Books, Inc.

Giddens, A. (1990) *The Consequences of Modernity*, Stanford, CA: Stanford University Press.

Gilroy, P. (1993) *The Black Atlantic*, Cambridge, MA: Harvard University Press.

Hein, L. and Selden, M. (eds) (2003) *Islands of Discontent*, Lanham, MD: Rowman & Littlefield Publishers, Inc.

Higashi, T. (1998) 'America no chicano, nippon no Okinawa. Bokutachi wa nippon no Los Lobos. Alberto Shiroma (Chicano in America, Okinawa in Japan. We are Japan's Los Lobos)' [interview], in DeMusik Inter. (ed.) *Oto no chikara –*

Okinawa: Amami/Yaeyama/Gyaku-ryû (Power of music – Okinawa: Amami/ Yaeyama/reversing the flow), Tokyo: Impact Shuppansha.

Hook, G. and Siddle, R. (eds) (2003) *Japan and Okinawa*, London and New York: RoutledgeCurzon.

Hosokawa, S. (2003) 'From Lima to Koza: Diamantes and the blurred identity of Okinawan-Peruvian "reverse migrants"', in S. Loza (ed.) *Musical Cultures of Latin America*, Proceedings of an International Conference, Department of Ethnomusicology and Systematic Musicology, University of California, Los Angeles.

Inoue, M. S. (2004) '"We are Okinawans but of a different kind:" new/old social movements and the U.S. military in Okinawa', *Current Anthropology*, vol. 45, no. 1: 85–104.

Isoda, K. (1995) 'Diamantes,' in K. Isoda and S. Kurokawa (eds) *Okinawan Music Guide for Beginners (in Japanese)*, Tokyo: Tôa Ongaku-sha.

Johnson, C. (ed.) (1999) *Okinawa: cold war island*, Cardiff, CA: Japan Policy Research Institute.

Johnson, H. (2001) 'Nationalisms and globalization in Okinawan popular music: Nenezu and their place in world music contexts', in R. Starrs (ed.) *Asian Nationalism in an Age of Globalization*, Japan Library.

Kaneshiro, A. (1997) *Yamatonchu no tame no Okinawa ongaku nyûmon* (Introduction to Okinawan music for the mainland Japanese), Tokyo: Ongakunotomosha.

Keil, C. and Feld, S. (1994) *Music Grooves*, Chicago and London: University of Chicago Press.

Kenko (2003) 'Okinawa beat goes on', in Tenkû Kikaku (ed.) *Okinawa Dream* [in Japanese], Tokyo: Kôbunsha.

Kerr, G. (1958) *Okinawa*, Rutland, VT, and Tokyo: Charles E. Tuttle.

Keyso, R. A. (2000) *Women of Okinawa*, Ithaca, NY, and London: Cornell University Press.

Kitanaka, M. (1998a) 'Yamatonchu ga fukikonda Uchinâ no uta (Uchinâ songs recorded by mainland Japanese)', in T. Fujita (ed.) *Uchinâ no uta* (Uchinâ songs), Tokyo: Ongakunotomosha.

——(1998b) 'Yamatonchu ga tsukutta Uchinâ kayô (Uchinâ songs made by mainland Japanese)', in T. Fujita (ed.) *Uchinâ no uta* (Uchinâ songs), Tokyo: Ongakunotomosha.

Kohama, T. (1991) 'Suiko Jizai' (Born to be wild), *Esquire*, vol. 5, no. 8: 92–5.

Kojima, S. (2003) 'Seimeiryoku ni michiafureta shima "Okinawa" (An island of life force, "Okinawa")', in H. Tanaka (ed.) *Okinawa Ongaku Disk Guide* (Guide to Okinawan music CDs), Tokyo: Tokyo FM Shuppan.

Kumada, S. (1998) '90 nendai Okinawa poppu ni okeru minzokusei hyôgen no shosô (Various expressions of ethnicity in 1990s Okinawan pop)', in Okinawa Prefectural Arts University, Department of Art Culture (ed.) *Okinawa kara geijutsu o kangaeru* (Thinking art from Okinawa), Ginowan: Yuju Shorin.

——(2000) 'Okinawa ekizochishizumu no genzai (Okinawa exoticism today)', *Kokusai Kôryû*: 89: 31–5.

Kumada, S. and Shinjô K. (2003) 'Okinawa pop to wa nan datta no ka, ushinawareta 90 nendai o megutte (What was Okinawan pop? On the lost 1990s)', *Wander* 34: 9–35.

Lipsitz, G. (1994) *Dangerous Crossroads*, London and New York: Verso.

Mathews, G. (2000) *Global Culture/Individual Identity*, London and New York: Routledge.

Matsumura, H. (1999) *Asia uta kaidô* (Asia highway song), Tokyo: Shinshokan.

——(2002) *Uta ni kiku Okinawa* (Listening to Okinawa in song), Tokyo: Hakusuisha.

Middleton, R. (1990) *Studying Popular Music*, Milton Keynes and Philadelphia: Open University Press.

Mitchell, T. (1996) *Popular Music and Local Identity*, London and New York: Leicester University Press.

Miyajima, O. (2004) 'Tokushû . . . Okinawa greatest hits 2K3 (Special issue . . . Okinawa greatest hits 2K3)', *Hands* 66: 22–37.

Negus, K. (1996) *Popular Music in Theory*, Cambridge: Polity Press.

Nishi, I. (1998) 'Yoseyama Sumiko Interview', in DeMusik Inter. (ed.) *Oto no chikara – Okinawa: Amami/Yaeyama/Gyaku-ryû* (Power of music – Okinawa: Amami/Yaeyama/reversing the flow), Tokyo: Impact Shuppansha.

Ogura, T. (1998) 'Ai to heiwa' o koeru Kyôretsu na rock o: Miyanaga Eiichi (Powerful rock beyond love and peace: Miyanaga Eiichi)' [interview]), in DeMusik Inter. (ed.) *Oto no chikara – Okinawa: Amami/Yaeyama/Gyaku-ryû* (Power of music – Okinawa: Amami/Yaeyama/reversing the flow), Tokyo: Impact Shuppansha.

——(2003) 'Military base culture and Okinawan rock 'n' roll', *Inter-Asia Cultural Studies*, vol. 4, no. 3: 466–70.

Okinawa City (1998) *Rock 'n' Koza*, revised edition*(in Japanese)*, Naha: Naha Shuppan.

Okinawa Prefecture (1995) *Okinawa Music Festival Jisshi Hôkokusho*, Naha: Okinawa Prefecture.

Okudaira, E. (1998) 'Hashiru shintai, tadayou me kokko (Running body, floating eyes and mind)', *Edge* 6: 44–6.

Ota, M. (2000) *Essays on Okinawa Problems*, Gushikawa City: Yui Shuppan Co.

Ota, Y. (1997) 'Appropriating media, resisting power: representations of hybrid identities in Okinawan popular culture,' in R. G. Fox and O. Starn (eds) *Between Resistance and Revolution*, New Brunswick, NJ, and London: Rutgers University Press.

Oyadomari, N. (1997) 'Special interview: idol shinkaron: Amuro o tsukutta otoko, Makino Masayuki, Okinawa Actors' School Kôchô (On the evolution of idol: the man who created Amuro, Makino Misayuki, the principal of the Okinawa Actors' School)', *Edge* 3: 44–58.

Potter, J. (2001) *The Power of Okinawa*, Kobe: S.U. Press.

Rabson, S. (1989) *Okinawa: two postwar novellas*, Berkeley, CA: Institute of East Asian Studies, University of California.

Radio Okinawa (1994) *Okinawa no uta 100-sen* (100 selected songs from Okinawa), Naha: Radio Okinawa.

Roberson, J. (2003) 'Uchinâ Pop: place and identity in contemporary Okinawan popular music', in L. Hein and M. Selden (eds) *Islands of Discontent*, Lanham, MD: Rowman & Littlefield Publishers, Inc.

——(n.d.) 'Singing diaspora: Okinawan songs of home, departure and return', unpublished manuscript.

Rosaldo, R. (1995) 'Foreword', in N. G. Canclini *Hybrid Cultures*, Minneapolis, MN: University of Minnesota Press.

Roth, J. (2002) *Brokered Homeland*, Ithaca, NY: Cornell University Press.

Shigeta, T. (2003) 'Roots o tadoreba Jazz ni ikitsuku! (Roots can be found in jazz)', in *Jazz Festa: Dai 13-kai Jazz in Urasoe* [pamphlet], Urasoeshi Bunka Shinkô Jigyô Jikkô Iinkai [and] Okinawa Jazz Kyôkai.

Stokes, M. (1994) 'Introduction: ethnicity, identity and music', in M. Stokes (ed.) *Ethnicity, Identity and Music*, Providence, RI: Berg.

Street Sounz (2003) *Okinawa Music Renaissance* (Special issue; in Japanese), Tokyo: Shinkô Music Pub. Co. Ltd.

Sunamori, K. (2000) *Okinawan Shout (in Japanese)*, Tokyo: Kôdansha.

Takahashi, E. (2003) 'Kiroro' [interview], in M. Tanaka (ed.) *Shimanchu damashî* (Island spirit), Tokyo: Shufu to Seikatsusha.

Takahashi, K. (2003) 'Okinawa music rekishi to sakuhin nenpyô (Okinawan music: its history and works)', *Street Sounz*, 30–3.

Tanaka, H. (ed.) (2003) *Okinawa Ongaku Disk Guide* (Guide to Okinawan music CDs), Tokyo: Tokyo FM Shuppan.

Tanaka, M. (ed.) (2003) *Shimanchu damashî* (Island spirit), Tokyo: Shufu to Seikatsusha.

Taylor, T. (1997) *Global Pop*, London and New York: Routledge.

Third Worldwide Uchinanchu Festival Executive Committee (2001) *Worldwide Uchinanchu Festival in Okinawa 2001 Guidebook* (English version), Naha: Third Worldwide Uchinanchu Festival Executive Committee Secretariat.

Tomlinson, J. (1999) *Globalization and Culture*, Chicago: University of Chicago Press.

Tonegawa, Y. (1988) *Kyan Marie no seishun* (Kyan Marie's adolescent years), Tokyo: Chikuma Shobô.

Tsuda, T. (2003) *Strangers in the Ethnic Homeland*, New York: Columbia University Press.

Wakanosuke (2003) 'IN-HI: Okinawa no identity o mochitsutsu zenkoku e shinshutsu (IN-HI: Going nationwide while maintaining Okinawan identity)', in M. Tanaka (ed.) *Shimanchu damashî* (Island spirit), Tokyo: Shufu to Seikatsusha.

Index